breaking through

Effective Instruction & Assessment for Reaching English Learners

Solution Tree | Press

a division of

Solution Tree

555 North Morton Street

Bloomington, IN 47404

800.733.6786 (toll free) / 812.336.7700

FAX: 812.336.7790

email: info@solution-tree.com

solution-tree.com

Printed in the United States of America

16 15 14 13 12   1 2 3 4 5

FSC
www.fsc.org
MIX
Paper from
responsible sources
FSC® C013483

Library of Congress Cataloging-in-Publication Data

Breaking through : effective instruction & assessment for reaching English learners / [edited by] Margarita Calderón.

   p. cm.

  Includes bibliographical references and index.

  ISBN 978-1-936765-36-2 (hardcover with dust jacket) 1. Linguistic minorities--Education--United States. 2. Education, Bilingual--United States. 3. English language--Study and teaching--Foreign speakers. 4. English language--Study and teaching--United States--Evaluation. I. Calderón, Margarita.

  LC3731.B657 2012

  371.829--dc23

                  2012006912

Solution Tree

Jeffrey C. Jones, CEO

Edmund M. Ackerman, President

Solution Tree Press

President: Douglas M. Rife

Publisher: Robert D. Clouse

Vice President of Production: Gretchen Knapp

Managing Production Editor: Caroline Wise

Senior Production Editor: Edward Levy

Proofreader: Linda Seifert

Text Designer: Amy Shock

Cover Designer: Rian Anderson

To Rebecca Fitch,
who has quietly done
so much for ELs!

Acknowledgments

Writing *Breaking Through* has been a pleasure and a dream come true, thanks to our editor, Ed Levy. His support and professional expertise expedited our collective process and end product. We would also like to acknowledge Robb Clouse, Jeff Jones, and Claudia Wheatley for their care and concern for all children in our schools.

∞

Solution Tree Press would like to thank Alex Wise for contributing his handwriting during the design of this book.

Table of Contents

About the Editor

Margarita Calderón

 Margarita Calderón, PhD, is professor emerita and senior research scientist at the Johns Hopkins University School of Education. Her research, training, and curriculum development for teaching language, reading comprehension, and content knowledge to K–12 English learners has been supported by the New York Carnegie Corporation Foundation, the U.S. Department of Education, the U. S. Department of Labor, the National Institutes of Health, and the Texas Education Agency. Her work has focused on effective instructional processes, two-way and dual-language programs, teacher learning communities, and professional development for schools with language-minority populations and striving adolescent readers.

The author of more than one hundred articles, chapters, books, and teacher training manuals, Dr. Calderón's most recent professional books are *Teaching Reading Comprehension to English Learners, K–5* and *Teaching Reading to English Language Learners, Grades 6–12*. She also developed RIGOR (Reading Instructional Goals for Older Readers), a series of intervention resources for older students reading at preliterate–grade 3 levels. RIGOR is being used in New York City, Boston, Houston, Louisville, Salt Lake City, and other major cities.

Dr. Calderón has also created and directed her own international institutes for administrators, teachers, and parents. She is an experienced classroom teacher, bilingual program director, professional development coordinator, professor of educational leadership graduate programs, and teacher supervisor.

Born in Juárez, Mexico, Dr. Calderón was educated in Mexico and the U.S., receiving a BA in English and MA in linguistics from the University of Texas at El Paso and her doctorate from Claremont Graduate School in Pomona, California.

Visit www.margaritacalderon.org to learn more about Dr. Calderón's work, and contact pd@solution-tree.com to book Dr. Calderón for professional development.

Introduction

Margarita Calderón

How does *Breaking Through: Effective Instruction & Assessment for Reaching English Learners* differ from other books in the upsurge of books on English learners (ELs)? One difference is that this book attempts to look at ELs from a larger perspective: it provides guidelines and recommendations for a whole-school approach to helping ELs achieve academically while learning English.

These recommendations are based on empirical studies that the contributors to this anthology describe in their respective chapters. However, beyond the evidence base, the contributors discuss the need to make a moral commitment to ELs—and to all other children who may be struggling in our schools. They draw attention to people who have already made such a commitment in ordinary schools and districts throughout the United States and Canada. The common trait of all these schools is that they have not given up hope. The school leaders constantly engage teachers, coaches, and specialists to make the minute-by-minute efforts that make a difference in children's lives.

The suggestions in this book stem from a new body of research, including field studies, emphasizing that language, literacy, and subject matter are learned faster when integrated, even in short periods of English as a second language (ESL) or language arts and bilingual education. Unless all the teachers in a school are well prepared to teach this way, the learning progress of ELs in that school will not change from the status quo.

In chapter 1, I discuss these two concepts in depth, providing examples of ongoing studies on the integration of language, literacy, and content, along with a look at implementation efforts. This chapter cautions against the use of certain practices stemming from the last few decades of the twentieth century, when knowledge about how to educate English learners was based mainly on guesswork. I also outline what courageous teachers and administrators do collaboratively to study their ELs. As these schools leaders take risks, study those risks, and continue working toward their goals, they are finding this process most rewarding, both for their students and themselves.

In chapter 2, Robert Slavin describes effective whole-school teaching for ELs. He stresses that good teaching for ELs is good teaching for *all* students, not the other way around, and he describes four strategies to reach all children: (1) teach well-organized, interesting lessons; (2) maximize opportunities for students to see, not just hear, key concepts; (3) maximize opportunities for them to verbally describe their current understandings to other students and to hear their peers' perspectives and feedback; and (4) maximize opportunities for students to "learn how to learn"—that is, to gain metacognitive skills to help them study, retain information, and apply new skills.

In chapter 3, Claude Goldenberg calls attention to the fact that there is remarkably little research documenting the achievement effects of many of the practices recommended for or used with ELs. Even when we do have evidence of effectiveness, the impact on student learning is at best modest. He suggests four important principles that can serve as a framework for designing effective instructional programs for ELs: (1) effective practices and programs for ELs and non-ELs overlap considerably; (2) ELs require additional instructional supports due to language limitations; (3) promoting English language proficiency must be a priority for ELs; and (4) ELs' home language is a valuable resource that can be used to promote their academic achievement. He cautions against quick fixes and urges comprehensive approaches that integrate multiple components and create a focused and coherent schoolwide approach to improving achievement for ELs.

Two concepts that have withstood the test of time are Jim Cummins's basic interpersonal communicative skills (BICS) and cognitive academic language proficiency (CALP). In chapter 4, Jim revisits those concepts and adds valuable information.

Guadalupe Valdés has given us great insights for the heart and mind through the years. In chapter 5, she takes her valuable perspectives into a new horizon with the empirical studies of her colleagues Sarah Capitelli and Laura Alvarez. Their one-on-one English project describes how it might look in practice for schools to move toward the common core standards.

In chapter 6, Liliana Minaya-Rowe discusses a way to integrate language, literacy, and subject-area instruction in middle and high schools. Her detailed description of the features of each component is coupled with the professional development designs that schools can adapt in order to prepare all teachers in a school to be teachers of academic language, reading, and writing when these are integrated into math, science, social studies, or language arts.

Okhee Lee addresses the emerging discipline of teaching science to ELs in chapter 7. She describes the types of approaches, such as collaborative teamwork, that make science interesting, relevant, and comprehensible to ELs. This chapter will serve the science education community well, as new science standards are currently being developed for all students, including ELs.

The education of ELs needs to start early—in preschool! In chapter 8, Maria Trejo outlines the research on early learning and the benefits for ELs of developing rich language, math, science, civics, social studies, and preliteracy skills simultaneously in English and the primary language.

In chapter 9, from a culturally responsive education perspective, Margo Gottlieb poses issues surrounding common instructional assessment for ELs as a whole-school initiative. She defines *common instructional assessment,* distinguishes it from other forms of assessment, and lays the foundation for the use of common instructional assessment data to counterbalance data from high-stakes testing.

In chapter 10, Alba Ortiz shares the essential components of response to intervention (RTI) for ELs and explores what effective instruction should look like. This chapter also stresses the importance of addressing system-level issues that contribute to student failure.

Of course, all of this is not possible without the commitment of and continuous learning by the adults in a school. In chapter 11, Elena Izquierdo looks at some of the old beliefs and myths that educators sometimes hold on to that need to be replaced, so that a school may transform.

Educational agencies and centers can become catalysts for professional learning. In chapter 12, Barbara Acosta, Kristina Anstrom, and Charlene Rivera, researchers and trainers from the George Washington University Center for Equity and Excellence in Education, share strategies and methods schools have adopted to create better learning systems for both adults and children.

In the final chapter, Joel Gómez and I highlight key messages from the authors and further elaborate on professional learning, and on what is required for it to have an impact on teachers and their ELs. This chapter also discusses new and sensible ways of addressing some of the more complex issues that have arisen around English learners.

Margarita Calderón

Margarita Calderón, PhD, is professor emerita at the Johns Hopkins University School of Education, where she continues to work with colleagues from the university's Talent Development Secondary Center (TDS). The TDS assists schools with organizational reform and provides significant curricular and instructional support designed to close the achievement gap and accelerate learning for struggling students.

Dr. Calderón assists with all components dealing with EL achievement and professional development for all teachers who come in contact with ELs.

Her work has been supported by the New York Carnegie Corporation Foundation, the U.S. Department of Education, the U. S. Department of Labor, the National Institutes of Health, and the Texas Education Agency.

Dr. Calderón has more than one hundred publications to her credit. In addition, she is an experienced classroom teacher, bilingual program director, professional development coordinator, professor of educational leadership graduate programs, and teacher supervisor.

In this chapter, Dr. Calderón debunks schools' old ways of helping ELs, which was to simply shift the responsibility to ESL teachers or bilingual schools; asserts that their education is a schoolwide responsibility; and points out that successful English learners have teachers who integrate language, literacy, and content and engage students in meaningful learning.

Chapter 1

Why We Need a New Way of Schooling Language-Minority Children

Margarita Calderón

In every state of the United States and throughout Canada and Great Britain, school districts have or will soon have English learners. As language-minority student populations grow, either through high birth rates or the arrival of refugee children and other newcomers, all schools must be prepared to teach them. In the past, outcomes for ELs were the responsibility of the lonely ESL teacher or the bilingual school down the road. For ELs in special education, outcomes were the responsibility of special education teachers. However, with the onset of response to intervention, the Common Core State Standards, and special funding—such as the funding schools are receiving from Race to the Top—all mainstream teachers and site administrators are now responsible for all students.

One trend in many schools for providing ESL services has been the use of "push-in" and "pull-out" approaches. However, when ELs are pulled out of class to learn English, they miss out on learning content and opportunities for socialization with mainstream students. When ESL teachers push in, to keep ELs in regular classrooms, the ELs feel singled out and frequently withdraw from meaningful learning. These programs create other problems as well—for example, when schools do not allow quality preparation time for mainstream, ESL, and bilingual teachers to meet and plan their co-teaching. As a result, team-teaching efforts can become disjointed and ineffective, as we see in the following two scenarios.

> Sharon, an elementary ESL teacher, pushes into the classroom quietly, going from one EL to another. She translates for one student for about four minutes, then helps another to understand his seat assignment. After five minutes, she answers some questions on a worksheet for a third student. Then she returns to the first and starts her rotation all over again until the thirty minutes are up, at which point she goes to the next class and follows the same routine.

> Jamil, a high school ESL teacher, pulls five ELs into a corner of the room and conducts an ESL lesson. This lesson is different from the core teacher's lesson and must be conducted quietly so as not to disturb the rest of the class. After a few explanations, the students begin their worksheet assignments or silent reading. As they read, they stop and quietly ask what a word means. Jamil asks them one or two questions, and one or two of the students answer softly.

The problem with both approaches is that they provide ELs with very little quality instructional time or English language development practice, and neither gives students very much opportunity for mastery of content. Oral production is key for ELs, yet these students have become a silent generation. Teachers tell us that their ELs are literally in their "silent period"—too shy, too embarrassed, to speak, and that in order to respect the students' silence, they do not hold them accountable for oral, reading, or writing production until the students are ready. By the time these students are in middle and high school, their teachers say, they are turned off to learning and don't want to respond to or ask questions.

When we interviewed students across the country, we discovered that they had never received explicit instruction in formulating questions or using sentence starters or discourse protocols for specific functions, such as math and science processes or historical events and their implications. Neither had they been exposed to comprehension skills development or writing strategies for those processes that the Common Core State Standards are now requiring. They knew how to decode, and they read aloud fairly fluently, but they could not comprehend what they were reading. This silent generation has gone through elementary and secondary school sitting quietly in the back of the room, barely passing from grade to grade, and being largely ignored.

Breaking the Cycle

What is turning some schools around and getting them to pay attention to the silent majority?

For all students to learn, particularly language-minority students, educators and their professional learning must be held to high standards. Challenging standards and high expectations have a positive effect on educator practice and student achievement (August & Shanahan, 2006). Student outcomes, in fact, are contingent on professional learning standards. When schools and school districts commit to educator performance standards that delineate the knowledge, skills, practices, and dispositions of highly effective educators of ELs, the whole school benefits. The standards that nest EL academic skills are professional growth and professional collaboration. That is why the whole school needs to do whatever it takes to break old habits and bring about professional development and collaboration (DuFour, DuFour, Eaker, & Karhanek, 2010) as intrinsic to EL achievement.

The Learning Forward standards specify what teachers need to know and do to deliver an effective, equitable education for every student. They also specify the leadership skills that support teachers as they make the transition into effective, equitable teaching informed by skills, dispositions, knowledge of pedagogy and content, assessment, an understanding of how students learn, and the engagement of students from diverse cultures, language, socioeconomic conditions, and exceptionalities (Learning Forward, 2011).

Without appropriate implementation of even small programs, there will be small effects. Without appropriate implementation of larger programs—for a hundred or more ELs—there will be dismal

> When the silent filling in of worksheets is replaced by interactive learning that integrates speaking, listening, reading, and writing, ELs learn throughout the day.

effects. What is called for is not only intensification of the implementation of early English language development (ELD), ESL, and sheltered programs, but also greater buy-in and extensive preparation for all core content teachers. When the silent filling in of worksheets is replaced by interactive learning that integrates speaking, listening, reading, and writing, ELs learn throughout the day.

Rigorous Attention and Instruction for ELs

As the Carnegie panel on adolescent ELs found, English learners have double the work compared to mainstream students (Short & Fitzsimmons, 2007). They have to simultaneously learn both language and content concepts from math, science, social studies, and language arts. A school's efforts must become even more intensive for students with interrupted formal education (SIFE) and students who received no education at all in their native countries; these newcomers have *triple* the work (Calderón, 2007b; Calderón & Minaya-Rowe, 2011). Along with learning English language and content concepts they have missed, they must also learn how to read and write. A well-prepared teacher should provide an intensive intervention for these students that integrates language, literacy, and content, and the students' other teachers must be prepared to engage them in meaningful learning within a sea of diverse learners in each classroom.

Why Are There So Many Long-Term ELs in Secondary Schools?

From teacher and student interviews, we found insufficient rigor in K–12 instruction to be one of the main reasons we have so many long-term ELs in the upper grades. English learners do not progress academically when:

- Teachers do most of the reading for them. If ELs rarely get to read during the early stages of language development, their exposure to academic language and subject matter concepts is delayed.

- ELs do mostly independent or silent reading of books that have been leveled using formulas for mainstream readers. This often results in "pretend reading" and trying to guess content from pictures. ELs need explicit instruction on reading—specific to their range of needs.

- Elementary schools are not teaching three thousand English words per year within the context of learning all subjects. There are too many silent classroom assignments and too few opportunities for interaction to practice vocabulary within oral discourse, reading, and writing.

- Schools that do teach vocabulary teach it in isolation, without connections to reading, writing, and content learning. These schools have forgotten that vocabulary is only a means to learning to read, write cohesively, and master content concepts.

- Writing consists of canned mini-workshops that water it down to meaningless guesswork. Writing needs to be developed in tandem with the vocabulary ELs are learning and the text they have been reading.

- Secondary teachers are not accustomed to teaching vocabulary and discourse, reading, and writing strategies within their content areas. They feel an urgency to "cover" their content. (Ways of integrating language, literacy and content are suggested throughout this anthology.)

- Bilingual programs keep students in the primary language throughout elementary grades without teaching sufficient English. Even in dual-language programs, there is insufficient rich language development in the home language (L_1) and the dominant language of the society (L_2). There are newer structures for organizing a balance of English and L_1.

- Only one ESL teacher or a handful of bilingual teachers are held responsible for ELs. When all teachers and administrators participate in year-long learning focused on ELs, all students improve, not just ELs.

- Professional learning around EL instruction is reduced to a couple of teachers attending a workshop and then training other teachers in one- or two-hour sessions. Comprehensive training for all teachers, follow-up systematic coaching, and continuous learning about ELs in the school's professional learning communities should be the goal in every school.

The authors in this book describe strategies, plans, and resources for addressing these issues.

Who Are Your ELs?

Given the wide range of English learners and their backgrounds, it is important to identify specific needs before implementing a program or intervention. ELs come with a range of language and literacy skills and with varying degrees of core subject knowledge.

Long-Term ELs

The majority of ELs in U.S. schools are long-term ELs (LT-ELs)—students who have been in our school systems for seven or more years, are usually below grade level in reading, writing, and math, and do poorly on standardized tests. These ELs have been in and out of various instructional programs without having benefited from continuous and sustained instructional support programs. They were born and raised in the United States and attended U.S. schools from kindergarten on. They may have been reclassified or exited from ESL/bilingual programs but are still struggling academically. Some may have never been identified as English learners.

> LT-ELs are often socially, psychologically, and educationally isolated from mainstream students and in urgent need of effective approaches that will help them catch up and compete.

Most LT-ELs have conversational, social fluency in English but lack the grade-level academic language proficiency to succeed in mainstream English classrooms. They are often socially, psychologically, and educationally isolated from mainstream students and in urgent need of effective approaches, strategies, and curriculum that will help them catch up and compete. Their motivation may have been hampered, but it can be brought back as soon as they see they can be successful students.

Newcomers

LT-ELs comprise anywhere from 60 to 85 percent of ELs in U.S. schools. The remaining ELs are newcomers—refugees or recent immigrants. Some newcomers have had no or very little schooling and need special interventions that support them in adjusting to classroom, school, and community cultural norms. Others are highly schooled, with strong literacy skills in their native language, and can benefit from accelerated language proficiency skills. These well-educated newcomers sometimes know more math, science, world history, and geography than their English-speaking peers. They *expect* to be challenged through a rigorous curriculum.

Students With Interrupted Formal Education

Students with interrupted formal education (SIFE) are students who come into the upper elementary, middle, or high schools having low levels of literacy and content background knowledge in their home language. They might have attended school in their home countries for only one or two years or not at all. Their needs surpass the resources of regular ESL or bilingual programs. Older SIFE will need intensive interventions to catch up with basic skills, in order to build background for content lessons.

Some SIFE may have migrated from state to state with their parents, following agricultural harvesting schedules, but missing many school days. In many cases, they are brilliant students who have so much worldly knowledge that they learn quickly and become the recipients of scholarships to top universities. Their parents have a focused goal of helping them succeed, no matter the cost. In other cases, the struggles for day-to-day living are too overwhelming, and they may not have the privilege of systematic school attendance. A migrant student might become an LT-EL, or he or she could turn out to be the class valedictorian.

Special Education Students

Like their mainstream counterparts, some ELs may have exceptional education needs. Recognized disabilities include specific learning disabilities, speech or language impairment, mental retardation, hearing impairment, serious emotional disturbance, multiple disabilities, visual impairment, deafness and blindness, and autism.

However, English learners continue to be overrepresented in special education, due not to learning disabilities but to lack of English proficiency. Issues of English language proficiency are entwined with perceptions of disability. Unlike physical conditions that are more objectively verifiable, many learning disabilities are still assessed through observation, subjective judgment, or ambiguous tests. Some ELs are therefore diverted from opportunities, while others fail to get the help they need.

Whole-School, Evidence-Based Instructional Interventions

Through our studies and work with schools, including our observation of many classrooms throughout the country for various studies, panels, and reports, we have found common instructional, professional development, and school effectiveness features that work across school settings, content areas, and grade levels (Calderón, 2007a; Calderón & Minaya-Rowe, 2003; Calderón & Minaya-Rowe, 2011; Calderón, Slavin, & Sánchez, 2011).

> Whether gifted or learning English as a second or third language, every student needs explicit and varied instruction in vocabulary to build solid word power.

This section describes (1) what the research says about vocabulary instruction, reading, and writing instruction; (2) what is typically observed in classrooms with regard to these foundational components; and (3) how schools are addressing each of them and achieving—and maintaining—positive results.

Vocabulary Instruction

Reading specialists, second-language-acquisition experts, and linguists agree that explicit instruction in vocabulary is necessary in order for students to have robust vocabularies to use throughout their daily learning routines. Whether gifted or learning English as a second or third language, every student needs explicit and varied instruction to build solid word power.

What the Research Says

Research on vocabulary has found that:

- Teachers need to provide rich language experiences and direct instruction in vocabulary and word-learning strategies to ensure that students learn from three thousand to five thousand words a year (Biemiller, 2011; Calderón, 2011a, 2011b; Graves, August, & Carlo, 2011).

- Effective vocabulary instruction has to start early, in preschool, and continue throughout the school years (Calderón et al., 2005; Carlo, August, & Snow, 2005; Grabe, 2009; Graves, 2006; Nagy, 2005).

- Teaching vocabulary helps develop both phonological awareness (Nagy, 2005) and reading comprehension (Beck, McKeown, & Kucan, 2002; Hiebert & Kamil, 2005; Zweirs, 2008).

- Robust instruction offers rich information about words and their uses, provides frequent and varied opportunities for students to think about and use words, and enhances students' language comprehension and production (Beck et al., 2002; Carlo et al., 2005; Graves, 2006).

- To help ELs catch up with the words they are missing and build reading comprehension, vocabulary instruction needs to be explicitly taught before, during, and after reading (Calderón et al., 2005; Calderón, 2007a; Calderón & Minaya-Rowe, 2003).

- Vocabulary instruction should include phonology and morphology for pronunciation and spelling; syntax for word order and collocation; and formal and informal discourse through academic and social linguistic functions. It should stem from texts students are about to read, discuss, write about, and most importantly, learn the content of (Bailey, 2007; Calderón, 2011a; Calderón, 2011b; Calderón & Minaya-Rowe, 2011).

What We Have Observed in Classrooms

Explicit vocabulary instruction is rare in most classrooms, in particular in secondary schools. Three approaches are most prevalent: (1) send the student to the dictionary with long lists of words; (2) spend fifteen to thirty minutes teaching one word by asking students to copy definitions and sentences and draw pictures, or by generating complicated word-webs that leave them more confused; and (3) offer no instruction in word knowledge before jumping into reading or writing, and instead offer only an after-reading activity using worksheets. The children do not practice using vocabulary orally with peers in any of these approaches. Students "help" each other by either copying or correcting, but not constructing, vocabulary.

Constructing vocabulary and oracy consists of students using the words that are key to comprehending the teacher's instruction and the text they will be reading, and the words they will be asked to use in their writing. Vocabulary instruction does not mean teaching only one word or learning word by word; more often, words come in clusters (for example, *stored energy, equivalent weight, over the course of, I agree with, after the fact, prime minister, direct proportion, commutative property*). It means knowing how to start a question or a sentence with those key words. Vocabulary is learned in the context of oracy—oral practice within the context of a sentence or text in which that word needs to be used.

When Vocabulary Instruction Comes Together in Schools

The sequence of steps for teaching vocabulary begins with preteaching key words, followed by reading those words in the context of content to be learned. ELs continue learning new words as they read and then finally use them in their writing. Preteaching entails explicit but brisk instruction for each word or cluster, during which students practice forming sentences orally with peers. Students use the new words as they partner read and summarize after each paragraph. Finally, they write brief summaries using five or six of the new words and recapitulating the content they have learned. Vocabulary is only the first step in developing oracy, literacy, and content learning. Chapter 6 describes this process in further detail.

Essentially, teaching vocabulary should be pervasive throughout each school. The more teachers are involved in systematic vocabulary instruction, the faster ELs, disadvantaged students, and special education students learn and succeed. In schools where all the teachers and administrators applied and sustained these principles, we have seen evidence of accelerated learning (Calderón & Minaya-Rowe, 2011).

> Teaching vocabulary should be pervasive throughout each school. The more teachers are involved in systematic vocabulary instruction, the faster ELs, disadvantaged students, and special education students learn and succeed.

Reading Instruction

Teaching basic reading along with reading comprehension is one of the most complex instructional endeavors. Without reading comprehension, students cannot read or learn core subject matter.

What the Research Says

Educating the full range of ELs and low-achieving students in intellectually demanding programs will require education professionals to learn new ways of teaching, with a strong focus on reading in the content areas, not just second-language acquisition through simple oral drills (August et al., 2008; Calderón, 2009; Calderón, Slavin, & Sánchez, 2011; Short & Fitzsimmons, 2007; Slavin, Madden, Calderón, Chamberlain, & Hennessey, 2009). Many ELs who sound like fluent readers because they have mastered the constrained skills of letter knowledge, concepts of print, and phonics do not understand what they are reading. These features of reading have been constrained because meaning has been left out of reading in most K–2 classrooms. By middle school, these children have developed superficial reading habits but no depth of comprehension (August & Hakuta, 2006; Calderón, Slavin, & Sánchez, 2011).

When ELs are given the opportunity to apply a strategy in all their subject areas—math, science, social studies, as well as language arts—knowledge of that strategy is reinforced. When all content teachers use these reading comprehension strategies. ELs and other low-level readers improve in language, reading, and content knowledge. One of those strategies is partner reading or reciprocal teaching, where students work in pairs to practice reading aloud. After reading each paragraph, reading partners should stop to verbally summarize what they read, so that they can retain the information, practice any new words and phrases, and work on any comprehension problems by rereading and questioning. Naturally, the teacher models how to go about doing all this beforehand.

What We Have Observed in Classrooms

We observed two prevalent reading approaches in most K–12 classrooms: silent independent reading and teacher reading. Silent reading does not work for ELs (Calderón & Minaya-Rowe, 2011; Francis, Rivera, Moughamian, & Lesaux, 2008; Slavin & Calderón, 2001) or for students at risk (Denton et al., 2011). One can never tell if they are comprehending or just "pretend reading." In other classrooms we saw teachers read aloud to students and students answering low-level questions. Some middle school teachers read novels to their students. This kept the students quiet, with their heads on their desks, until the teacher asked a question. Some teachers asked students to take notes while being read to. This was followed by a handful of students sharing from their notes. In these classrooms, the students were also expected to write without having read good models of text to emulate. In all these cases, students were not reading, nor were they being taught to read.

Most language arts textbooks for both ELs and non-ELs currently in use recommend teaching them the following reading comprehension skills:

- Predict
- Determine important information
- Summarize
- Make inferences
- Use graphic and semantic organizers
- Visualize
- Ask and answer questions

- Make connections and use schema

- Monitor comprehension

All of these skills are useful in helping ELs develop reading strategies. The ones we observed most frequently in classrooms were making predictions, using graphic organizers, and answering questions on worksheets. ELs cannot be expected to make predictions and inferences or to visualize if they don't know 85–90 percent of the words necessary to describe that prediction or inference or to describe what they visualize (August & Shanahan, 2006). We also observed that newcomers and SIFE had difficulty making connections to areas of prior knowledge that were not part of their culture or schooling experiences (Calderón, 2007b). This background knowledge needs to be explicitly taught along with vocabulary before they can participate in these discussions.

When Reading Comes Together in Schools

Essentially, it is easier for ELs to begin with this sequence of skills:

1. Ask and answer questions.

2. Determine important information.

3. Summarize.

4. Make connections and use schema.

5. Monitor comprehension.

These cognitive and verbal processes are best practiced during partner reading and discussions only after a teacher presents them with academic discourse protocols, sentence starters, and subject-related common phrases. Chapter 3 of this book elaborates on background building; chapters 5 and 6 describe integrated approaches to language, literacy, and content.

Writing Instruction

Writing can be used as a means of personal expression, as a means to communicate knowledge, as evidence of comprehension, or as an audience-focused activity. Each of

Writing is the most difficult domain for ELs and their high school teachers.

these purposes has different assessment criteria (Graham, Harris, & Hebert, 2011). Writing is also the most difficult domain for ELs and their high school teachers. A newcomer may have good writing skills in the primary language, while a student who has been in a North American school since kindergarten may have oral fluency yet no writing skills in either the first or second language.

What the Research Shows

Although the research of Steve Graham, Karen Harris, and Michael Hebert (2011) and Steve Graham and Dolores Perin (2007) on students' difficulty with writing did not focus on ELs, their findings have implications for them nevertheless. Writing workshops, they discovered, have the smallest effect sizes of all writing approaches they studied (Graham & Hebert, 2010; Graham & Perin, 2007). They also identified certain methods that some of our schools have adapted and applied. The ones teachers of ELs find most useful are collaborative writing, summarization, the study of models, and writing for content knowledge.

What We Have Observed in Classrooms

Middle and high school teachers and administrators report that their greatest concern is students' low writing skills. In part, this is because the kinds of writing demands and the nature of instruction in science, history, and math vary from those of ESL and language arts classes. In fact, the writing we observed consisted of either filling in worksheets that accompany textbooks or "doing writing workshops" that show no evidence of being effective with ELs. We rarely observed explicit writing instruction, with all its basic steps, or writing connected to what students had been reading. Explicit word and discourse instruction in preparation for writing was negligible. When we visited second-grade classrooms with large numbers of ELs, we looked at student writing posted around the walls and read examples such as, "I like my pet. I like the ears. I like the nose. I like the color brown." When we visited ninth-grade classrooms with ELs, we read examples such as, "I like photosynthesis. I like analyses. I like procedures." The posted writing samples in Spanish were lengthier but contained many grammatical, punctuation, and spelling errors. The higher the grade, the larger the number of errors on student papers.

The lessons we observed on writing did little to generate quality writing from ELs. Teachers typically asked students to pick a topic from the board or gave them a topic to write on. Teachers then walked around trying to provide additional individual help to all students, but this approach became overwhelming when so many hands kept going up. There is precious little time allocated to writing, and that time is not being used in an efficient and effective way.

How Writing Comes Together In Schools

Writing comes together in schools when teachers model the type of writing they are requiring (for example, expository, procedural, persuasive, argumentative, essay, or research), explain how to edit for each type, and understand how the teacher will grade according to proficiency levels. An approach to writing we have adapted from previous research with good results for ELs (Graham & Hebert, 2010; Graham & Perin, 2007) follows a seven-step sequence (Calderón, 2011a; 2011b):

1. **Preteach the most important vocabulary**—Select key words that you want to see students use for writing assignments and grading.

2. **Develop background knowledge**—Students from different cultures approach writing differently and they also have different schooling experiences. Develop background knowledge or explanations of unfamiliar concepts, structures, and mechanics for writing by using the text they are reading.

3. **Describe it**—Discuss and present the strategy, its purpose, benefits, and goals, and the grading rules for finished products. Consider differentiated grading scales for ELs, depending on their level of English proficiency.

4. **Model it**—Model the writing you want them to emulate. Model each phase of the strategy. Show examples from the text they are reading.

5. **Support it**—Support or scaffold the student's use of the strategy until he or she can apply it with few or no supports. Model self-regulated learning and the use of mnemonic devices.

6. **Make ample use of student interaction**—Model and implement collaborative and cooperative writing strategies to plan, draft, revise, and edit compositions.

7. **Use differentiated assessment**—Assess the point of entry for writing (not just oral production), and continue measuring the learning progression of writing, since the oral, reading, and writing proficiencies for ELs vary dramatically.

Summary

Language and literacy development in K–3 has typically been relegated to how fast children can decode, with little attention given to depth of comprehension, with which children can interpret facts and integrate information from different sources. Very little time is given to science, civics, history, and current events. Everything seems centered on children's literature. When these children get to middle school, their marginal reading skills become the responsibility of the ESL or English/language arts teachers. No one actually teaches them to read math, science, and social studies, or schools them in the language structures they will need to discuss those subjects.

Reading, writing, and oral language proficiency are best developed simultaneously through rigorous but caring instruction. All students across the country need further development in reading, writing, and oracy—not just the English learners. Success leaps out when a whole school commits to this attainment.

References and Resources

August, D., Beck, I. L., Calderón, M., Francis, D.J., Lesaux, N. K., & Shanahan, T. (2008). Instruction and professional development. In D. August & T. Shanahan (Eds.), *Developing reading and writing in second-language learners: Lessons from the report of the National Literacy Panel on Language-Minority Children and Youth* (pp. 131–250). New York: Routledge.

August, D., & Calderón, M. (2006). Teacher beliefs and professional development. In D. August & T. Shanahan (Eds.), *Developing literacy in second-language learners: Report of the National Literacy Panel on Language-Minority Children and Youth* (pp. 555–582). Mahwah, NJ: Lawrence Erlbaum.

August, D., & T. Shanahan (Eds.). (2008). *Developing literacy in second-language learners: Report of the National Literacy Panel on Language-Minority Children and Youth.* Mahwah, NJ: Lawrence Erlbaum.

Bailey, A. (2007). *The language of school: Putting academic English to the test.* New Haven, CT: Yale University Press.

Beck, I., McKeown, M., & Kucan, L. (2002). *Bringing words to life: Robust vocabulary development.* New York: Guilford Press.

Biemiller, A. (2011). What words should we teach? *Better: Evidence-based Education, 3*(2), 10–11.

Calderón, M. E. (2007a). *Teaching reading to English language learners, grades 6–12: A framework for improving achievement in the content areas.* Thousand Oaks, CA: Corwin Press.

Calderón, M. E. (2007b). *RIGOR! Reading instructional goals for older readers: Reading program for 6th–12th students with interrupted formal education.* New York: Benchmark Education.

Calderón, M. (2009). Language, literacy and knowledge for ELLs. *Better: Evidence-based Education,* 1(1), 14–15.

Calderón, M. E. (2011a). *Teaching reading and comprehension to English learners, K–5.* Bloomington, IN: Solution Tree Press.

Calderón, M. (2011b). Teaching writing to ELLs in high schools. *Better: Evidence-based Education, 3*(2), 8–9.

Calderón, M., August, D., Slavin, R., Cheung, A., Durán, D., & Madden, N. (2005). Bringing words to life in classrooms with English language learners. In Hiebert, A & M. Kamil (Eds.), *Research and development on vocabulary pp..* Mahwah, NJ: Lawrence Erlbaum.

Calderón, M. E., & Minaya-Rowe, L. (2003). *Designing and implementing two-way bilingual programs: A step-by-step guide for administrators, teachers, and parents.* Thousand Oaks, CA: Corwin Press.

Calderón, M., & Minaya-Rowe, L. (2011). *Preventing long-term English language learners: Transforming schools to meet core standards.* Thousand Oaks, CA: Corwin Press.

Calderón, M., Slavin, R. E., & Sánchez, M. (2011). Effective instruction for English Language Learners. In M. Tienda & R. Haskins (Eds.). *The future of immigrant children (pp. 103–128).* Washington, DC: Brookings Institute/Princeton University.

Carlo, M. S., August, D., & Snow, C. E. (2005). Sustained vocabulary-learning strategy instruction for English language learners. In E. H. Hiebert & M. L. Kamil (Eds.), *Teaching and learning vocabulary: Bringing research to practice* (pp. 137–154). Mahwah, NJ: Lawrence Erlbaum.

Denton, A. C., Barth, A. E., Fletcher, J. M., Wexler, J., Vaughn, S., Cirino, P. T. et al. (2001). The relations among oral and silent reading fluency and comprehension in middle school: Implications for identification and instruction of students with reading difficulties. *Scientific Studies of Reading, 15*(2), 109–145.

DuFour, R., DuFour R., Eaker, R., & Karhanek, G. (2010). *Raising the bar and closing the gap: Whatever it takes.* Bloomington, IN: Solution Tree Press.

Francis, D. J., Rivera, M. O., Moughamian, A. C., & Lesaux, N. K. (2008). *Effective interventions for reaching reading to English language learners and English language learners with disabilities: Guidance document.* Portsmouth, NH: RMC Research, Center on Instruction.

Grabe, W. (2009). *Reading in a second language: Moving from theory to practice.* New York: Cambridge University Press.

Graham S., Harris, K., & Hebert, M. (2011). *Informing writing: The benefits of formative assessment: A report from Carnegie Corporation of New York.* Washington, DC: Alliance for Excellent Education.

Graham, S., & Hebert, M. (2010). *Writing to read: Evidence for how writing can improve reading.* Washington, DC: Alliance for Excellent Education.

Graham, S., & Perin, D. (2007). *Writing next: Effective strategies to improve writing of adolescents in middle and high schools.* Washington, DC: Alliance for Excellent Education.

Graves, M. F. (1986). Vocabulary learning and instruction. *Review of Research in Education, 13,* 49–89.

Graves, M. F. (2006). *The vocabulary book: Learning and instruction.* New York: Teachers College Press.

Graves, M. F., August, D., & Carlo, M. (2011). Teaching 50,000 words. *Better: Evidence-based Education, 3*(2), 6–7.

Hiebert, E. H., & Kamil, M. L. (Eds.). (2005). *Teaching and learning vocabulary: Bringing research to practice.* Mahwah, NJ: Lawrence Erlbaum.

Learning Forward. (2011). *Standards for professional learning.* Oxford, OH: Author.

Nagy, W. (2005). Why vocabulary instruction needs to be long-term and comprehensive. In E. H. Hiebert & M. L. Kamil (Eds.), *Teaching and learning vocabulary: Bringing research to practice* (pp. 27–44). Mahwah, NJ: Lawrence Erlbaum.

Nagy, W. E., & Herman, P. A. (1987). Breadth and depth of vocabulary knowledge: Implications for instruction. In M. G. McKeown & M. E. Curtis (Eds.), *The nature of vocabulary acquisition* (pp. 19–35). Mahwah, NJ: Lawrence Erlbaum.

Short, D. J., & Fitzsimmons, S. (2007). *Double the work: Challenges and solutions to acquiring language and academic literacy for adolescent English language learners.* Washington, DC: Alliance for Excellent Education.

Slavin, R. E., & Calderón, M. (Eds.). (2001). *Effective programs for Latino students.* Mahwah, NJ: Lawrence Erlbaum.

Slavin, R. E., Madden, N., Calderón, M., Chamberlain, A., & Hennessy, M. (2009). *Fifth-year reading and language outcomes of a randomized Evaluation of transitional bilingual education: Report to IES.* Washington, DC: Institute for Education Sciences, U.S. Department of Education.

Zwiers, J. (2008). *Building academic language: Essential practices for content classrooms, grades 5–12.* San Francisco: Jossey-Bass.

Robert E. Slavin

Robert Slavin is currently director of the Center for Research and Reform in Education at Johns Hopkins University, part-time professor at the Institute for Effective Education at the University of York, England, and Chairman of the Success for All Foundation. He received his BA in psychology from Reed College in 1972 and his PhD in Social Relations in 1975 from Johns Hopkins University.

Dr. Slavin has authored or coauthored more than three hundred articles and book chapters and twenty-four books, including *Educational Psychology: Theory Into Practice; Cooperative Learning: Theory, Research, and Practice; Show Me the Evidence: Proven and Promising Programs for America's Schools; Effective Programs for Latino Students; Educational Research in the Age of Accountability;* and *Two Million Children: Success for All.*

He has received the American Educational Research Association's Raymond B. Cattell Early Career Award for Programmatic Research, the Charles A. Dana Award, the James Bryant Conant Award from the Education Commission of the States, the Outstanding Leadership in Education Award from the Horace Mann League, the Distinguished Services Award from the Council of Chief State School Officers, and the AERA Review of Research Award and has twice received the Palmer O. Johnson award for the best article in an American Educational Research Association journal.

Dr. Slavin was appointed to the National Academy of Education in 2009 and became an AERA Fellow in 2010.

In this chapter, Dr. Slavin describes effective whole-school teaching for ELs, stresses that good teaching for ELs is good teaching for all students, and explains why teachers must create well-organized, interesting lessons, with opportunities for students to see key concepts, verbally describe their current understandings, receive feedback, and gain metacognitive skills.

Chapter 2

Effective Whole-School Teaching for English Learners

Robert E. Slavin

One of the fastest-growing groups of students in North American schools consists of students who are learning to speak English. They face serious difficulties in achieving the goals we expect for all, for they must learn literacy, numeracy, science, and social studies just like other students, but they must also become proficient enough in English to benefit from ordinary English instruction.

Not very long ago, the debate about teaching English learners revolved primarily around what their language of instruction should be. Advocates of transitional bilingual education argued that children should be taught to read in their native language and transitioned to English-only instruction gradually. Others argued for structured immersion, according to which ELs were taught only in English, with appropriate supports. Dual-language programs have long been popular in theory but difficult to put into practice. Politically, a reaction against bilingual education has greatly reduced the likelihood that ELs will receive much if any native language instruction. In any case, research has found few differences in English outcomes for Spanish-dominant ELs taught initially in Spanish or in English (Slavin, Madden, Calderón, Chamberlain, & Hennessy, 2011).

For all these reasons, it is more important than ever that teachers have solid strategies to help English learners succeed in the classroom. Once localized in parts of the United States, ELs are now found everywhere in North America. Teachers in every type of school can expect to encounter students who are not fully proficient in English, and they must be ready to help them succeed.

Good Teaching for ELs Is Good Teaching for All

The topic of effective teaching for English learners is complicated by such factors as students' home languages, levels of English proficiency, experiences with English outside of school, and social classes. For these and other reasons, generalizations about teaching ELs need to be made with caution. Obviously, the child of middle-class, educated parents who emigrated to the United States or Canada has a very different experience than a child whose immigrant parents are not literate in their home language; similarly, a teacher with a class full of Spanish-dominant children faces a different challenge from a teacher of children speaking many languages. Students who enter school with little or no English, either at preschool or kindergarten, and those entering with little English in the later grades have distinct needs, and even after English learners do have basic English, there is a long process of solidifying and extending their school language and learning the school's curriculum.

For those who have progressed beyond understanding the rudiments of English, the good news is that the evidence generally finds that effective strategies for ELs are broadly effective for English-proficient students as well. The result is that, while there are common-sense points of emphasis or adaptation to the needs of particular groups of children, teachers can be reasonably confident that whatever they do to help their English learners succeed in classroom instruction will be beneficial to all of their students. Teachers throughout elementary and secondary schools can learn and apply proven classroom and school strategies with confidence that they are benefiting the ELs as well as other students (Cheung & Slavin, 2005, 2012).

What Should Teachers Do?

Teachers of English learners should ensure that they do the following in daily instruction (Calderón, 2001; Calderón et al., 2004; Carlo et al., 2004; Cheung & Slavin, 2012; Slavin, 2012):

- Teach well-organized, interesting lessons.
- Maximize opportunities for students to see, not just hear, key concepts.
- Maximize opportunities for students to verbally describe their current understandings to other students and to hear their peers' perspectives and feedback.
- Maximize opportunities for students to "learn how to learn" by gaining metacognitive skills that help them study, retain information, and know how to apply new skills.

Let's look at each of these in turn.

Teach Well-Organized, Interesting Lessons

English learners depend on the clarity and organization of lessons even more than other students. They need to see the structure of a lesson and be very clear about where it is going, where they are on that path, and what is being asked of them.

Imagine, for example, that a teacher is presenting a lesson on the three branches of the U.S. government. It is easy for ELs to get confused if the teacher zigzags among the three branches, making it unclear which is being discussed. Pictorial graphics showing each of the branches are likely to give ELs mental categories in which to file information (and unfamiliar language). Instead of just saying, "The executive branch is responsible for security, education, and international affairs," a teacher can show pictures of policemen, soldiers, schools, and images of other countries linked with a picture of the White House, so students can file the words and pictures together in their minds.

> English learners depend on the clarity and organization of lessons even more than other students. They need to see the structure of a lesson and be very clear about where it is going and what is being asked of them.

Teachers should also verbally or symbolically mark transitions from one topic to another, perhaps saying, "We've been talking about the *legislative branch,* the Congress, which passes the laws. Now we'll learn about the *executive branch,* which makes sure the laws are carried out."

One of the most common mistakes teachers make in working with English learners is failing to be clear about exactly what they are asking them to do. Using clear, simple language assignments or questions helps. Teachers may also model a good response for students and check to be sure they know what to do.

Another common mistake is teaching too slowly. Just like everyone else, ELs get bored when things are moving slowly. Using many examples, giving many opportunities to respond, and teaching clear, well-organized lessons with many visuals allows teachers to go at a faster rate, which both engages students and covers more material.

Maximize Opportunities to See Key Concepts

All children can benefit from more visual input to illustrate auditory input. English learners need this even more, however. Whenever possible, they need to see pictures or videos of essential objects or ideas behind lesson content. This provides not only excellent language development, but also mental "markers" that children can return to when in doubt. For example, in a lesson on adaptations to the environment among animals, showing a spotted leopard in a dappled jungle not only reinforces the word *camouflage,* it also anchors the concept of why it is useful for the leopard to have spots, and why the leopard evolved that way. Showing a clearly visible leopard disappearing into a dappled forest further anchors the word and the concept.

Today, still and video images are readily available online for just about any subject, to be shown on DVDs, interactive whiteboards, video monitors, or other devices. It is well worth finding images to drive home the key points of any lesson for ELs.

There are a few cautions to note, however. Research on the use of video and still images finds that they can be useless or detrimental if they do not support, or worse, if they distract from the main points (Mayer, 2009). Images or information that distract are known as *seductive details.* Video or still images must lead to the lesson objective. The images should simplify or unify the key ideas, not add further complications.

Maximize Opportunities to Verbally Describe and Hear Feedback

This is perhaps the most important of the principles described in this chapter. Anyone who has ever successfully learned a language knows how important it is to use it many times, in new ways, to solve real problems. This is why people who study languages in school for many years may learn little in comparison to those who live in a foreign country for even a few months.

Some ELs are brave and confident in using their new English, but many are shy and unsure of themselves, not wanting to be laughed at. Teachers have long noted how quickly most ELs learn playground English but how slowly they learn school English. The reason is that, in an integrated school or in daily life, ELs are likely to use their burgeoning English skills casually with their peers on the playground, but they may be too silent and shy in class to get much practice with formal English. If you travel in a foreign country and have partial skill with the language spoken there, think about how much easier it is to order food (a skill you are likely to practice often) than it would be to discuss science or literature (a skill in which you are unlikely to have had much verbal practice).

The solution for this problem is regular, daily use of cooperative learning strategies (Slavin, 1995, 2012; Webb, 2008). These are methods in which children work in teams (usually of four to five) and help each other learn academic content. The success of the team depends on the individual learning of all team members. For example, in a technique called *random reporter,* each team member has a secret number. At regular intervals, the teacher calls on "number threes," for example, to represent their teams. Teams earn points toward weekly recognition based on these responses. Since students do not know who will be called, they must prepare all team members to answer any question.

Well-structured cooperative learning methods improve the learning of English learners as well as that of other students of all ages and in many subjects.

In the process of preparing each other, teaching each other, asking each other questions, and so on, team members get plenty of opportunities to express their current understandings, obtain feedback, and most importantly, use their school English in meaningful contexts. A great deal of research has found that well-structured cooperative learning methods of this kind improve the learning of English learners as well as that of other students of all ages and in many subjects (Calderón, Hertz-Lazarowitz, & Slavin, 1998; Slavin, 1995; Webb, 2008).

Maximize Opportunities to Gain Metacognitive Skills

Long ago, it was believed that some students just knew how to learn and others didn't, and there wasn't much one could do about it. Today, research has identified many strategies for learning that all children can learn and apply (Bransford et al., 2005; Slavin, 2012). English learners appear to benefit in particular from these metacognitive skills (Cheung & Slavin, 2012).

One metacognitive skill used across many subjects is particularly useful for English learners. This is the use of graphic organizers, such as webs, charts, outlines, and so on. Graphic organizers help students sort out their thinking on a given topic and identify linkages, major and minor points, and so on.

Figure 2.1 (page 33) shows a partially filled out idea tree, which is a type of graphic organizer.

Another useful strategy for reading narrative or expository text is called *clarification*. When students read, they often encounter words or phrases they do not understand. To avoid blocking the flow, students are encouraged to mark difficult words with a sticky note and then go back at regular intervals to figure them out. Sometimes the words have been made clear by later content, but if not, students are taught a set of strategies, such as using context, background knowledge, and electronic or print dictionaries.

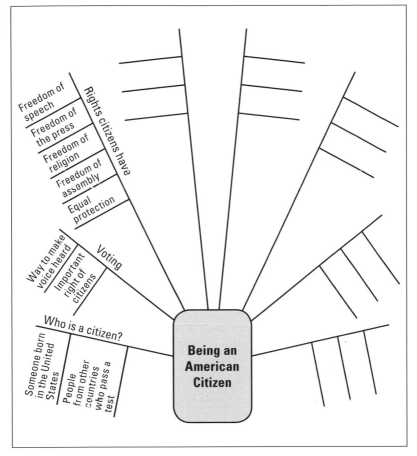

Figure 2.1: A partially completed idea tree.

Prediction is a useful strategy, especially for narrative text, and *summarization* is useful for all sorts of text. These and other metacognitive strategies, practiced many times with cooperative groups, give students a sense of mastery over their reading, writing, and content learning—a confidence that they don't merely know things but know how to learn anything they encounter (Bransford et al., 2006; Pressley, 2003; Schunk & Zimmerman, 2003).

Comprehensive School Reform

Any teacher of English learners (and other students) can use the strategies just discussed, and for most teachers, they may be all that is needed. However, in schools serving many disadvantaged students, ELs or not, more comprehensive solutions are available. The most widely used and extensively evaluated is Success for All, a program that works with all students in grades preK to 8. Success for All provides extensive professional development in:

- Cooperative learning

- Teaching of metacognitive, learning-to-learn skills

- Embedded multimedia (video content to illustrate key concepts)

- Fast-paced, exciting lessons

- Frequent formative assessments and feedback

- Computer-assisted small-group or individualized tutoring for struggling readers

- Parent involvement and solution of out-of-school problems

Success for All has been particularly successful in schools serving English learners, in all types of communities (Borman et al., 2007; Calderón, Hertz-Lazarowitz, & Slavin, 1998; Cheung & Slavin, 2005, 2012; Slavin, Madden, Chambers, & Haxby, 2009). It was one of the few programs awarded scale-up funding by the U.S. Department of Education's Investing in Innovation program, which helps schools adopt programs that have met a high standard of evidence of effectiveness.

Uniting to Improve Schools for English Learners

Implementing a schoolwide strategy to improve learning outcomes for English learners should involve all teachers and administrators in the school. Staff members should agree on goals, look at summaries of research on effective programs, and then formulate a plan for professional development and implementation of proven approaches. They might consider seeking information on comprehensive reform models that will deal with all key issues in improving outcomes, or they may decide to assemble their own set of approaches. Whichever initial strategies are suggested, subgroups may volunteer to explore options, find out about costs and time requirements, and investigate district, state, and Title I resources to support professional development. Providers of comprehensive reform or other professional development approaches might be invited to present at the school, and a delegation might visit other schools to see models of proven, replicable programs in practice.

The process of forming a plan for professional development should be informed by evidence of effectiveness for various programs and approaches. That is, the emphasis should be on programs that have met the following standards (Slavin, 2008):

1. The program has been evaluated in comparison to a well-matched control group.

2. Studies have taken place over periods of at least twelve weeks, involving many schools.

3. Studies used fair and reliable measures of skills taught in all classes.

4. Learning in the groups using the program was significantly higher than learning in control groups.

Reviews of studies on effective programs for English learners and other students appear on the Best Evidence Encyclopedia (BEE), at www.bestevidence.org.

Conclusion

Effective teaching of English learners is mainly a question of adapting proven approaches for students in general for the particular needs of students learning English. All students benefit from well-structured lessons, supportive visuals, cooperative learning, and metacognitive skills, but English learners appear to have particularly strong needs for these strategies, in order to help them build the language, confidence, strategies, and motivation needed by all. Research on effective methods for English learners gives every indication that teachers can enable these students to achieve at much higher levels than those that are currently typical.

References and Resources

Borman, G., Slavin, R. E., Cheung, A., Chamberlain, A., Madden, N. A., & Chambers, B. (2007). Final reading outcomes of the national randomized field trial of Success for All. *American Educational Research Journal, 44*(3), 701–703.

Bransford, J., Vye, N., Stevens, R., Kuhl, P., Schwartz, D., Bell, P., et al. (2006). Learning theories and education: Toward a decade of synergy. In P. Alexander & P. Winne (Eds.), *Handbook of Educational Psychology* (2nd ed., pp. 209–244). Mahwah, NJ: Erlbaum.

Calderón, M. (2001). Curricula and methodologies used to teach Spanish-speaking limited English proficient students to read English. In R. Slavin & M. Calderón (Eds.), *Effective programs for Latino students* (pp. 251–305). Mahwah, NJ: Erlbaum.

Calderón, M., August, D., Slavin, R. E., Duran, D., Madden, N. A., & Cheung, A. (2004). *The evaluation of a bilingual transition program for Success for All.* Baltimore: Johns Hopkins University, Center for Research on the Education of Students Placed at Risk.

Calderón, M., Hertz-Lazarowitz, R., & Slavin, R. E. (1998). Effects of bilingual cooperative integrated reading and composition on students transitioning from Spanish to English reading. *Elementary School Journal, 99*(2), 153–166.

Calderón, M. E., & Minaya-Rowe, L. (2003). *Designing and implementing two-way bilingual programs.* Thousand Oaks, CA: Corwin Press.

Carlo, M. S., August, D., McLaughlin, B., Snow, C. E., Dressler, C., Lippman, D., et al. (2004). Closing the gap: Addressing the vocabulary needs of English language learners in bilingual and mainstream classrooms. *Reading Research Quarterly, 39*(2), 188–215.

Cheung, A., & Slavin, R. E. (2005). Effective reading programs for English language learners and other language-minority students. *Bilingual Research Journal, 29*(2), 241–267.

Cheung, A., & Slavin, R. E. (2012). *Effective reading programs for Spanish-dominant English language learners in the elementary grades: A synthesis of research.* Baltimore: Center for Research and Reform in Education.

Fashola, O. S., Slavin, R. E., Calderón, M., & Durán, R. (2001). Effective programs for Latino students in elementary and middle schools. In R. E. Slavin and M. Calderón (Eds.), *Effective programs for Latino students* (pp. 1–54). Mahwah, NJ: Lawrence Erlbaum.

Mayer, R. E. (2009). *Multimedia learning* (2nd ed.). New York: Cambridge University Press.

Pressley, M. (2003). Psychology of literacy and literacy instruction. In W. M. Reynolds & G. E. Miller (Eds.), *Handbook of Psychology, Volume 7* (pp. 333–356). Hoboken, NJ: Wiley.

Schunk, D. H., & Zimmerman, B. J. (2003). Self-regulation and learning. In W. M. Reynolds & G. E. Miller (Eds.), *Handbook of Psychology, Volume 7* (pp. 59–78). Hoboken, NJ: Wiley.

Slavin, R. E. (2008). What works? Issues in synthesizing educational program evaluations. Educational Researcher, *37*(1), 5–14.

Slavin, R. E. (2012). *Educational psychology: Theory into practice* (10th ed.). Boston: Allyn & Bacon.

Slavin, R. E., & Calderón, M. (Eds.). (2001). *Effective programs for Latino students.* Mahwah, NJ: Lawrence Erlbaum.

Slavin, R. E., & Cheung, A. (2004). How do English language learners learn to read? *Educational Leadership, 61*(6), 52–57.

Slavin, R. E., & Cheung, A. (2005). A synthesis of research on language of reading instruction for English language learners. *Review of Educational Research, 75*(2), 247–284.

Slavin, R. E., & Madden, N. A. (1999). Effects of bilingual and English as a second language adaptations of success for all on the reading achievement of students acquiring English. *Journal of Education for Students Placed at Risk, 4*(4), 393–416.

Slavin, R. E., Madden, N. A., Calderón, M. E., Chamberlain, A., & Hennessy, M. (2011). Reading and language outcomes of a five-year randomized evaluation of transitional bilingual education. *Educational Evaluation and Policy Analysis, 33*(1), 47–58.

Slavin, R. E., Madden, N. A., Chambers, B., & Haxby, B. (2009). *Two million children: Success for all.* Thousand Oaks, CA: Corwin Press.

Webb, N. M. (2008). Learning in small groups. In T. L. Good (Ed.), *21st century education: A reference handbook* (pp. 203–211). Los Angeles: SAGE.

Claude Goldenberg

A native of Argentina, Claude Goldenberg is professor of education at Stanford University. He was previously at California State University, where he was professor of teacher education, associate dean of the College of Education, and executive director of the Center for Language Minority Education and Research.

Dr. Goldenberg received his AB in history from Princeton University and MA and PhD from the Graduate School of Education, University of California at Los Angeles. He has taught junior high school in San Antonio, Texas, and first grade in a bilingual elementary school in the Los Angeles area.

Dr. Goldenberg was a National Academy of Education Spencer Fellow from 1986–88. He has received the Albert J. Harris Award (along with Ronald Gallimore) from the International Reading Association and the Distinguished Faculty Scholarly and Creative Activities Award from California State University, Long Beach.

In 1997, he produced *Settings for Change,* a video describing a five-year school improvement project that raised literacy achievement in a largely Latino, bilingual elementary. The book based on this project, *Successful School Change: Creating Settings to Improve Teaching and Learning,* led to research (in collaboration with Bill Saunders, Ronald Gallimore, and Brad Ermeling) that won the Best Research Award from Learning Forward.

Dr. Goldenberg's books include *Promoting Academic Achievement Among English Learners: A Guide to the Research,* coauthored with Rhoda Coleman, and *Language and Literacy Development in Bilingual Settings,* coedited with Aydin Durgunoglu.

In this chapter, Dr. Goldenberg calls attention to how little research exists to document the effects of many of the instructional practices currently used with ELs and suggests four important principles that can serve as a framework for instruction. These approaches integrate multiple components and acknowledge the importance of a focused and coherent schoolwide approach.

Chapter 3

Research on English Learner Instruction

Claude Goldenberg

The number of professional publications aimed at improving instruction for English learners has exploded since the early 2000s. Dozens of books, articles, and reports were published in the space of a few years following the appearance of two major research reviews in 2006 (August & Shanahan, 2006; Genesee, Lindholm-Leary, Saunders, & Christian, 2006). According to one count, nearly fifteen books on the topic of English learning were published in 2010 alone (Gold, 2010), most aimed at professional audiences.[1]

Yet there is surprisingly little research on common practices and recommendations for practice with ELs. This absence of adequate research applies to all areas, including promoting English language development and instruction in content areas such as math and history. In 2006, Genesee et al. commented that there is "a dearth of empirical research on instructional strategies or approaches to teaching content" for ELs (p. 190). Janzen (2008) echoed the same theme in a subsequent review of research on content area instruction for ELs. Rather than providing a list of instructional practices specifically validated by research as effective with ELs—which would be

---

[1] My thanks to Norm Gold, who is heroically attempting to help us all keep up with this spate of publications.

a very short list—I instead identify four important principles based in the research. These are:

1. Generally effective practices are likely to be effective with ELs.

2. ELs require additional instructional supports.

3. ELs need early and ample opportunities to develop proficiency in English.

4. The home language can be used to promote academic development.

For each principle, I provide specific examples from research on ELs.

Generally Effective Practices Are Likely to Be Effective With ELs

There is a vast literature on effective teaching practices. Educational research over more than a half-century has yielded a number of reasonably consistent findings about the features of teaching likely to result in improved student learning.[2] These include:

- Clear goals and objectives

- Appropriate and challenging material

- Well-designed instruction and instructional routines

- Clear input and modeling

- Active student engagement and participation

- Informative feedback to learners

- Application of new learning and transfer to new situations

- Practice and periodic review

- Structured, focused interactions with other students

- Frequent assessments, with reteaching as needed

- Well-established classroom routines and behavior norms

---

[2] Two useful references that provide somewhat contrasting, but in many respects overlapping, perspectives can be found in Darling-Hammond and Bransford (2005) and Marzano (2007).

Virtually all published studies that have demonstrated positive effects on ELs' achievement have at least several of these features incorporated into the instructional procedures. For example, Gómez, Parker, Lara-Alecio, and Gómez (1996) found that structured writing instruction—including teacher instruction, error correction and feedback, and a focus on building writing skills— had more positive effects on fifth-grade ELs' writing than did a free writing approach with no explicit instruction or error correction other than teachers responding to student writing through written comments. Both groups were allowed to write in either Spanish or English. Another writing study with native Cantonese speakers in Hong Kong reported similar findings—explicit teaching of revision strategies helped improve the quality of student writing and helped students learn to write so that readers could understand them (Sengupta, 2000).

Many other studies illustrate the value of well-known elements of effective instruction to promote the learning of ELs, whether in vocabulary instruction (Carlo et al., 2004; Collins, 2005), early reading interventions (Vaughn et al., 2006), English language development (Tong, Lara-Alecio, Irby, Mathes, & Kwok, 2008), or science education (Lee, Deaktor, Hart, Cuevas, & Enders, 2005). In fact, several studies have shown similar effects on both ELs and non-ELs (Carlo et al., 2004; Lee et al., 2005), again suggesting that there is considerable overlap between what is effective instruction for ELs and what is effective for students already proficient in English.

Cheung and Slavin reviewed many of the same studies as the National Literacy Panel (August & Shanahan, 2006) and concluded that "the programs with the strongest evidence of effectiveness in this review are all programs that have also been found to be effective with students in general" (Cheung & Slavin, 2005, p. 262) and modified for ELs (see the next section, on instructional supports and modifications). These programs include various versions of Success for All, a schoolwide program that involves far more than classroom instruction (see chapter 2 of this volume), Direct Instruction (DISTAR), and phonics instruction programs. Other programs with at least some evidence of effectiveness included vocabulary instruction programs (Carlo et al., 2004), a comprehensive language arts program combining direct teaching and literature study (Saunders, 1999; Saunders & Goldenberg, 1999), a program that promoted reading between parents and kindergarten children (Goldenberg, 1990), a Spanish version of Reading Recovery (Escamilla, 1994), an English tutoring program (Denton, Anthony, Parker, & Hasbrouck, 2004), and cooperative learning (Calderón, Hertz-Lazarowitz, & Slavin, 1998).

> Effective instruction in general is the foundation of effective instruction for ELs. However, while "generic" effective instruction is almost certainly a necessary base, it is probably not sufficient.

The key message is that what we know about effective instruction in general is the foundation of effective instruction for ELs. However, as we'll see in the next section, while "generic" effective instruction is almost certainly a necessary base, it is probably not sufficient to promote accelerated learning among ELs.

ELs Require Additional Instructional Supports

ELs in an English instructional environment will almost certainly need additional supports so that instruction is meaningful and productive. Aside from the pedagogical need, there is also the legal requirement mandated by the Supreme Court's decision in *Lau v. Nichols* (1974) that classroom instruction must be meaningful to students even if their English language proficiency is limited (see chapters 4, 5, and 6). The need for additional supports is particularly true for instruction aimed at higher-level content and comprehension of academic texts. One of the most important findings of the National Literacy Panel (August & Shanahan, 2006) was that the effects of reading instruction on ELs' reading comprehension were uneven and often nonexistent even when comprehension skills were taught directly. This is in contrast to studies with English-proficient students, for whom reading instruction helps improve reading comprehension (National Reading Panel [NRP], 2000).

Why does improving reading comprehension for English learners instructed in English appear so elusive? A likely explanation is that lower levels of English proficiency interfere with comprehension and can blunt the effects of otherwise effective instruction. Bill Saunders and I conducted a study that suggests this possibility (Saunders & Goldenberg, 2007). We randomly assigned a group of ELs either to an instructional conversation group (interactive teacher-led discussions designed to promote better understanding of what students read) or a control condition, where the teacher used comprehension questions in the teacher's guide. We found that instructional conversations had no overall effect on ELs' story comprehension—students in both groups understood the story about equally. We did find that instructional conversations produced deeper understandings of a complex concept at the heart of a story the students read, but this is different from story comprehension.

However, when we looked at the results for students with different English proficiency levels, we found something striking: for the highest–English proficient students, participation in instructional conversations did have an impact on story comprehension—91 percent accuracy versus 73 percent accuracy for students in the comparison group. The middle-level students also did better with instructional conversations, but the results were not statistically significant. The lowest-level English speakers did worse with instructional conversations, although also not to a statistically significant degree. These results suggest that instruction aimed at improving ELs' comprehension is likely to be more effective when ELs have relatively higher English skills, but less effective, or even *in*effective, when their English skills are lower.

One obvious implication is that we need to focus on English language development for ELs, particularly those least proficient in English. This is the topic of the next section of this chapter (see also chapters 1 and 6 of this volume). But what can teachers do to help ELs who are developing their English skills as they simultaneously learn advanced academic content and skills in English?

Sheltered Instruction

To meet this challenge, educators and researchers have proposed a set of instructional supports or modifications that are sometimes referred to as *sheltered instruction* (Echevarria, Vogt, & Short, 2008).

The goal of sheltered strategies is to facilitate the learning of grade-level academic content and skills for students being instructed in English but who have limited proficiency in the language. Sheltered instruction can be expected to contribute to English language development, but its real focus is academic content and skills.

Some of the supports and modifications that have been proposed for instructing ELs include:

- Building on student experiences and using material with familiar content

- Providing students with necessary background knowledge

- Using graphic organizers (tables, webs, Venn diagrams)

- Making instruction and learning tasks extremely clear

- Using pictures, demonstrations, real-life objects

- Providing hands-on, interactive learning activities

- Providing redundant information (gestures, visual cues)

- Giving additional practice and time for discussion of key concepts

- Designating language *and* content objectives for each lesson

- Using sentence frames and models to help students talk about academic content

- Providing instruction differentiated by students' English language proficiency

There are also sheltered strategies that involve strategic use of students' home language—for example, cognates and other L_1 support. These will be discussed in the fourth section, on use of the home language for classroom instruction.

The problem, however, is that we do not have a great deal of evidence that these strategies actually help English learners overcome the challenges they face in learning advanced academic content and skills. There are virtually no data to suggest that sheltered instruction or any of these modifications and supports help ELs keep up with non-ELs or help close the achievement gap between them. For some of the items on the list, such as the use of content and language objectives, sentence frames, and differentiating instruction by English proficiency levels, there are no published data at all about their effects on ELs' learning.

Even the most popular sheltered model in existence and one that brings together many disparate elements into a useful and coherent model—the Sheltered Instruction Observation Protocol (SIOP) (Echevarria et al., 2008)—has yet to demonstrate more than a very modest effect on student learning (Echevarria, Short, & Powers, 2006). A recent study showed stronger effects than did Echevarria et al. (2006), but unfortunately researchers excluded from the analysis classrooms with lower implementation levels (McIntyre, Kyle, Chen, Muñoz, & Beldon, 2010).

We also have compelling portraits of teachers who incorporate many of the supports included in the SIOP into their teaching in order to make instruction more meaningful for English learners and to promote academic language skills. Dong (2002), for example, describes high school biology teachers who integrate language and content instruction; use hands-on activities, pictures, and diagrams; build on student background and experiences; and provide opportunities and time for discussion and language use. But we do not know the extent to which these supports actually compensate for students' lack of proficiency in English, particularly in the sort of English language skills required for academic success. (See also chapter 6, which describes the combination of instructional strategies in the ExC-ELL approach.)

> We have compelling portraits of teachers who incorporate supports into their teaching, but we do not know the extent to which these supports can actually compensate for students' lack of proficiency in English.

Some Evidence of Benefits

There is some evidence that these supports and modifications do benefit ELs. For example, studies reviewed by the National Literacy Panel (August & Shanahan, 2006) find that building on student experiences and using material with familiar content can facilitate ELs' literacy development and reading comprehension. One ethnographic study finds that the writing development of young English learners is helped by the teacher's incorporating literacy activities and materials from home and community into classroom activities (Kenner, 1999). Another set of studies shows that second-language learners' reading comprehension improves when they read material with familiar content (Abu-Rabia, 1996; Lasisi, Falodun, & Onyehalu, 1988).

It is generally true that what we know and are already familiar with can influence new learning and the comprehension of what we read (McNamara & Kintsch, 1996; Tobias, 1994). Teachers should therefore use materials with some degree of familiarity to students. If students are to read material with unfamiliar content, it is important to help them acquire the necessary background knowledge. Building background or building on prior experience and familiar content might be especially important for ELs, since they face the double challenge of learning academic content and skills as they learn the language of instruction. However, like all students, ELs must learn to read and comprehend unfamiliar material.

There is also a substantial literature on graphic displays and organizers, which facilitate and support learning by clarifying content and making explicit the relationships among concepts (Nesbit & Adesope, 2006). Tang (1992) found that graphic representations helped improve seventh-grade Canadian ESL students' comprehension and academic language, but this appears to be the only study of its kind with second-language learners (Jiang & Grabe, 2007). Nussbaum (2002) also described the use of graphic organizers to help sixth-grade ELs write a historical argument, although he concluded that students would have benefited from additional explicit instruction in historical writing.

Perhaps these and other instructional supports, which are applicable to learners generally, are especially important or helpful for ELs. That certainly makes intuitive sense, but we have scant evidence either way. In fact, there is some evidence that these supports are equally effective for ELs and non-ELs. Lee et al. (2005) taught students explicitly about the science inquiry method by using pictures to illustrate the process, employing multiple modes of representation (for example, verbal, gestural, graphic, or written), and incorporating students' prior linguistic and cultural knowledge into the instruction. Carlo et al. (2004) built their intervention around the topic of immigration, which presumably had considerable resonance for the ELs, who were themselves or had parents who were immigrants from Latin American or the Caribbean. Carlo et al. (2004) also used supports in the home language. Neither study found any difference in learning outcomes for ELs and non-ELs.

A study by Silverman and Hines (2009) represents a new development. These researchers found that "multimedia-enhanced instruction" (videos used as part of lessons) helped make read-aloud vocabulary instruction more effective for ELs in preschool to second grade, but had no effect on the learning of non-ELs. Teachers used videos related to the topics in books they read aloud to their students as part of the science curriculum on habitats (for example, coral reefs or deserts). The ELs who saw the videos as part of the vocabulary instruction learned more of the target words and made greater gains on a general vocabulary measure than those who did not. The videos helped either greatly diminish or eliminate the gap in vocabulary knowledge between ELs and non-ELs. This suggests a potentially very effective strategy that improves ELs' vocabulary learning while not compromising the learning of students already proficient in English.

In short, we have many promising leads but not a very good understanding of how to help ELs learn high-level academic content and skills despite limited English proficiency. What Janzen (2008, p. 1015) says about instruction focusing on language in addition to academic content—"the published research is at an early stage"—is equally true for other supports intended to help ELs achieve at high academic levels.

ELs Need Early and Ample Opportunities to Develop Proficiency in English

Bill Saunders and I reviewed available research to derive principles to guide the teaching of English to ELs (Saunders & Goldenberg, 2010). As in the other areas discussed in this chapter, there is a shortage of research on many vital questions having to do with English

> The foreign language literature is useful and informative, but we must be careful about generalizing from Hong Kong businessmen learning English to sixth-grade ELs in Chicago.

language development (ELD) instruction for ELs. We know, in fact, surprisingly little about the relative effects, benefits, and disadvantages of different approaches to promoting ELD for ELs in K–12 schools. There is considerable research on second-language instruction conducted with university and adult populations learning a foreign language for professional or academic reasons, but far less for students whose second language is the majority language of the school and the society. The foreign language literature is useful and informative, but we must be careful about generalizing from research, for example, on Hong Kong businessmen learning English to sixth-grade ELs in Chicago.

With these cautions in mind, we proposed a number of guidelines for providing ELD instruction for English learners. The guidelines have varying degrees of research support, and some are based on research in other curriculum areas. But they are the most grounded we have, based on research that attempts to relate particular approaches or strategies to student learning outcomes.

1. Providing ELD instruction is better than not providing it.

2. ELD instruction should include interactive activities among students, but they must be carefully planned and carried out.

3. A separate, daily block of time should be devoted to ELD instruction.

4. ELD instruction should emphasize listening and speaking, although it can incorporate reading and writing.

5. ELD instruction should explicitly teach elements of English (e.g., vocabulary, syntax, grammar, functions, and conventions).

6. ELD instruction should integrate meaning and communication to support explicit teaching of language.

7. ELD instruction should provide students with corrective feedback on form.

8. Use of English during ELD instruction should be maximized; the primary language should be used strategically.

9. Teachers should attend to communication and language-learning strategies and incorporate them into ELD instruction.

10. ELD instruction should emphasize academic language as well as conversational language.

11. ELD instruction should continue at least until students reach level 4 (early advanced) and possibly through level 5 (advanced).

12. ELD instruction should be planned and delivered with specific language objectives in mind.

13. English learners should be carefully grouped by language proficiency for ELD instruction; for other portions of the school day they should be in mixed classrooms and not in classrooms segregated by language proficiency.

14. The likelihood of establishing and/or sustaining an effective ELD instructional program increases when schools and districts make it a priority.

(Saunders & Goldenberg, 2010, pp. 35–36)

Space does not permit a thorough discussion of all the guidelines, so I will make just a few key points. To begin, it might seem odd to include the first guideline, suggesting that students should be provided with instruction. Of the many controversies in the ELD field, perhaps the most fundamental is whether a second language can actually be *taught* as opposed to acquired through actual use. Although it is true that it is impossible to become a competent second-language speaker without ample opportunities to use the language for communicative purposes (in contrast, say, to using it in contrived classroom lessons), it is also the case that instruction in how to use a second language contributes to promoting second-language competence. What that instruction should comprise, of course, is another matter.

Second, there are many controversies over how to approach second-language instruction. (See Lightbown and Spada, 2006, for an excellent discussion.) For example, some researchers and practitioners advocate a communicative approach, in which language is not the object of instruction but is rather used for authentic communication, which then leads to second-language acquisition. The contrasting perspective is to focus on formal aspects of a second language, more along the lines of traditional language instruction in "correct" usage—grammar, vocabulary, idioms, and so on. Another controversy has to do with the use of feedback: one view holds that explicit feedback disrupts communication and is demotivating to second-language learners; another says that feedback provides second-language learners with important information about language conventions that would be missed by learners if not pointed out to them.

There is probably merit to both sides of these and other controversies in second-language teaching. At the moment, we do not have research that would rule definitively in favor of one or the other. Consequently, teachers must adopt a pragmatic and nondogmatic perspective. It is probably the case that both communicative and formal approaches to ELD instruction make important contributions to second-language learning and acquisition. The same is true for feedback. Some strategic feedback is almost certainly helpful, but too much or poorly timed feedback can be counterproductive. However, we do not know where the balance lies in either case. Researchers and practitioners have more work to do in helping identify what the balance is and how it varies for different learners under different circumstances.

Third, and related to the first point, whether a second language can be taught, there is some, although limited, evidence to support the claim that efforts by teachers and schools to promote ELD can probably have a substantial impact on students' acquisition of language proficiencies critical for school success. The study by Tong et al.

(2008) found that kindergarten and first-grade students provided with an "English-oracy intervention" experienced more accelerated ELD growth compared to students in control schools who received typical ESL instruction. The effects were seen in schools using English immersion (all-English instruction) and in schools with bilingual education programs. The ELD intervention consisted of (1) daily English tutorials with a published ELD program; (2) storytelling and retelling with authentic, culturally relevant literature and questions leveled from easy to difficult; and (3) an academic oral language activity using a "question of the day." Students who participated in the experimental treatment also received more ELD instructional time. It is therefore possible that the additional time explains the results. Nonetheless the study is important in that it is the first to demonstrate accelerating ELD growth through intensive, organized instruction.

> Some strategic feedback is almost certainly helpful, but too much or poorly timed feedback can be counterproductive.

The Home Language Can Be Used to Promote Academic Development

We turn, finally, to the most controversial topic in instructing ELs—the role of the home language. There are two aspects to the issue: teaching academic content and skills, such as reading and mathematics, in the home language; and using the home language as support in an otherwise all-English instructional environment—for example, providing definitions or brief explanations in the home language, but keeping instruction overwhelmingly in English.

Teaching academic skills in the home language is at the core of the great "bilingual education" debate. Proponents of bilingual education have long argued that students should be taught in their home language (although certainly not exclusively) and that doing so strengthens the home language and creates a more solid foundation for acquiring academic skills in English. Opponents of bilingual education argue that instruction in a student's home language is a waste of time, depresses achievement in English, and simply delays an EL's entrance into the academic (and social) mainstream. Crawford (2004) provides an excellent history of the political and ideological debates around bilingual education.

These debates over bilingual education are typically framed in terms of outcomes in English. English outcomes are without a doubt important, but there is an additional reason to consider primary language instruction for English learners. That is the inherent advantage of knowing and being literate in two languages. No one should be surprised to learn that all studies of bilingual education have found that teaching children in their primary language promotes achievement in the primary language. Achievement in the primary language should be seen as a value in and of itself. Of course, if primary language achievement comes at the expense of achievement in English, this might not be a worthwhile tradeoff. As we will see, however, bilingual education tends to produce better outcomes in English; at worst it produces outcomes in English equivalent to those produced by English immersion. In other words, bilingual education helps students become bilingual—something that is valuable for anyone, not just ELs (Bialystok, 2001; Saiz & Zoido, 2005). This should not be lost amid the controversy over bilingual education and English immersion.

What the Research Tells Us

Although bilingual education continues to be a politically charged issue (Gándara & Hopkins, 2010), there are some things we can say from the research.

Reading Instruction in the Home Language Can Be Beneficial

Numerous experimental studies have been conducted over the past forty years, and the consensus—although it is by no means unanimous—is that learning to read in their home language helps ELs boost reading skills in English. Learning to read in the home language also maintains home language literacy skills; there is no controversy over this. To date there have been five meta-analyses conducted since 1985 by researchers from different perspectives (see chapter 2 in Goldenberg and Coleman [2010], for a more detailed discussion of the meta-analyses). All five reached the same conclusion—namely, that bilingual education produced superior reading outcomes in English compared to English immersion.

A more recent study, and probably the strongest methodologically, reached a different conclusion. Slavin, Madden, Calderón, Chamberlain, and Hennessy (2011) randomly assigned Spanish-speaking ELs to either transitional bilingual education or English immersion. All students were in the Success for All program (see chapter 2). This is very important, since previous studies of bilingual education had not controlled for instruction, curriculum, or other factors that could have compromised the findings. The authors found that in first grade, children in English immersion did significantly better on English achievement measures than did children in bilingual education. By fourth grade, English immersion students' scores were somewhat higher than that of the bilingual education students, but the differences were not significant. Slavin et al. (2011) contend that these results support neither side in the bilingual education controversy. Instead, they argue, quality of instruction is a more important determinant of ELs' achievement than language of instruction.

> Five meta-analyses conducted since 1985 reached the same conclusion—that bilingual education produced superior reading outcomes in English compared to English immersion.

The Effects Are Small to Moderate

The effects of home language instruction on English achievement are fairly modest, even if we disregard the findings of Slavin et al. (2011). The five meta-analyses mentioned in the previous section found that, on average, teaching reading in the home language could boost children's English literacy scores by approximately 12 to 15 percentile points in comparison to children in the control conditions. This is not a trivial effect, but neither is it as large as many proponents of bilingual education suggest. Of course, if we add in the results of the Slavin study, the average effect would be reduced. But we should keep in mind that there is no controversy over the positive effect of home language instruction *on home language skills*. This should be seen as an important outcome in itself, given the many possible advantages—intellectual, cultural, and economic—of bilingualism and biliteracy (Bialystok, 2001; Saiz & Zoido, 2005).

The Data on Length of Time in Primary Language Instruction Are Insufficient

The soundest studies methodologically focus on relatively short-term transitional bilingual education. In transitional programs, children generally receive instruction in the home language from one to three years and then transition to all-English instruction. Among this group of studies, there is no evidence that more or less time spent in bilingual education is related to student achievement (Goldenberg & Coleman, 2010).

Another type of bilingual education is two-way or dual-language (Lindholm-Leary, 2001). The goal of two-way bilingual education is bilingualism and biliteracy, in contrast to transitional bilingual education, which uses the home language only to help students transition to all-English instruction and then stops instruction in the home language. Two-way programs use the home language for far longer, at least through elementary school and often into middle school and beyond (K–12 two-way programs are rare). Two-way programs were virtually excluded from the five meta-analyses. The reason is that these longer-term studies do not meet the methodological requirements set by the meta-analyses. For example, they do not control for possible differences in the types of students in different programs, who vary considerably in terms of language, literacy, and education levels (Reese, Goldenberg, & Saunders, 2006). If we don't control for these factors, we are likely to get misleading results.

Our knowledge about the effects of two-way programs is unfortunately very limited. Nonetheless, two-way bilingual education offers a promising model for the education of ELs. It also offers a way to promote bilingualism and biliteracy for non–English learners, since two-way programs include English-speaking students as well as students from language-minority backgrounds (for example, Spanish speakers). This is an area in great need of additional research and rigorous evaluation.

Virtually No Data Exist on Bilingual Education in Other Curriculum Areas

Reading is by far the curriculum area that has received most attention in studies of bilingual education. A small number of studies have found positive effects in math (see Greene's 1997 meta-analysis). We know very little about the effects of bilingual education in other areas of the curriculum.

Instructional Support in the Home Language

Students' home language can play a role even in an all-English instructional program. This is referred to as home language or primary language support. There is no teaching of content and academic skills in the home language; instead, the home language is used to help facilitate learning content and skills in English. The home language can be used to support learning in an English instructional environment in the following ways:

- Cognates (words with shared meanings that have common etymological roots, such as *geography* and *geografía*).

- Brief explanations in the home language (not direct concurrent translations, which can cause students to "tune out").

- Lesson preview and review (lesson content is previewed in students' home language to provide some degree of familiarity when the lesson is taught; following the lesson there is a review in the home language to solidify and check for understanding).

- Strategies taught in the home language (reading, writing, and study strategies are taught in the home language but then applied to academic content in English).

Cognates have been used with a number of vocabulary and reading programs (Carlo et al., 2004). No study has ever isolated the specific effects of cognate instruction, but more successful second-language learners do make use of cognates when trying to understand material in the second language (Dressler, Carlo, Snow, August, & White, 2011).

Ulanoff and Pucci (1999) report a study in which teachers previewed difficult vocabulary in Spanish before reading a book in English; the teacher then reviewed the material in Spanish afterward. This produced better comprehension and recall than either reading the book in English or doing a simultaneous Spanish translation while reading. The program reported by Carlo et al. (2004) also made use of a similar technique. Before the class read a written passage, Spanish speakers were given written and audiotaped versions to preview in Spanish.

We also have evidence that reading strategies can be taught in students' home language, then applied in English. Fung, Wilkinson, and Moore (2002) found that teaching comprehension strategies in students' primary language improved reading comprehension when students afterward read in English.

Concluding Comments

There is certainly good news in the current interest in developing, studying, and evaluating effective practices for ELs. Educators should also consider it positive that we are coming to understand that ELs are not "a breed apart," but instead are students first and foremost. Much of what we know about effective instructional practices for students in general also applies to ELs in particular.

But the challenge remains great. We have inadequate evidence for many current and recommended practices. Even when we do have evidence of effective practices, their effects on ELs' learning is quite modest, far too modest to make sizable inroads into the substantial achievement gap that exists between many ELs and their English-proficient peers. A key question for which we do not as yet have a clear answer is whether this achievement gap can be bridged if students do not become fully proficient in the English skills required for school success. So far, there is little evidence that strategies and techniques that have been evaluated will help ELs close the gap.

There are no simple answers to these challenges. Meeting them will require comprehensive solutions that combine and integrate multiple components in schools and districts, where entire faculties and administration are involved in focused and coherent efforts to improve achievement systematically (see chapters 2 and 14 in this volume and chapter 6 in Goldenberg & Coleman, 2010). Moreover, these challenges will not be met exclusively through additional research, as necessary as additional research is. The issues practitioners face on a daily basis far outstrip what researchers can decisively address and resolve. If educators were to wait until all the research was in, they would be immobilized. Rather, they must address the challenges they face as effectively as possible using a combination of the evolving research base, what they learn from their own practice and that of others, and their best guesses and intuitions about how to meet the needs of their students. At a minimum, however, practitioners should have as firm a grasp as possible of what is—and is not—in the published research.

In the end, progress in this area will require continued research, certainly, but also thoughtful reflective practice and small-scale experimentation to see what works in classrooms. An extraordinary opportunity exists for practitioners to contribute to our general knowledge base about effective practices for ELs. We should put aside the ideological debates that have defined this field for too long and work as a profession to seek and try out approaches that will afford ELs full access to success in school and beyond.

References

Abu-Rabia, S. (1996). Druze minority students learning Hebrew in Israel: The relationship of attitudes, cultural background, and interest of material to reading comprehension in a second language. *Journal of Multilingual and Multicultural Development, 17*(6), 415–426.

August, D., & Shanahan, T. (Eds.). (2006). *Developing literacy in second-language learners: Report of the National Literacy Panel on Language-Minority Children and Youth.* Mahwah, NJ: Erlbaum.

Bialystok, E. (2001). *Bilingualism in development: Language, literacy, & cognition.* New York: Cambridge University Press.

Calderón, M., Hertz-Lazarowitz, R., & Slavin, R. E. (1998). Effects of bilingual cooperative integrated reading and composition on students making the transition from Spanish to English reading. *Elementary School Journal, 99*(2), 153–165.

Carlo, M. S., August, D., McLaughlin, B., Snow, C. E., Dressler, C., Lippman, D. N., et al. (2004). Closing the gap: Addressing the vocabulary needs of English language learners in bilingual and mainstream classrooms. *Reading Research Quarterly, 39*(2), 188–215.

Cheung, A., & Slavin, R. E. (2005). Effective reading programs for English language learners and other language-minority students. *Bilingual Research Journal, 29*(2), 241–267.

Collins, M. F. (2005). ESL preschoolers' English vocabulary acquisition from storybook reading. *Reading Research Quarterly, 40*(4), 406–408.

Crawford, J. (2004). *Educating English learners: Language diversity in the classroom* (5th ed.). Los Angeles, CA: Bilingual Education Services.

Darling-Hammond, L., & Bransford, J. (Eds.). (2005). *Preparing teachers for a changing world: What teachers should learn and be able to do.* San Francisco: Jossey-Bass.

Denton, C. A., Anthony, J. L., Parker, R., & Hasbrouck, J. E. (2004). Effects of two tutoring programs on the English reading development of Spanish-English bilingual students. *Elementary School Journal, 104*(4), 289–305.

Dong, Y. R. (2002). Integrating language and content: How three biology teachers work with non-English speaking students. *International Journal of Bilingual Education and Bilingualism, 5*(1), 40–57.

Dressler, C., Carlo, M. S., Snow, C. E., August, D., & White, C. E. (2011). Spanish-speaking students' use of cognate knowledge to infer the meaning of English words. *Bilingualism: Language and Cognition, 14*(2), 243–255.

Echevarria, J., Short, D., & Powers, K. (2006). School reform and standards-based education: A model for English-language learners. *Journal of Educational Research, 99*(4), 195–210.

Echevarria, J., Vogt, M., & Short, D. J. (2008). *Making content comprehensible for English learners: The SIOP model* (3rd ed.). Boston: Allyn & Bacon.

Escamilla, K. (1994). Descubriendo la lectura: An early intervention literacy program in Spanish. *Literacy, Teaching, and Learning, 1*(1), 57–70.

Fung, I. Y. Y., Wilkinson, I. A. G., & Moore, D. W. (2002). L_1-assisted reciprocal teaching to improve ESL students' comprehension of English expository text. *Learning and Instruction, 13*(1), 1–31.

Gándara, P., & Hopkins, M. (Eds.). (2010). *Forbidden language: English learners and restrictive language policies.* New York: Teachers College Press.

Genesee, F., Lindholm-Leary, K., Saunders, W., & Christian, D. (2006). *Educating English language learners: A synthesis of research evidence.* New York: Cambridge University Press.

Gold, N. (2010). *Educating English learners: English learner brief 10.1.* Unpublished bibliography.

Goldenberg, C. (1990, April). *Evaluation of a balanced approach to literacy instruction for Spanish-speaking kindergartners.* Paper presented at the annual meeting of the American Educational Research Association, Boston.

Goldenberg, C., & Coleman, R. (2010). *Promoting academic achievement among English learners: A guide to the research.* Thousand Oaks, CA: Corwin Press.

Gómez, R., Jr., Parker, R., Lara-Alecio, R., & Gómez, L. (1996). Process versus product writing with limited English proficient students. *Bilingual Research Journal, 20*(2), 209–233.

Greene, J. P. (1997). A meta-analysis of the Rossell and Baker review of bilingual education research. *Bilingual Research Journal, 21*(2–3), 103–122.

Janzen, J. (2008). Teaching English language learners in the content areas. *Review of Educational Research, 78*(4), 1010–1038.

Jiang, X., & Grabe, W. (2007). Graphic organizers in reading instruction: Research findings and issues. *Reading in a Foreign Language, 19*(1), 34–55.

Kenner, C. (1999). Children's understandings of text in a multilingual nursery. *Language and Education, 13*(1), 1–16.

Lasisi, M. J., Falodun, S., & Onyehalu, A. S. (1988). The comprehension of first- and second-language prose. *Journal of Research in Reading, 11*(1), 26–35.

Lau v. Nichols, 414 U.S. 563, [1974].

Lee, O., Deaktor, R. A., Hart, J. E., Cuevas, P., & Enders, C. (2005). An instructional intervention's impact on the science and literacy achievement of culturally and linguistically diverse elementary students. *Journal of Research in Science Teaching, 42*(8), 857–887.

Lightbown, P. M., & Spada, N. (2006). *How languages are learned* (3rd ed.). New York: Oxford University Press.

Lindholm-Leary, K. J. (2001). *Dual language education.* Clevedon, UK: Multilingual Matters.

Marzano, R. J. (2007). *The art and science of teaching: A comprehensive framework for effective instruction.* Alexandria, VA: Association for Supervision and Curriculum Development.

McIntyre, E., Kyle, D., Chen, C., Muñoz, M. & Beldon, S. (2010). Teacher learning and ELL reading achievement in sheltered instruction classrooms: Linking professional development to student development. *Literacy Research and Instruction,* 49, 334–351.

McNamara, D. S., & Kintsch, W. (1996). Learning from texts: Effects of prior knowledge and text coherence. *Discourse Processes, 22*(3), 247–288.

National Reading Panel. (2000). *Report of the National Reading Panel: Teaching children to read: An evidence-based assessment of the scientific research literature on reading and its implications for reading instruction.* Washington, DC: National Institute of Child Health and Human Development.

Nesbit, J. C., & Adesope, O. O. (2006). Learning with concept and knowledge maps: A meta-analysis. *Review of Educational Research, 76*(3), 413–448.

Nussbaum, E. M. (2002). Scaffolding argumentation in the social studies classroom. *The Social Studies, 93*(2), 79–83.

Reese, L., Goldenberg, C., & Saunders, W. (2006). Variations in reading achievement among Spanish-speaking children in different language programs: Explanations and confounds. *Elementary School Journal, 106*(4), 362–366.

Saiz, A., & Zoido, E. (2005). Listening to what the world says: Bilingualism and earnings in the United States. *Review of Economics and Statistics, 87*(3), 523–538.

Saunders, W. M. (1999). Improving literacy achievement for English learners in transitional bilingual programs. *Educational Research and Evaluation, 5*(4), 345–381.

Saunders, W. M., & Goldenberg, C. (1999). *The effects of a comprehensive language arts transition program on the literacy development of English language learners.* Santa Cruz: Center for Research on Education, Diversity, and Excellence, University of California.

Saunders, W., & Goldenberg, C. (2007). The effects of an instructional conversation on English language learners' concepts of friendship and story comprehension. In R. Horowitz (Ed.), *Talking texts: How speech and writing interact in school learning* (pp. 221–252). Mahwah, NJ: Erlbaum.

Saunders, W. M., & Goldenberg, C. (2010). Research to guide English language development instruction. In D. Dolson & L. Burnham-Massey (Eds.), *Improving education for English learners: Research-based approaches* (pp. 21–81). Sacramento: California Department of Education.

Sengupta, S. (2000). An investigation into the effects of revision strategy instruction on L2 secondary school learners. *System, 28*(1), 97–113.

Silverman, R., & Hines, S. (2009). The effects of multimedia-enhanced instruction on the vocabulary of English-language learners and non-English-language learners in pre-kindergarten through second grade. *Journal of Educational Psychology, 101*(2), 305–314.

Slavin, R. E., Madden, N., Calderón, M., Chamberlain, A., & Hennessy, M. (2011). Reading and language outcomes of a multiyear randomized evaluation of transitional bilingual education. *Educational Evaluation and Policy Analysis, 33*(1), 47–58.

Tang, G. (1992). The effect of graphic representation of knowledge structures on ESL reading comprehension. *Studies in Second Language Acquisition, 14*(2), 177–195.

Tobias, S. (1994). Interest, prior knowledge, and learning. *Review of Educational Research, 64*(1), 37–54.

Tong, F., Lara-Alecio, R., Irby, B., Mathes, P., & Kwok, O. (2008). Accelerating early academic oral English development in transitional bilingual and structured English immersion programs. *American Educational Research Journal, 45*(4), 1011–44.

Ulanoff, S. H., & Pucci, S. L. (1999). Learning words from books: The effects of read-aloud on second language vocabulary acquisition. *Bilingual Research Journal, 23*(4), 409–422.

Vaughn, S., Mathes, P., Linan-Thompson, S., Cirino, P., Carlson, C., Pollard-Durdola, S., et al. (2006). Effectiveness of an English intervention for first-grade English language learners at risk for reading problems. *Elementary School Journal, 107*(2), 153–181.

Jim Cummins

Jim Cummins received his PhD from the University of Alberta in the area of educational psychology. He is currently a Canada Research Chair in the Department of Curriculum, Teaching, and Learning of the Ontario Institute for Studies in Education at the University of Toronto. His research focuses on literacy development in multilingual school contexts as well as on the potential roles of technology in promoting language and literacy development. In recent years, Dr. Cummins has been working actively with teachers to identify ways of increasing the literacy engagement of learners in multilingual school contexts. He has served as a consultant on language planning in education to numerous international agencies.

Dr. Cummins's publications include *Language, Power, and Pedagogy: Bilingual Children in the Crossfire; Negotiating Identities: Education for Empowerment in a Diverse Society; The International Handbook of English Language Teaching* (co-edited with Chris Davison); *Literacy, Technology, and Diversity: Teaching for Success in Changing Times* (with Kristin Brown and Dennis Sayers); and *Identity Texts: The Collaborative Creation of Power in Multilingual Schools* (with Margaret Early).

In this chapter, Dr. Cummins discusses academic language proficiency as it relates to the whole school and contrasts cognitive academic language proficiency (CALP) and basic interpersonal communicative skills (BICS). He shows why teachers must understand the nature of the language English learners are required to learn in school and the instructional approaches that are most effective in teaching it.

Chapter 4

Whole-School Approaches to Academic Language Proficiency Among English Learners

Jim Cummins

The construct of cognitive academic language proficiency (CALP) was introduced (Cummins, 1979) to draw educators' attention to the timelines and challenges that second-language learners encounter as they attempt to catch up to their peers in academic aspects of the school language. CALP refers to students' ability to understand and express, in both oral and written modes, concepts and ideas that are relevant to success in school. Academic language draws on low-frequency (less-often used) vocabulary and specific discourse and grammatical structures (for example, passive voice) that reflect the increasing conceptual and linguistic complexity of subject matter content taught beyond the primary grades. CALP was contrasted with basic interpersonal communicative skills (BICS), which refer to conversational fluency in a language. Conversational language typically relies on high-frequency vocabulary and relatively common grammatical and discourse structures. The terms *conversational fluency* and *academic language proficiency* are used interchangeably with BICS and CALP in the remainder of this chapter.

The BICS/CALP distinction assumes relevance for policy and practice for the simple reason that if we're going to teach English effectively, we need to know what it is we are trying to teach. Thus, it is imperative to understand the nature of the language we require students to learn in school and the instructional approaches that are most effective in teaching this language. This point was made forcefully by Lily Wong Fillmore in her 2005 deposition to the California State Legislature. She pointed out that academic language is "used in school for learning about and discussing the ideas, information, and skills that comprise the content of the school's curriculum" (2005, p. 2). She defined academic language as follows:

> It is extended, reasoned discourse—it is more precise in reference than ordinary spoken language, and makes frequent use of grammatical devices that allow speakers/writers to pack as much information as necessary for interpretation into coherent and logical sequences. (2005, p. 3)

We find this language most obviously in written text. As noted by David Corson, there are major lexical differences between the language of text and the language of social interaction:

> For example, even children's books contained 50% more rare words than either adult prime-time television or the conversations of university graduates; popular magazines had three times as many rare words as television and informal conversation. (1997, p. 677)

He notes that "most of the specialist and high-status terminology of English is Graeco-Latin in origin, and most of its more everyday terminology is Anglo-Saxon in origin" (Corson, 1993, p. 13).[1] Nation (1990) estimates that about two-thirds of the low-frequency words in English derive from Latin or Greek origins. He points out:

> High-frequency vocabulary consists mainly of short words which cannot be broken into meaningful parts. Low-frequency vocabulary, on the other hand, while it consists

---

[1] Contemporary English reflects a merger of the Germanic Anglo-Saxon language spoken in Britain roughly between the fifth and eleventh centuries and the variety of French brought in by the conquering Normans when they invaded in 1066.

of many thousands of words, is made from a much smaller number of word parts. The word *impose,* for example, is made of two parts, *im* and *pose,* which occur in hundreds of other words—*imply, infer, compose, expose, position.* This has clear implications for teaching and learning vocabulary. (1990, p. 18)

We seldom use low-frequency words in everyday conversation. Our everyday social interactions are characterized by the use of high-frequency words and a limited range of grammatical structures. A considerable amount of meaning in face-to-face situations is also conveyed by nonverbal cues such as facial expressions and gestures. Thus, precise linguistic reference is generally not necessary to communicate effectively in these contexts. The quickest way to lose friends (on or off Facebook) is to use low-frequency vocabulary and academic language structures in social contexts.

Gibbons has similarly expressed the difference between the everyday language of face-to-face interaction and the language of schooling in outlining the distinction between what she terms *playground language* and *classroom language*:

This playground language includes the language which enables children to make friends, join in games and take part in a variety of day-to-day activities that develop and maintain social contacts. . . . But playground language is very different from the language that teachers use in the classroom, and from the language that we expect children to learn to use. The language of the playground is not the language associated with learning in mathematics, or social studies, or science. The playground situation does not normally offer children the opportunity to use such language as: *if we increase the angle by 5 degrees, we could cut the circumference into equal parts.* Nor does it normally require the language associated with the higher order thinking skills, such as hypothesizing, evaluating, inferring, generalizing, predicting or classifying. Yet these are the language functions which are related to learning and the development of cognition; they occur in all areas of the curriculum, and without them a child's potential in academic areas cannot be realized. (1991, p. 3)

It is important to note that the BICS/CALP distinction was not proposed as an overall theory of language proficiency but as a very specific conceptual distinction that has important implications for policy and practice. It has proved helpful in interpreting patterns of second-language development among minority group students and in drawing attention to potentially prejudicial psychological and educational assessment practices experienced by second-language learners. These applications of the BICS/CALP distinction are considered in subsequent sections.

> The BICS/CALP distinction has proved helpful in drawing attention to potentially prejudicial psychological and educational assessment practices experienced by second-language learners.

Acquisition Trajectories for BICS and CALP

In view of the obvious differences between conversational and academic language, it is not surprising that they follow different acquisition trajectories for both first- and second-language learners. Native speakers of every language acquire conversational fluency through interaction with parents or caregivers. Usually by age five or so, children have acquired the ability to converse easily about immediate everyday issues or experiences. Yet they typically spend an additional twelve years at school expanding this conversational fluency into academic spheres, acquiring the ability to read and interpret complex text and understand classroom instruction in subject areas such as science, mathematics, and language arts. Second-language learners whose home language is different from the dominant language of the society usually acquire conversational fluency to a functional or peer-appropriate level within about two years of initial exposure in the school or wider society. However, a much longer period of time is required for minority group students to catch up to grade expectations in L_2 academic language.

The different acquisition trajectories for BICS and CALP were first highlighted by a reanalysis of language performance data involving 25 percent of the students in grades 5, 7, and 9 in the

Toronto school system (Cummins, 1981). Within this sample, it was possible to compare the performance of immigrant students who were learning English as L₂ to that of native speakers of English. These data showed that a period of five to seven years was required, on average, for immigrant students to approach grade norms in academic aspects of English. Students' scores on the vocabulary measure administered in the study are plotted in figure 4.1 according to the length of residence (LOR) and age on arrival (AOA) of each group. Students who had been in Canada for only one year were performing almost two standard deviations (equivalent to thirty standard score points) below grade norms. After three years length of residence, there was still a gap of about one standard deviation.

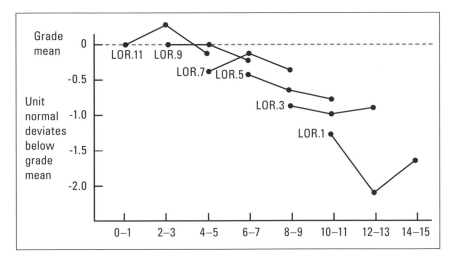

Figure 4.1: Age on arrival (AOA), length of residence (LOR), and picture vocabulary test (PVT) scores for immigrant students in the Toronto Board of Education (Cummins, 1981).

The differential time periods required to attain peer-appropriate L₂ conversational fluency as compared to meeting grade expectations in academic language proficiency have been corroborated in many subsequent research studies carried out over decades in Canada (Klesmer, 1994), Europe (Snow & Hoefnagel-Hohle, 1978), Israel (Shohamy et al., 2002), and the United States (Collier, 1987; Hakuta, Butler, & Witt, 2000; Thomas & Collier, 2002). Particularly relevant for current policy issues in the United States is the finding that after three years of English-only instruction, a mere 12 percent of English learners in California had acquired sufficient academic English to be redesignated as English proficient (Parrish, Merickel, Perez, & Linquanti, 2006).

The different acquisition trajectories for BICS and CALP derive partially from the nature of academic language in comparison to conversational language. Academic language reflects the increasing linguistic and conceptual complexity of the school curriculum, and it is found predominantly in two places—written texts and classrooms. Access to conversational language through social interaction is generally much less restricted, and students can function effectively in these contexts with a much smaller linguistic repertoire. However, equally relevant to understanding the length of time ELs require to catch up academically is the fact that they are trying to hit a moving target. Native speakers are not standing still waiting for English learners to catch up. Every year, they make significant gains in vocabulary knowledge and in their ability to read and write for a variety of purposes. As a result, ELs have to run faster to bridge the gap. Collier and Thomas (1999) have estimated that in order to catch up to grade norms within six years, ELs must make fifteen months' gain in every ten-month school year compared to the ten-month gain expected for the typical native-speaking student.

It should be noted that the academic catch-up trajectory reported in numerous studies (at least five years) represents the typical pattern English learners experience. However, this figure is not in any sense fixed. There is likely to be considerable variation among individual students, depending on factors such as level of L_1 literacy, socioeconomic status, and so on. The quality of the instruction that students experience will also affect the rate of academic progress. This is illustrated in the research reported by Slavin and Calderón (chapters 2 and 1, respectively, of this volume), which documents that English learners caught up to grade norms within four years in a school program that aimed to implement evidence-based instructional strategies across the curriculum.

Relevance of the BICS/CALP Distinction for Policy and Practice

Many of the challenges currently faced by educators and policymakers in boosting achievement among English learners can be traced to misunderstandings about the nature of academic language proficiency and how long it takes for students to catch up to their native-speaking peers. As illustrated in the sections that follow, effective instruction for ELs requires that educators and policymakers understand the nature of academic language proficiency and how it develops.

Traditional School-Based Practice

The potential for teachers to confound BICS and CALP is highlighted by Carolyn Vincent (1996), who conducted an in-depth study of second-generation Salvadorean students in Washington, DC. She reported that the students began school in an English-speaking environment and "within their first two or three years attained conversational ability in English that teachers would regard as native-like" (p. 195). Vincent suggested, however, that this fluency is largely deceptive:

> The children seem to have much greater English proficiency than they actually do because their spoken English has no accent and they are able to converse on a few everyday, frequently discussed subjects. Academic language is frequently lacking. Teachers actually spend very little time talking with individual children and tend to interpret a small sample of speech as evidence of full English proficiency. (1996, p. 195)

Under these circumstances, teachers who are unaware of the typical acquisition trajectory for CALP may consider that students' below-grade-level academic performance is caused by some form of learning difficulty that might benefit from special education intervention. The potential for inappropriate placement or intervention when students are referred for psychological assessment was highlighted in an analysis of more than four hundred teacher referral forms and psychological assessments carried out in a school system in western Canada (Cummins, 1984). One student, whom we will call PR, was referred in first grade by the school principal, who noted that "PR is experiencing considerable difficulty with grade-one work. An intellectual assessment would help her teacher to set realistic learning expectations for her and might provide some clues as to remedial assistance that might be offered" (Cummins, 1984, p. 38). No mention was made of the fact that the child did not speak English at home. This emerged only when the child was referred again by the second-grade teacher in the following year. Thus, the psychologist did not consider it a possible factor in accounting for the discrepancy between PR's verbal IQ of 64 and performance (nonverbal) IQ of 108. The assessment report read as follows:

> Although overall ability level appears to be within the low average range, note the significant difference between verbal and nonverbal scores. . . . It would appear that PR's development has not progressed at a normal rate and consequently she is, and will continue to experience much difficulty in school. Teacher's expectations at this time should be set accordingly. (Cummins, 1984, p. 39)

Rather than lowering expectations for English learners, teachers need to implement instruction that simultaneously provides high challenge accompanied by high support—what has been termed learning in the challenge zone.

The relevance of the BICS/CALP distinction to interpretation of this assessment derives from the fact that the child's oral English conversational skills were presumably sufficiently well developed that the psychologist—and possibly the teacher—were not alerted to her linguistic background. This led the psychologist to set low academic expectations for her. Clearly, low expectations can become self-fulfilling. Rather than lowering expectations for English learners, teachers need to implement instruction that simultaneously provides high challenge (tasks students cannot do unaided) accompanied by high support (the scaffolding that enables students to complete these tasks successfully)—what Pauline Gibbons (2010) has termed *learning in the challenge zone*. As argued later in this chapter, this will involve promoting high levels of literacy engagement together with an explicit focus on extending students' awareness of how language works across the curriculum.

Educational Policy

There is currently intense pressure on teachers and school administrators in the United States to boost students' performance on standardized tests. This pressure is felt particularly in schools serving students from low income and minority group backgrounds, because these students experience disproportionate school failure. International comparisons of the reading performance of fifteen-year old students carried out by the Organisation for Economic Co-operation and Development (OECD, 2010b) show that the gap between high- and low-income students in the United States is extremely high. Students in schools with less than 10 percent of students eligible for free or reduced-price lunch scored an average of 551 on the reading measure while those in schools with 75 percent or more students eligible for free or reduced-price lunch scored 446, a difference of more than 100 points. The U.S. mean was 500, slightly higher than the OECD average of 493.

Thus, overall school improvement is directly related to the extent to which educational policies are effective in closing the achievement gap between rich and poor and across social and linguistic groups (Darling-Hammond, 2010). In this regard, policymakers have unfortunately largely ignored the evidence that poverty is a major contributor to low achievement, preferring to focus instead on using high-stakes standardized tests to measure not only the progress of students but also the effectiveness of teachers and the teacher education programs that certified them. A "no excuses" discourse has been directed at educators who point to the influence of poverty or the challenges faced by English learners.

For policymakers who adhere to this ideological orientation, the time periods required for EL students to attain academic grade expectations represents an inconvenient truth. These policy makers have ignored the fact that ELs are catching up to a moving target (native speakers of English), and rather than being assigned the dubious status of long-term English learner, they need instruction that focuses on accelerating their acquisition of CALP.

This can be illustrated by Proposition 227, the referendum passed by the voters of California in 1998 with the aim of eliminating bilingual education for English learners. Some bilingual programs have survived, but for a large majority of bilingual students, Proposition 227's English-only instructional mandate effectively eliminated any instructional use of these students' L_1. Proposition 227 was premised on the assumption that one year of intensive English instruction would be sufficient to enable ELs to become integrated into mainstream classrooms with minimal additional support. The referendum was initiated by millionaire Ron Unz, who claimed on the CNN program *TalkBack Live* (2000) that ELs learned English in "well under one year" when they were immersed in English-only programs. He further claimed that "all of the bilingual researchers . . . claim that it takes five to seven years for a child to learn English" and "everybody knows that's nonsense" (2000). Unz's claim that English is acquired in less than one year might have had some limited plausibility if he had specified that he was talking about conversational fluency. Instead, he conflated conversational and academic proficiency into "learning English," which conveniently ignores the issue of how long it takes ELs to learn sufficient *academic* English to understand instruction and attain grade expectations. As noted, the investigation into the effects of Proposition 227 showed that only 12 percent of EL students had acquired sufficient English for reclassification as fluent English speakers after *three* years.

Clearly, based on these data, the expectation that EL students can transition to mainstream English-medium programs after just one year is totally unrealistic. Unz's dismissal of bilingual and dual-language programs is also evidence free. A finding common to all forms of bilingual education is that spending instructional time through two languages entails no long-term adverse effects on students' academic development in the majority language (August & Shanahan, 2006; Cummins, 2001; Genesee, Lindholm-Leary, Saunders, & Christian, 2006; Lindholm-Leary & Hernández, 2011; Rolstad, Mahoney, & Glass, 2005). This pattern emerges among both majority and minority language students, across widely varying sociolinguistic and sociopolitical contexts, and in programs with very different organizational structures. In some studies, an overall positive effect of bilingual education on academic outcomes was reported. For example, the August and Shanahan (2006) meta-analysis of research suggested "a positive effect for bilingual instruction that is moderate in size… [a] conclusion [that] held up across the entire collection of studies and within the subset of studies that used random assignment of students to conditions" (Francis, Lesaux, & August 2006, p. 397). More recent research using randomized assignment of students to programs (bilingual/dual language versus structured English immersion) suggests that the quality of instruction rather than medium of instruction is the crucial variable. These studies reported that although students in bilingual programs experienced an initial lag in English reading development, they caught up by the end of elementary school (Cheung & Slavin, 2005; Slavin et al., 2011).

Current Testing Policies

The same kind of unrealistic and evidence-free thinking in relation to English learners has infused educational policy throughout the United States since the implementation of No Child Left Behind (NCLB, 2002). Under the provisions of NCLB, schools were required to demonstrate "adequate yearly progress" (AYP) on standardized tests administered to all students between grades 3 and 8. EL students were exempted from testing only in their first year of learning English. After that, their scores were interpreted, along with the scores of other students, as reflective of the quality of instruction in a particular school. In other words, the provisions of NCLB totally ignored the fact that only a small fraction of English learners are likely to attain grade norms after one year of instruction, regardless of how effective that instruction might be. To attribute ELs' failure on the test to ineffective teaching is not simply bad policy, it is also ethically problematic, given the strong potential for that failure to have a negative impact on students' academic self-image and on teacher morale.

Despite the fact that English learners' "underachievement" on standardized tests administered during the period when they are on the normal four-to-seven-year catch-up trajectory reveals nothing about the quality of instruction they have received, policymakers have refused to acknowledge this reality. They have continued to interpret ELs' poor performance as a failure of schools and teachers.

In short, policymakers have tended to pay lip service to the implications of CALP for EL students' academic success. While they have typically endorsed the importance of promoting academic language across the curriculum, many have refused to acknowledge that current AYP expectations are totally evidence free when applied to ELs. They have also failed to acknowledge the fact that, if academic language is predominantly found in written text and classroom discourse, then extensive access to and engagement with written text is likely to play a significant role in boosting student achievement. Thus, failure on the part of policymakers to understand the nature of CALP represents a major reason why the ambitious policies of "leaving no child behind" have produced virtually no improvement in students' reading achievement.

> To attribute ELs' failure on the standardized test to ineffective teaching is not simply bad policy, it is also ethically problematic.

The remainder of this chapter outlines how educators can use what we know about the nature of academic English and the way it is acquired to accelerate English learners' academic progress and extend their awareness and knowledge of the English language. I present an empirically based framework for promoting students' academic language proficiency and, based on this synthesis of research, a guide for self-study and collaborative inquiry designed to enable the entire school to articulate options for implementing evidence-based instructional directions.

Literacy Instruction for ELs: A Pedagogical Framework

When we understand the nature of CALP, it becomes obvious that the promotion of literacy engagement must be a key ingredient in educational efforts to promote reading achievement and close the achievement gap. As noted previously, academic language is found predominantly in written text. Corson has emphasized this point:

> Academic Graeco-Latin words are mainly literary in their use. Most native speakers of English begin to encounter these words in quantity in their upper primary school reading and in the formal secondary-school setting. So the words'

introduction in literature or textbooks, rather than in conversation, restricts people's access to them. (1997, p. 667)

Several research studies have reinforced the fact that students from lower-income communities have significantly less access to books and other forms of print in their schools and homes than students from middle-income communities (Duke, 2000; Neuman & Celano, 2001). Without access to print, literacy engagement is unlikely.

The role of literacy engagement was not examined in depth in either the National Reading Panel (NRP, 2000) or the National Literacy Panel on Language-Minority Children and Youth (August & Shanahan, 2006). However, other reviews of the research have highlighted its relevance (Guthrie, 2004; Krashen, 2004; Lindsay, 2010). Guthrie (2004), for example, points out that the construct of *literacy engagement* incorporates notions of *time on task* (reading and writing extensively), *affect* (enthusiasm and enjoyment of literacy), *depth of cognitive processing* (strategies to deepen comprehension), and *active pursuit of literacy activities* (amount and diversity of literacy practices in and out of school). He cites the OECD's data from the Programme for International Student Achievement (PISA) as showing that students

whose family background was characterized by low income and low education, but who were highly engaged readers, substantially outscored students who came from backgrounds with higher education and higher income, but who themselves were less engaged readers. Based on a massive sample, this finding suggests the stunning conclusion that engaged reading can overcome traditional barriers to reading achievement, including gender, parental education, and income. (OECD, 2004, p. 5)

The OECD authors are careful to point out that "engagement in reading can be a consequence, as well as a cause, of higher reading skill, but the evidence suggests that these two factors are mutually reinforcing" (OECD, 2004, p. 8).

Lindsay's (2010) meta-analysis of 108 studies similarly concluded that print access plays a causal role in the development of reading skills. He summarizes the findings of the most rigorous (that is, experimental and quasi-experimental) studies as follows:

> Separate meta-analytic procedures performed on just those effects produced by "rigorous" studies suggest that children's access to print materials plays a *causal* role in facilitating behavioral, educational, and psychological outcomes in children—especially attitudes toward reading, reading behavior, emergent literacy skills, and reading performance. (p. 85)

The more recent PISA findings (OECD, 2010a) confirm these trends. Engagement in reading was assessed through measures of time spent reading various materials, enjoyment of reading, and use of various learning strategies. Across OECD countries, reading engagement was significantly related to reading performance, and approximately one-third of the association between reading performance and students' socioeconomic background was mediated by reading engagement.

The framework presented in figure 4.2 (page 77) incorporates these data and posits a direct relationship between literacy attainment and print access and literacy engagement. It also specifies the interrelated dimensions of instruction for EL students that are particularly important in promoting literacy engagement. These dimensions essentially express what teachers need to do in order to promote literacy engagement.

Let's examine each of these.

Scaffold Meaning

The term *scaffolding* refers to the provision of temporary supports that enable learners to carry out tasks and perform academically at a higher level than they would be capable of without these supports. Activation of students' prior knowledge and building background knowledge represent forms of scaffolding that operate on students' internal cognitive structures. Other forms of scaffolding focus on modifying the input so that it becomes more comprehensible to students. These include the use of visuals, demonstrations, dramatization, acting out meanings, and explanation of words and linguistic structures. Development of effective learning strategies

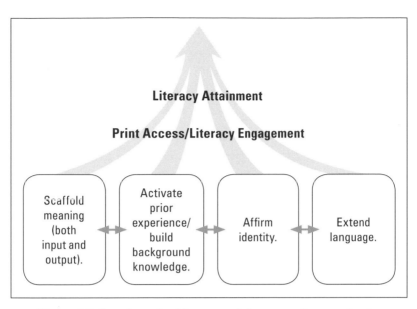

Figure 4.2: A pedagogical framework for promoting academic development among English learners.

(such as summarizing, predicting, and so on) also represents a form of scaffolding. In addition, scaffolding can be used to support students in using the target language in both written and oral modes. For example, students from the same language group might be encouraged to brainstorm in their L_1 to clarify ideas or draft an initial response before presenting to the large group in English. Research suggests that encouraging students to use their L_1 when necessary to complete a group task can result in higher quality of L_2 output than when students are prohibited from L_1 use (Swain & Lapkin, 2005).

> Research suggests that encouraging students to use their L_1 when necessary to complete a group task can result in higher quality of L_2 output than when students are prohibited from L_1 use.

Activate Prior Experience and Build Background Knowledge

The cognitive science research on learning highlights the centrality of students' experience and existing knowledge (Bransford, Brown, & Cocking 2000). Snow, Burns, and Griffin (1998) express the centrality of background knowledge as follows:

> Every opportunity should be taken to extend and enrich chil-
> dren's background knowledge and understanding in every
> way possible, for the ultimate significance and memorabil-
> ity of any word or text depends on whether children possess
> the background knowledge and conceptual sophistication to
> understand its meaning. (p. 219)

This implies that when students' background knowledge is encoded in their L_1, they should be encouraged to use their L_1 to activate and extend this knowledge (for example, by brainstorming in groups). This is true even when instruction is being conducted primarily through L_2 (Cummins, 2007a; Lucas & Katz, 1994).

Affirm Identity

One of the most frustrating initial experiences for English learners being educated exclusively through the majority language is not being able to express their intelligence, feelings, ideas, and humor to teachers and peers. Under these conditions, it is easy to underestimate what students are capable of and what they aspire to achieve in school and with their lives. By contrast, when students feel that their intelligence, imagination, and multilingual talents are affirmed in the school and classroom context, they invest their identities much more actively in the learning process. Creation of dual-language books that can be published on the web and shared with a variety of audiences (including peers, sister classes, parents, and teachers) are a highly effective way of affirming English learners' academic and personal identities (see Cummins & Early, 2011, for examples). The affirmation of minority students' identity in the context of teacher-student interactions explicitly challenges the frequent devaluation of student and community identity in the wider society. Considerable research suggests that the degree of minority student engagement is directly related to the patterns of teacher-student identity negotiation within the school (see Cummins, 2001, for a review).

Extend Language

As noted previously, students encounter low-frequency academic vocabulary and more complex grammatical and discourse structures predominantly through reading written text. Therefore, students who read extensively in a variety of genres both inside and outside school have far greater opportunities to acquire academic language than those whose reading is limited. However, it is also essential for teachers to focus directly on demystifying how academic language works, constantly drawing students' attention to how language can be used in powerful ways (Wong Fillmore, 2005). Encouraging students to use their L_1 as a cognitive tool in acquiring L_2 and to compare and contrast their languages contributes to extending students' awareness of language. Translation in the context of literacy tasks to which students are committed (such as writing and publishing dual-language books) can also extend students' awareness and knowledge of language in significant ways. This is illustrated in Kanta's reflection on the process of creating with two of her friends, Madiha and Sulmana, a dual-language book *The New Country,* which told about how difficult it was to leave Pakistan and come to a new country:

> Students encounter low-frequency academic vocabulary and more complex grammatical and discourse structures predominantly through reading written text.

> It helped me a lot to be able to write it in two languages and especially for Madiha, who was just beginning to learn English because the structure of the two languages is so different. So if you want to say something in Urdu it might take just three words but in English to say the same thing you'd have to use more words. So for Madiha it helped the differences between the two languages become clear. (Cummins, 2007b)

Whole-School Change Through Collaborative Inquiry

Planned change in educational systems always involves choice. Thus, the first step for educators interested in pursuing the pedagogical directions implied by the literacy engagement framework as a means of supporting students in developing academic language proficiency is to articulate and reflect critically on the instructional choices they make on a daily basis and to examine alternative possibilities. Individual educators always exercise agency—they are never powerless, although they frequently work in conditions that are constrictive and challenging, both for them and their students. While they rarely have complete freedom, educators do have choices in the way they structure the interactions in their classrooms, and they determine the social and educational goals they want to achieve with their students. There are always options with respect to educators' orientation to students' language and culture, in the forms of the parent and community participation they encourage, and in the ways they implement pedagogy and assessment. Thus, educators individually and collectively have the potential to work toward the creation of contexts of empowerment, understood as the *collaborative creation of power* (Cummins, 2001).

The framework presented in table 4.1 provides a starting point for in-school discussion among educators about how they can implement evidence-based instructional approaches to accelerate ELs' academic development.

Table 4.1: Implementing Whole-School Change Through Collaborative Inquiry

Instructional Options	Current Realities: Where Are We?	Vision for the Future: Where Do We Want to Be?	Getting It Done: How Do We Get There?
Content How do we adapt curriculum materials to link with students' prior knowledge and cultural background? How do we scaffold students' access to these materials? How do we promote language awareness and critical thinking about academic and social issues?			
Cognition How can we modify instruction to evoke higher levels of literacy engagement and critical thinking?			

Tools How can we use technological tools such as computers, digital cameras, camcorders, and web pages to support project-based work and academic inquiry among students?			
Assessment How can we complement mandated standardized assessments in order to present to students, parents, and administrators a more valid account of student progress? (For example, is there a role for portfolio assessment?)			
Language and Culture What messages are we giving students and parents about home language and culture? How can we enable students to use their L_1 as a powerful tool for learning? Can we increase students' identity investment by means of bilingual instructional strategies (that is, teaching for two-way transfer)?			
Parental Involvement How can we engage parents as co-educators in such a way that their linguistic and cultural expertise is harnessed to support their children's academic progress?			

Educators may want to add additional categories or modify the categories specified in table 4.1 according to their educational priorities or particular contexts. By highlighting the centrality of collaborative pedagogical inquiry as a tool for educational change, the framework provides a starting point for educators to articulate their instructional choices and align their practice with the research evidence. This process enables educators to *reclaim agency*—the power to act—and push back against evidence free-policies that limit their students' opportunities to learn.

References

August, D., & Shanahan, T. (Eds.). (2006). *Developing literacy in second-language learners: Report of the National Literacy Panel on Language-Minority Children and Youth*. Mahwah, NJ: Lawrence Erlbaum.

Bransford, J. D., Brown, A. L., & Cocking, R. R. (2000). *How people learn: Brain, mind, experience, and school*. Washington, DC: National Academies Press.

Calderón, M. E. (2011). *Teaching reading and comprehension to English learners, K–5*. Bloomington, IN: Solution Tree Press.

Cheung, A., & Slavin, R. E. (2005). Effective reading programs for English language learners and other language minority students. *Bilingual Research Journal, 29*(2), 241–267.

Collier, V. P. (1987). Age and rate of acquisition of second language for academic purposes. *TESOL Quarterly, 21,* 617–641.

Collier, V. P. and Thomas, W. P. (1999). Making U.S. schools effective for English language learners, Part 1. *TESOL Matters,* 9(4) (August/September), pp. 1, 6.

Corson, D. (1993). *Language, minority education and gender: Linking social justice and power*. Clevedon, UK: Multilingual Matters.

Corson, D. (1997). The learning and use of academic English words. *Language Learning, 47,* 671–718.

Cummins, J. (1979). *Cognitive/academic language proficiency, linguistic interdependence, the optimum age question and some other matters. Working papers on bilingualism, No. 19*. Toronto: Bilingual Education Project, Ontario Institute for Studies in Education.

Cummins, J. (1981). Age on arrival and immigrant second language learning in Canada: A reassessment. *Applied Linguistics, 11,* 132–149.

Cummins, J. (1984). *Bilingualism and special education: Issues in assessment and pedagogy*. Clevedon, UK: Multilingual Matters.

Cummins, J. (2000). *Language, power and pedagogy: Bilingual children in the crossfire*. Clevedon, UK: Multilingual Matters.

Cummins, J. (2001). *Negotiating identities: Education for empowerment in a diverse society* (2nd ed.). Los Angeles: California Association for Bilingual Education.

Cummins, J. (2007a). Pedagogies for the poor? Re-aligning reading instruction for low-income students with scientifically based reading research. *Educational Researcher, 36,* 564–572.

Cummins, J. (2007b). Rethinking Monolingual Strategies in Multilingual Classrooms. *Canadian Journal of Applied Linguistics, 10*, 221–240. Accessed at www.aclacaal.org/Documents/10-2-abstracts.pdf on February 25, 2012.

Cummins, J., & Early, M. (2011). *Identity texts: The collaborative creation of power in multilingual schools*. Stoke-on-Trent, England: Trentham Books.

Darling-Hammond, L. (2010). *The flat world and education: How America's commitment to equity will determine our future*. New York: Teachers College Press.

Duke, N. (2000). For the rich it's richer: Print experiences and environments offered to children in very low and very high-socioeconomic status first-grade classrooms. *American Educational Research Journal, 37*(2), 441–478.

Francis, D., Lesaux, N., & August, D. (2006), Language of instruction. In D. August & T. Shanahan (Eds.),. *Developing literacy in second-language learners. Report of the National Literacy Panel on Language-Minority Children and Youth* (pp. 365–413). Mahwah, NJ: Lawrence Erlbaum.

Genesee, F., Lindholm-Leary, K, Saunders, W. M., & Christian, D. (Eds.). (2006). *Educating English language learners: A synthesis of research evidence*. New York: Cambridge University Press.

Gibbons, P. (1991). *Learning to learn in a second language*. Newtown, AUS: Primary English Teaching Association.

Gibbons, P. (2010). *English language learners, literacy and thinking: Learning in the challenge zone in the middle years*. Portsmouth, NH: Heinemann.

Guthrie, J. T. (2004). Teaching for literacy engagement. *Journal of Literacy Research, 36*(1), 1–30.

Hakuta, K., Butler, Y. G., & Witt, D. (2000). *How long does it take English learners to attain proficiency?* Santa Barbara: University of California Linguistic Minority Research Institute.

Is it time to end bilingual education? [Television series episode]. (2000). In *CNN talkback live*. New York: Turner Broadcasting System.

Klesmer, H. (1994). Assessment and teacher perceptions of ESL student achievement. *English Quarterly, 26*(3), 8–11.

Krashen, S. D. (2004). *The power of reading: Insights from the research* (2nd ed.). Portsmouth, NH: Heinemann.

Lindsay, J. (2010). *Children's access to print material and education-related outcomes: Findings from a meta-analytic review*. Naperville, IL: Learning Point.

Lindholm-Leary, K. & Hernández, A. (2011). Achievement and language proficiency of Latino students in dual language programmes: Native English speakers, fluent English/previous ELLs, and current ELLs. *Journal of Multilingual & Multicultural Development, 32*, 531–545.

Literacy and Numeracy Secretariat, Ministry of Education, Ontario. (n.d.). Webcast on *Teaching and Learning in Multilingual Ontario*. Accessed at http://www.curriculum.org/secretariat/archive.html on March 30, 2007.

Lucas, T., & Katz, A. (1994). Reframing the debate: The roles of native languages in English-only programs for language minority students. *TESOL Quarterly, 28*(3), 537–562.

Nation, I. S. P. (1990). *Teaching and learning vocabulary*. Boston: Heinle & Heinle.

National Reading Panel. (2000). *Teaching children to read: An evidence-based assessment of the scientific research literature on reading and its implications for reading instruction*. Washington, DC: National Institute of Child Health and Human Development.

Neuman, S. B., & Celano, D. (2001) Access to print in low-income and middle-income communities: An ecological study of four neighbourhoods. *Reading Research Quarterly, 36*(1), 8–26.

No Child Left Behind Act of 2001, Pub. L. No. 107–110. § 115, Stat. 1425 (2002).

Organisation for Economic Co-operation and Development. (2004). *Messages from PISA 2000*. Paris: Author.

Organisation for Economic Co-operation and Development. (2010b). *PISA 2009 results: Learning to learn—Student engagement, strategies and practices,* Vol. 3. Paris: Author.

Organisation for Economic Co-operation and Development. (2010a). *Strong performers and successful reformers in education: Lessons from PISA for the United States*. Accessed at www.oecd.org/dataoecd/32/50/46623978.pdf on December 27, 2010.

Parrish, T., Merickel, A., Perez, M., & Linquanti, R. (2006). *Effects of the implementation of Proposition 227 on the education of English learners, K–12: Findings from a five-year evaluation* (Final report). San Francisco: American Institutes for Research and WestEd.

Rolstad, K., Mahoney, K., & Glass, G. V. (2005). The big picture: A meta-analysis of program effectiveness research on English language learners. *Educational Policy, 19,* 572–594.

Slavin, R. E., Madden, N., Calderón, M., Chamberlain, A., & Hennessy, M. (2009). *Fifth-year reading and language outcomes of a randomized evaluation of transitional bilingual education: Report to IES*. Washington, DC: Institute for Education Sciences, U.S. Department of Education.

Shohamy, E., Levine, T., Spolsky, B., Kere-Levy, M., Inbar, O., & Shemesh, M. (2002). *The academic achievements of immigrant children from the former USSR and Ethiopia*. Report in Hebrew submitted to the Ministry of Education, Israel.

Slavin, R., Madden, N., Calderón, M., Chamberlain, A., & Hennessy, M. (2011). Reading and language outcomes of a multiyear randomized evaluation of transitional bilingual education. *Educational Evaluation and Policy Analysis, 33,* 47–58.

Snow, C. E., Burns, M. S., & Griffin, P. (Eds.). (1998). *Preventing reading difficulties in young children.* Washington, DC: National Academies Press.

Snow, C. E., & Hoefnagel-Hohle, M. (1978). The critical period for language acquisition: Evidence from second language learning. *Child Development, 49,* 1114–1128.

Swain, M., & Lapkin, S. (2005). The evolving sociopolitical context of immersion education in Canada: Some implications for program development. *International Journal of Applied Linguistics 15,* 169–186.

Thomas, W. P., & Collier, V. P. (2002). *A national study of school effectiveness for language minority students' long-term academic achievement.* Accessed at http//www.crede.ucsc.edu on April 12, 2004.

Vincent, C. (1996). *Singing to a star: The school meanings of second generation Salvadorean students.* Unpublished doctoral dissertation, George Mason University, Fairfax, VA.

Wong Fillmore, L. (2005, March 2). *Academic English learning.* Submission to Hearing on English Learners, California State Capitol.

Sarah Capitelli

Sarah Capitelli, PhD, is an assistant professor in teacher education at the University of San Francisco (USF). She also coordinates the Bilingual Authorization Program at USF. She received her MA in early childhood education and a Spanish-bilingual teaching credential from Mills College, in Oakland, California, and earned her doctorate in educational linguistics from Stanford University. Dr. Capitelli's research interests include the English language development of young English learners and the development of teaching practices that support ELs. Prior to her time at Stanford, she taught first and second grades in a Spanish bilingual program in Oakland, California.

Dr. Capitelli is coauthor (with Guadalupe Valdés and Laura Alvarez) of *Latino Children Learning English: Steps in the Journey.*

Laura Alvarez

Laura Alvarez, PhD, is a program associate with the Teacher Professional Development program at WestEd—a research, development, and service agency—where she works with the Quality Teaching for English Learners (QTEL) initiative. She received an MA in education from Mills College and a doctorate in educational linguistics from Stanford University.

Dr. Alvarez's research interests include academic language and children's bilingual language and literacy development. Prior to her time at Stanford, she taught fourth and fifth grades in a Spanish bilingual program in Oakland, California. She has also taught, supervised, and mentored preservice teachers at Mills College and Stanford with a focus on supporting English learners and teaching in bilingual classrooms. She is coauthor (with Guadalupe Valdés and Sarah Capitelli) of *Latino Children Learning English: Steps in the Journey.*

Guadalupe Valdés

Guadalupe Valdés, PhD, is professor of education at Stanford University. Her work has focused on English-Spanish bilingualism of Latinos in the United States. Dr. Valdés' investigations of Latino students has led to more than seventy articles and six books, including *Con respeto: Bridging the Distance Between Culturally Diverse Families and Schools* and *Bilingualism and Testing: A Special Case of Bias.* She is coauthor (with Sarah Capitelli and Laura Alvarez) of *Latino Children Learning English: Steps in the Journey.*

Dr. Valdés is a member of the American Academy of Education, a fellow of the American Educational Research Association (AERA), and a member of the board of trustees of the Educational Testing Service. She serves on the editorial boards of a number of journals, including *Review of Educational Research, Bilingual Review, Written Communication, Modern Language Journal,* and *Hispanic Journal of the Behavioral Sciences.* In May 2000, she received an honorary doctorate from the University of Arizona for her work on the use of Spanish in the United States. In 2012, she was the recipient of AERA's Henry T. Trueba Award for Research Leading to the Transformation of the Social Contexts of Education.

In this chapter, the authors explain the school contexts and language learning conditions that many Latino ELs confront and highlight findings from their own study that inform classroom practices. They describe how it would look for schools to move toward common core standards, how the integrated approach to teaching ELs looks different from what they are currently experiencing, and why this approach is so critical for the ELs' academic success.

Chapter 5

Educating English Learners: An Integrated Perspective

Sarah Capitelli, Laura Alvarez, and Guadalupe Valdés

As the number of English learners grows across North America, questions about the best ways to meet their language and learning needs continue to arise. What are the most effective teaching strategies when working with ELs? What do language proficiency assessments tell us—and not tell us—about an EL's language development? How do we make grade-level content accessible to beginning and intermediate proficiency ELs? What are the most advantageous learning conditions for developing a second language, and if these learning conditions are not available, is it possible to modify conditions to provide ELs with a more advantageous learning environment? These questions, among others, illustrate how complex and diverse the challenge of educating EL students is and demonstrate how much work remains to better meet the complex needs of this population of students.

A long-term design experiment we conducted aimed at providing access to English for young ELs in linguistically segregated schools through regular interactions with volunteer English speakers. Based on what we learned from that experiment, we will discuss what we believe schools need to consider when educating ELs. We will describe an integrated approach to teaching ELs, how it looks different from what ELs are currently experiencing in schools, and why we believe this approach is so critical for these students' academic success.

Challenging Learning Contexts Confronting ELs

One-on-One English grew out of our concerns regarding the learning contexts and pedagogies that many ELs, particularly Latinos, encounter in public schools. Of particular concern to us is the linguistic segregation that many Latino ELs contend with. In these school settings, the vast majority of their classmates are also ELs and speak Spanish as their primary language. Across the country, 70 percent of young ELs are being educated in 10 percent of all elementary schools, creating hypersegregated schools in which ELs make up more than 50 percent of the total school population (Cosentino de Cohen & Clewell, 2007). The reality is that most Latino ELs find themselves in schools surrounded by other ELs and with very little access to English (Gifford & Valdés, 2006). Beyond the linguistic status of these students, linguistically segregated schools also differ in terms of student ethnicity, student poverty, and school location (Consentino de Cohen et al., 2005; Gándara & Rumberger, 2002; Rogers et al., 2009). Additionally, teachers in these schools have less academic preparation and are less likely to be fully certified (Gándara & Hopkins, 2010, Gándara, Maxwell-Jolly, & Rumberger, 2008).

> Academic language is often conceptualized as formal, written language, neglecting the importance of speaking and listening in academic learning and language development.

In these contexts, much emphasis is placed on ELs' development of "academic language," or the language needed to succeed in school. However, there is a lack of clarity about what in fact academic language is, how it develops, and how it can be taught (Alvarez, 2008; Valdés, 2004; Valdés, MacSwan, & Alvarez, 2009). As we will see, academic language is often conceptualized as formal, written language, neglecting the importance of speaking and listening in academic learning and language development.

One-on-One English: A Design Experiment

In response to the challenging linguistic and learning contexts we have described, as well as to a national context in which volunteers were often seen as a potential solution to educational problems, we developed an intervention program aimed at training and supporting volunteers to provide access to English for young ELs in school contexts where they have few opportunities to interact with fluent speakers of the language. Volunteers—English buddies—spent forty-five minutes twice a week after school looking at books and playing games one-on-one with a young EL, with the hope of providing the student with rich English input and access to the language. One-on-One English was conceptualized as a design experiment (Reinking & Bradley, 2008) informed by second-language acquisition research that sought to generate knowledge about the kinds of input that can be provided to children by English-speaking volunteers, the degree of English language growth that occurs from exposure to increased input, and the most effective methods of preparing volunteers to provide rich language input to young ELs. In this chapter, we will highlight two findings that we believe are particularly relevant for teachers of ELs: (1) change over time in the development of English learners and (2) the kinds of affordances that support this development.

Over the course of a five-year period, we identified the kindergarten through second-grade students at a linguistically isolated school who were most in need of an English language intervention. Initial oral productive and receptive English-language baseline data were collected on each student, as well as data at the beginning and end of each year the student participated in the program. Students were paired with an English buddy, and a segment of every forty-five-minute session between students and English buddies was videotaped. We provided ongoing training and support to the English buddies. This training and support was informed both by second-language acquisition theory, primarily the work of Wong Fillmore (1976, 1982, 1985a, 1985b, 1991), and by our ongoing observations of the sessions and reflections on the videotapes.

Change Over Time

As mentioned, an important goal of One-on-One English was to generate knowledge about the impact of exposure to increased input of English over time for young ELs. We want to acknowledge that children who participated in the program had regular access to ordinary speakers of English, who in varying degrees engaged them in talk that involved interesting and colorful age-appropriate literature. Therefore, we are not claiming that participation was the exclusive or primary contributing factor in the growth we saw over time.

An important lesson from One-on-One English is that the change we saw in children's language over time was not uniform. Although all of the children were classified as "beginners" by the state-mandated English-language proficiency assessment,[1] there was a great deal of variation between their language development at the beginning as compared to the end of the program. In addition, students' language development did not follow the sequential trajectory expected by many English language proficiency assessments and English language development (ELD) curricula. These assume a straightforward upward trajectory in terms of interactional competencies and the use of linguistic forms (vocabulary, grammatical tenses, parts of speech, and so on) considered to be more or less advanced. In the California context, this is made evident in ELD instructional programs that almost exclusively focus on the explicit and sequential teaching of grammar, phonics, and vocabulary (Thompson, 2009) that "will move English learners as quickly as possible through stages of language proficiency" (California State Board of Education, 2007, p. 274, as cited in Thompson, 2009).

However, our experience with the children who participated in One-on-One English indicates that quick movement through stages of language proficiency was not the path that young ELs took and that change over time was a far more complex and multifaceted

---

[1] In California, the state mandated English language proficiency assessment is the California English Language Development Test (CELDT). Students in kindergarten through twelfth grade whose home language is not English are required to take the test. The test assesses the four language modalities: speaking, listening, reading, and writing.

matter than simply being taught a series of language structures they were meant to master. For example, over time we observed that children were able to produce more independent and structured oral narratives. This was made evident through longer turns that were independent of the examiner's language, as well as use of a greater variety of linguistic forms. (For a more complete description and discussion of the change and growth in the children's language, as well as a description of the analysis, please refer to Valdés, Capitelli, and Alvarez [2011]).

> Quick movement through stages of language proficiency was not the path that young ELs took and that change over time was a far more complex and multifaceted matter than simply being taught a series of language structures.

At the same time, students did not learn and master linguistic structures in a sequential manner, and their speech did not necessarily become more accurate as they began using more linguistic forms and communicating more complex meanings, as expected in English language proficiency assessments.

The Role of Affordances

As we have mentioned, another important goal of One-on-One English was to generate knowledge about the kinds of input that can be generated by English-speaking volunteers for young ELs. The children in the program had available a range of affordances that we hypothesized would be of benefit to them and their English language development. These included a socially defined situation (after-school sessions), interaction with an adult English-speaking volunteer, literacy tools (such as books, games, and puzzles), and embodied tools (for example, gestures, eye gaze, and pantomines).

Over the course of the five-year project, we developed a greater understanding of how these affordances worked differently for children depending on, for instance, their volunteer, the materials their volunteer used, and the affect of the student. Although we do not go into great detail regarding everything we learned about the role of affordances in the development of English for these young children, for the purposes of this chapter it is critical to underscore the importance of the affordance being embedded in rich and engaging language activities.

Implications for Practice

One-on-One English grew out of our concerns regarding the learning contexts of and pedagogies being used with young ELs. We were particularly concerned with the growing focus on prescriptive reading curricula used with young ELs, their focus on phonics and vocabulary development, and the lack of emphasis on oral language development. This concern motivated our design of One-on-One English and the hope of providing increased access to oral English for young ELs who had limited access to English speakers. Our learnings from One-on-One English challenge many current policies and pedagogical practices that expect the rapid English-language development of ELs.

What Kind of English Must Be Acquired to Succeed in School?

Supporting the education of ELs requires clarity about the kind of academic language that students need to acquire at different grade levels. Academic language has often been vaguely defined in contrast to conversational or everyday language (Bailey, 2007; Francis & Rivera, 2007; Scarcella, 2003). The focus has been on linguistic features found in academic writing, which, in states like California, has led to ELD instruction comprised of sequential and explicit instruction in vocabulary and grammar (Thompson, 2009). As Lily Wong Fillmore and Catherine Snow (2002) assert, although academic language is often described in terms of a dichotomy between oral and written language, academic English proficiency encompasses a broad range of language abilities. Conversational or everyday language plays an essential role in school learning, supporting students' engagement with academic content and bridging to formal academic language (Bunch, 2006; Warren, Ballenger, Ogonowski, Rosebery, & Hudicourt-Barnes, 2001). Focusing solely on the features of formal academic writing therefore leads to a narrow definition of academic language, which can constrain students' opportunities to learn both language and content.

In addition to recognizing the role that both oral and written language play in academic work, it is important to consider the overlapping and relational uses of oral and written language in academic contexts (Horowitz, 2007). Within a single academic task, students are often called upon to engage with or produce both spoken and written language. For example, students as well as academics who are experts in their fields talk from texts they have read, produce written work incorporating information gleaned through a lecture or discussion, and speak in both formal and informal settings from written notes.

An Integrated Perspective

Our position that oral language is critical for classroom participation, engagement, collaboration, and ultimately academic success, leads us to propose a working framework that includes and recognizes the value and necessity of conversational and interactional competencies in school, as well as the importance of receptive and productive proficiencies (that is, reading and writing). It is our hope that such a framework can help guide instructional practices away from narrow conceptions that dichotomize oral language and literacy. We will describe what this integrated perspective might look like in practice.

Most ELD curriculum and language proficiency assessments focus on and separate the four language modalities (speaking, listening, reading, and writing). For example, children who take the CELDT test in California take separate speaking, listening, reading, and writing portions of the test, and as they move higher up in the grades, the reading and writing portion of the assessment is weighted more heavily. Similarly, ELD instructional blocks are often focused on the development of the four language modalities. Although children might sing songs, recite chants, and listen to a short story during ELD in kindergarten and first grade, as students move to higher grades, they spend less time talking and hearing English and more time focused on language forms, with the result that much of English class might be done in silence completing worksheets. Implicit in this type of instructional activity is the belief that the purpose of "English time" is practicing English rather than communicating meaning to your teacher or peers.

An integrated perspective on the dimensions of school communication highlights the three types of communication required to participate and achieve in classroom settings: interpersonal, interpretive, and presentational (table 5.1). Each takes into account the number and arrangement of the interlocutors involved (one-on-one or one-to-many, and face-to-face or at a distance), as well as the types of skills (receptive or productive) required for the particular skills or tasks. An integrated perspective puts content learning at the center rather than focusing on language learning for its own sake. The language demands of learning academic content and literacy in school include oral language proficiencies as well as proficiencies in reading and writing texts.

> An integrated perspective on the dimensions of school communication highlights the three types of communication required to participate and achieve in classroom settings: interpersonal, interpretive, and presentational.

Table 5 1: An Integrated Perspective on the Dimensions of School Communication

	Interpersonal Communication	Interpretive Communication	Presentational Communication
Oral language	Used in face-to-face oral communication	Used in comprehending spoken communication as a member of a class, audience, or other group (for example, understanding the talk in partner work or cooperative groups)	Used in communicating orally with a group face-to-face or at a distance (for example, small-group work or class presentation)
Written language	Used in informal written communication between individuals who come into personal contact	Used in comprehending written communication as a member of a general readership	Used in communicating in writing with an audience or general readership

Working with the integrated perspective we have outlined in conjunction with the Common Core State Standards (CCSS),[2] we highlight one strand recommended for third grade and describe the instructional practices that might support ELs in meeting some of the grade-level standards under that strand.

A third-grade strand for English/language arts consists of Reading Standards for Informational Text. This includes four strand areas: (1) Key Ideas and Details; (2) Craft and Structure, (3) Integration of Knowledge and Ideas, and (3) Range of Reading and Level of Text Complexity. Under each of these are a number of standards that support the development of the critical skills and understandings needed to meet the content and language demands of school. For example, standard R1.3.1, under Key Ideas and Details, reads:

> Ask and answer questions to demonstrate understanding of a text, referring explicitly to the text as the basis for the answers. (National Governors Association Center for Best Practices & Council of Chief State School Officers [NGA & CCSSO], 2010a, p. 14)

Clearly, standards such as this require students to do more than practice correct grammatical structures and vocabulary, as is common with most ELD instruction. They require that students be engaged in rich instructional experiences that incorporate the multiple dimensions of communication. One activity or task will not "teach" students Standard R1.3.1. Rather, learning the standard will be accomplished through a series of well planned and executed units of study and lessons over time.

The infusion of rich, age-appropriate content knowledge and vocabulary requires a diversity of classroom experiences for ELs, so that they are able to develop the required interpersonal, interpretive, and presentational skills.

The CCSS emphasize that exposure and reading of "complex informational texts should begin at the very earliest elementary school grades" (NGA & CCCSO, 2010b, p. 3). Furthermore, the standards underscore the

---

[2] See www.corestandards.org for a complete discussion of the CCSS, including the process of development as well as a detailed description of the strands and standards.

importance of infusing language arts instruction with rich, age-appropriate content knowledge and vocabulary. The CCSS highlight exemplar texts on the human body that can be used across the grade levels to support both content and vocabulary development as well as the complex skills needed to make sense of the content and vocabulary. This infusion of rich, age-appropriate content knowledge and vocabulary requires a diversity of classroom experiences for ELs, so that they are able to develop the required interpersonal, interpretive, and presentational skills.

In table 5.2 (page 99), we take a closer look at the following standard in the Reading Standards for Informational Text, R.1.3.3:

> Describe the relationship between a series of historical events, scientific ideas or concepts, or steps in technical procedures in a test, using language that pertains to time, sequence, and cause/effect, and give examples of how the Integrated Perspective on the Dimensions of School Communication is helpful in interpreting the CCSS. (NGA & CCSSO, 2010)

In looking at the activities that would support the development of Standard R.1.3.3, it is clear that there is no single lesson that would accomplish developing the standard, but rather a series of experiences that build on one another that enable students to develop both the content and language skills needed to describe the digestive system and the important ideas and concepts associated with, and the cause-and-effect relationship inherent in, the digestive system. Ideally, these experiences would build on classroom experiences ELs have had previously and will build upon in the future. It is important to note that these experiences do not begin with a series of oral language experiences culminating with a written experience, but rather incorporate and depend upon oral and textual experiences throughout.

Two Critical Issues

Given the challenges facing ELs in schools that we have highlighted, and building on our work with One-on-One English and our articulation of an integrative practice for educating ELs, we close with two critical issues.

**Table 5.2: Using the Third-Grade Common Core
State Standards: The Digestive System**

	Interpersonal Communication	Interpretive Communication	Presentational Communication
Oral language	Participate in comprehension-check pair-shares during read-alouds, video watching, and pictorial and vocabulary input activities. Ask clarifying questions of teacher and peers. Answer questions from teacher and peers.	Listen to (and watch) teacher's pictorial and vocabulary input on the digestive system. Listen to a read-aloud of *What Happens to a Hamburger* (Showers,1985). Watch a video of *Digestive System: The Magic School Bus for Lunch* (Scholastic, 1994). Listen to online sources about the digestive system (for example, http://kidshealth.org/kid/htbw/digestive_system.html). Listen to and participate in small-group work on the digestive system. Listen to classroom presentations from peers. Practice a script for small-group presentation.	Construct a labeled pictorial with a small group for presentation. Present small-group work on the digestive system to the class.

Continued →

Written language	Write in an interactive science journal with the teacher. Write a reflection on classmates' presentations in a science journal.	Gather and record information from the pictorial and vocabulary input, video, and read-aloud. Read books like *The Digestive System,* by Kristin Petrie (2006). Read online sources about the digestive system (for example, www .enchantedlearning .com/subjects/anatomy /digestive).	Write an individual report on the digestive system for a group report. Write a script for a small-group presentation.

First, in order to achieve in schools, ELs must develop the requisite communicative competencies. All of the instruction directed at ELs must be aimed at the development of the productive and receptive skills that are essential to fully participate in the life of schools. They will not reach these critical levels of competencies with instruction and instructional goals focused solely on grammatical structures, vocabulary, and bits and pieces of language. ELs must be engaged in rich academic tasks that incorporate meaningful experiences—with both oral and written language—that are essential to academic achievement. This means that ELs must learn and have opportunities to share ideas with their teachers and peers, work collaboratively in groups, and engage in discussions about content that is interesting and compelling. Additionally, they must develop the communicative competencies to learn from their teachers and texts. This means they must learn how to read and understand textbooks, how to take notes during and learn from teacher explanations and lectures, and how to gather information from various sources of information (for example, videos, the Internet, and primary sources).

Second, in order for ELs to develop these communicative competencies, teacher education and ongoing teacher professional development need to prepare and support teachers in structuring their instruction and classrooms to provide maximum access to

English. Currently, teacher education and professional development tend to separate content instruction from preparing and supporting teachers to work with ELs. However, as the both the Integrated Perspective and CCSS highlights, language instruction and content instruction cannot be separated. Rather, teachers need to learn how to teach content while simultaneously developing the interpersonal, interpretive, and communicative abilities students need to participate in the high level discourse of schooling. Regardless of the approach they take to teaching ELs (GLAD, SIOP, SDAIE, or some other),[3] teachers need to learn that the emphasis needs to be on developing particular aspects of interpersonal, interpretive, and communicative abilities. For example, in the third-grade science unit highlighted earlier, a teacher may be using GLAD strategies during her science unit on the digestive system, as evident from the pictorial and vocabulary input chart she introduces, as well as the chants and songs she utilizes. However, these GLAD strategies are not enough to ensure that her students develop the communicative competencies needed to engage completely in the unit. In order to develop students' understanding of cause-and-effect relationships, the teacher would also need to design and implement a series of lessons aimed at teaching (building on students' prior experiences) about the elements of cause-and-effect relationships. Students might have the opportunity to brainstorm in small groups about cause-and-effect relationships they are familiar with (thus developing interpersonal communication skills). Additionally, they might have the opportunity to hear read-alouds about the digestive system that highlight cause-and effect-relationships (while developing interpretive communication skills). They might then create posters that they share with the rest of the class demonstrating what happens to a particular meal when they eat it (building presentational communication skills).

We have only touched on a few of the important areas that schools need to consider when educating ELs. However, by addressing the ways in which instruction needs to be reconceptualized to

---

[3] Like SIOP, GLAD (Guided Language Acquisition Design and SDAIE (Specially Designed Academic Instruction in English) are popular approaches to teaching and developing English in ELs.

create experiences that permit ELs to develop their interpersonal, interpretive, and presentational skills, schools and teachers will be more able to fully meet their needs.

References

Alvarez, L. (2008). *Examining academic language in process and in practice.* Unpublished doctoral dissertation proposal, Stanford University, California.

Bailey, A. (2007). *The language of school: Putting academic English to the test.* New Haven, CT: Yale University Press.

Bunch, G. C. (2006). "Academic English" in the 7th grade: Broadening the lens, expanding access. *Journal of English for Academic Purposes, 5,* 284–301.

California State Board of Education. (2007). *Reading/language arts framework for California public schools.* Sacramento: California Department of Education.

Consentino de Cohen, C., & Clewell, B. C. (2007). *Putting English language learners on the educational map.* Washington, DC: Urban Institute.

Cosentino de Cohen, C., Deterdin, N., & Clewell, B. C. (2005). *Who's left behind? Immigrant children in high- and low-LEP schools.* Washington, DC: Urban Institute.

Francis, D., & Rivera, M. (2007). Principles underlying English language proficiency tests and academic accountability for ELs. In J. Abedi (Ed.), *English language proficiency assessment in the nation: Current status and future practice* (pp. 13–32). Davis: University of California Press

Gándara, P., & Hopkins, M. (2010). The changing linguistic landscape of the United States. In P. Gándara & M. Hopkins (Eds.), *Forbidden language: English learners and restrictive language policies* (pp. 7–19). New York: Teachers College Press.

Gándara, P., Maxwell-Jolly, J., & Rumberger, R. W. (2008). *Resource needs for English learners: Getting down to policy recommendations.* Santa Barbara: University of California Linguistic Minority Research Institute.

Gándara, P., & Rumberger, R. (2002). *The inequitable treatment of English learners in California's public schools.* Los Angeles: University of California, Los Angeles, Institute for Democracy, Education, and Access.

Gifford, B. R., & Valdés, G. (2006). The linguistic isolation of Hispanic students in California's public schools: The challenge of reintegration. In A. Ball (Ed.), *With more deliberate speed: Achieving equity and excellence in education— Realizing the full potential of Brown v. Board of Education: The 105th yearbook of the National Society for the Study of Education,* Part II (pp. 125–154). Malden, MA: Wiley-Blackwell.

Horowitz, R. (Ed.). (2007). *Talking texts: How speech and writing interact in school learning awareness.* Mahwah, NJ: Lawrence Erlbaum.

National Governors Association Center for Best Practices & Council of Chief State School Officers. (2010). *Common core state standards for English language arts & literacy in history/social studies, science, and technical subjects.* Accessed at www.corestandards.org/assets/CCSSI_ELA%20Standards.pdf on August 8, 2011.

Petrie, K. (2006). *The digestive system.* Edina, MN: Checkerboard Books.

Reinking, D., & Bradley, B.A. (2008). *Formative and design experiments: Approaches to language and literacy research.* New York: Teachers College Press.

Rogers, J., Fanelli, S., Medina, D., Zhu, Q., Freelon, R., Bertrand, M. et al. (2009). *California Educational Opportunity Report: Listening to Public School Parents.* Los Angeles: University of California, Los Angeles, Institute for Democracy, Education, and Access /University of California All Campus Consortium on Research for Diversity.

Scarcella, R. (2003). *Academic English: A conceptual framework* (Technical Report No. 20031). Santa Barbara, CA: Linguistic Minority Research Institute.

Scholastic. (1994). *Magic school bus: For lunch (Digestion).* Accessed at www.gamequarium.org/dir/SqoolTube_Videos/Science/Human_Body/Digestive_System/magic_school_bus_for_lunch_9673.html on October 28, 2011.

Showers, P. (1985). *What happens to a hamburger?* New York: Harper & Row.

Thompson, K. (2009). *The role of research-based ideas about language acquisition in California's curriculum materials for English language development.* Unpublished qualifying paper, Stanford University, California.

Valdés, G. (2004). Between support and marginalisation: The development of academic language in linguistic minority children. *International Journal of Bilingual Education and Bilingualism, 7*(2–3), 102–132.

Valdés, G., Capitelli, S., & Alvarez, L. (2011). *Latino children learning English: Steps in the journey.* New York: Teachers College Press.

Valdés, G., MacSwan, J., & Alvarez, L. (2009, October). *Deficits and differences: Perspectives on language and education.* Paper presented at the National Research Council workshop on the Role of Language in School Learning: Implications for closing the Achievement Gap, Menlo Park, CA. Accessed at www.nationalacademies.org/cfe/Role_of_Language_Workshop_Agenda_October_15–16_2009.html on January 31, 2012.

Warren, B., Ballenger, C., Ogonowski, M., Rosebery, A. S., & Hudicourt-Barnes, J. (2001). Rethinking diversity in learning science: The logic of everyday sense making. *Journal of Research in Science Teaching, 38,* 529–552.

Wong Fillmore, L. (1976). *The second time around: Cognitive and social strategies in second language acquisition.* Unpublished doctoral dissertation, Stanford University, Palo Alto, CA.

Wong Fillmore, L. (1982). Language minority students and school participation: What kind of English is needed? *Journal of Education, 164*(2), 143–156.

Wong Fillmore, L. (1985a, July). *Second language learning in children: A proposed model.* Paper presented at the Issues in for Minority Language Education conference, Arlington, VA.

Wong Fillmore, L. (1985b). When does teacher talk work as input. In S. Gass & C. Madden (Eds.), *Input in second language acquisition* (pp. 17–50). Rowley, MA: Newbury.

Wong Fillmore, L. (1991). When learning a second language means losing the first. *Early Childhood Research Quarterly, 63*(3), 323–347.

Wong Fillmore, L., & Snow, C. (2002). *What teachers need to know about language.* Washington, DC: Center for Applied Linguistics.

Liliana Minaya-Rowe

Liliana Minaya-Rowe, PhD, a native of Peru, is an educational consultant and researcher in the areas of teacher education, literacy, two-way bilingual and ESL program design and development, educational leadership, and first- and second-language acquisition and teaching methodology. She is professor emerita of the Neag School of Education at the University of Connecticut, where she implemented a graduate program of specialization in bilingual multicultural education. Between 1980 and 2001, she administered twenty-six U.S. Department of Education Grants with multimillion-dollar funding. She has also directed over forty-two doctoral dissertation research studies in education and graduated more than three hundred students at the masters, post-masters, and doctoral levels.

Dr. Minaya-Rowe was coprincipal investigator with Margarita Calderón of the Johns Hopkins University/Carnegie Corporation's *Project ExC-ELL: Expediting Comprehension for English Learners,* an initiative to design, implement, and refine a staff development program for middle and high school teachers with English learners in their classrooms. She has edited *Teacher Training and Effective Pedagogy in the Context of Student Diversity,* coauthored with Margarita Calderón *Preventing Long-Term ELs: Transforming Schools to Meet Core Standards* and *Designing and Implementing Two-Way Bilingual Programs,* and with Virginia González and Thomas Yawkey *English as a Second Language Teaching and Learning: Pre-K–12 Classroom Applications for Students' Academic Achievement and Development.* She has published over three hundred articles, chapters, books, teacher-training manuals and guidebooks.

In this chapter, Dr. Minaya-Rowe discusses how to integrate language, literacy, and subject-area instruction in middle and high schools and shows what professional development designs schools can use to prepare all teachers, whether in math, science, social studies, or language arts, to be teachers of vocabulary, reading, and writing.

Chapter 6

Effective Teaching for ELs and All Students: Vocabulary, Reading, and Writing Within All Subjects

Liliana Minaya-Rowe

The current trend of globalization and the necessity to compete in a "flattened" world within an increasingly integrated world economic system has prompted a profound shift in education (Friedman, 2005). To meet these needs, schools in North America are broadening their goals to encompass equity, access, and the need to help students become critical thinkers and compete effectively in the global marketplace (Darling-Hammond, 2010).

School improvement is mainly concerned about the effectiveness of teachers and schools and how they affect student outcomes. Administrators play an important role in this change process, which requires both leadership skills and academic knowledge of content. Their role in school improvement and reform efforts includes managing the process, providing professional development resources, and developing innovative solutions to the day-to-day problems of implementing change (DuFour & Marzano, 2011).

What Do ELs Need?

As ELs progress through school, they need the tools to comprehend ever more complicated texts, and they require development in one or more of the following areas: vocabulary, grammar, basic reading (including decoding and fluency), reading comprehension, and writing skills (August & Shanahan, 2006, 2008). Furthermore, they need to learn and apply the vocabulary and reading and writing in the content areas (Calderón, 2007, Calderón & Minaya-Rowe, 2011; Calderón et al., 2005). If one component is not present, then the foundation will not be solid enough for academic English proficiency.

Language, literacy, and content learning are an integrated approach to learning for ELs that supports schools' efforts to respond to the high demand for quality literacy and differentiated instruction to address the diversity of student needs (Calderón & Minaya-Rowe, 2011). Since most ELs are in heterogeneous classrooms that include English-only students, this chapter is designed as a tool for teachers to use in providing effective instruction for ELs and all other students in their classrooms, particularly those reading below grade level and needing extensive vocabulary development for comprehending subject-matter texts.

Academic English

ELs need academic English to acquire a deeper understanding of discipline content related to the grade-level curriculum and to communicate that understanding to others. It is also the language students need to acquire and produce appropriately through oral and written modes in order to participate effectively in the classroom environment. Academic language spans several linguistic levels: the word level, or vocabulary; the sentence level, or grammar; and the extended text level, or discourse. It is the language students need to succeed at school and in life. Table 6.1 (page 109) presents a description of each of these linguistic levels.

Figure 6.1 (page 110) illustrates the cycle that includes vocabulary mastery, reading comprehension, and fluency, and writing for core content grade-level standards.

Table 6.1: Academic English-Language Proficiency Components

Level	Description
Word or vocabulary	Words, phrases, and expressions, including general vocabulary in classroom routines; nonspecialized, general academic vocabulary encountered across the disciplines (for example, *analysis, predict, as a matter of fact*) and specialized discipline-specific vocabulary (such as *Bill of Rights* in social studies, *personification* in literature, *Pythagoras' theorem* in mathematics)
Sentence or grammar	Language patterns and grammatical structures specific to individual discipline contents. These may be highly complex and may be encountered primarily in print form (for example, "There have been several longitudinal comprehensive studies that have shown how to simultaneously work on school structures, teacher support mechanisms, and effective instruction for ELs").
Extended text discourse	Discussions and reading of academic structures in discipline-specific genres, such as compare-and-contrast essays, summaries, cause-and-effect text structures, oral and written reports on the amendments to the Constitution, and precise word definitions

Academic Vocabulary Mastery

For ELs, learning vocabulary in the content areas often means learning entirely new concepts. Teachers build on the word selection from texts and on recommendations by a number of researchers in the field about when and how to teach these concepts, and to what degree their ELs should know them (Calderón et al., 2005; Calderón & Minaya-Rowe, 2011) have contributed to our understanding on what words ELs need in order to succeed in school and have developed steps to teach them before, during, and after reading. Calderón (2007, 2011) has posited that vocabulary mastery is a precursor for reading and writing and must therefore be a priority. Vocabulary strategies are applicable not only for ELs and struggling readers but for all students.

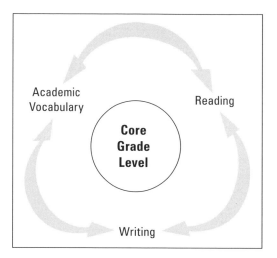

Figure 6.1: Vocabulary, reading, and writing within subject areas.

Vocabulary plays a major role in improving reading comprehension in classrooms with ELs. English learners need to master academic vocabulary in order to understand the language of content areas. They need to know the literal meaning of the word, its various connotations, and the relationships between words (syntactic constructions), and they must develop a rich array of associations, including synonyms and antonyms (Nagy, 2005). Depth and breadth of word knowledge are an important goal of vocabulary mastery. *Depth of word knowledge* refers to multiple meanings for the same word, roots, affixes, and polysemous (multiple meaning), and cognate status. *Breadth of word knowledge* refers to large numbers of academic words. A high-achieving twelfth grader learns fifteen words a day in each content area, over five thousand words a year (Stahl, 2005).

The more words ELs know, understand, and apply accurately, the easier it is for them to make connections in their reading. Vocabulary strategies are multifaceted and encompass the following research-based instructional practices:

- Teach the words that are critical to new content in a direct and sustained way.

- Concentrate on key concepts in each lesson or unit.

- Connect new vocabulary to student experiences through schema activators.

- Provide word practice through listening, speaking, reading, and writing.

- Teach word parts or prefixes, suffixes, and roots.

- Incorporate visuals with caution to teach new words—for example, when matching definitions and new key terms on a circulatory system chart.

- Cross-reference words to other content areas when appropriate; for example, *root* in both science and math.

- Use cognates to teach new words wherever possible.

Cognates are used for vocabulary instruction for ELs whose first language is Spanish in order to expand on word relationships between Spanish and English. There are also false cognates that need to be clarified—for example, *exit* does not have the same meaning as *éxito* (success); rather, the correct translation for *exit* is *salida;* the word for *embarrassed* in Spanish is not *embarazada* (pregnant), it is *avergonzada(o).*

Isabel Beck and her colleagues Margaret McKeown and Linda Kucan describe how teachers can work with their students to improve their vocabularies by (1) selecting words for instruction, (2) explaining the new words with meaningful learning activities, and (3) getting students involved in thinking about, using, and noticing new words. The goal is for students to have the vocabulary they need in order to understand what they read.

Margarita E. Calderón has customized these three strategies for English learners (and any other students) who need to become academic English proficient. She incorporates them into a differentiation framework to address the listening, speaking, reading, and writing needs of second-language learners. To (1), selecting words for instruction, she adds:

- Parsing or "chunking" of text

- English-Spanish cognates and false cognates

- Phrases, idioms, connectors, clusters, transition words, and homophones

To (2), explaining new words with meaningful learning activities, she adds:

- A seven-step strategy to pre-teach key vocabulary before reading

- Targeting oracy development, word structure, and depth and breadth of meaning

- Use of the EL criteria of (1) above—for example, whether the word is an English-Spanish cognate

To (3), how to get students involved in thinking about, using, and noticing new words, Calderón adds:

- Oral strategies of EL engagement with the word during pre-teaching

- Oral and written student involvement strategies during reading

- Oral and written student involvement after reading

Beck, McKeown, and Kucan's (2002, 2005) premise for teaching words is based on three vocabulary tiers. Each tier is predicated on the following dimensions: the nature of the word (is it concrete, or can it be demonstrated?), its cognate status, the depth of word meaning, and its utility. A summary of the three tiers follows with a specific description for each tier as it applies to ELs.

Tier 1: Everyday Words

Tier 1 words, according to Beck et al., are basic words that ELs need for everyday speech and for scaffolding academic conversations, explanations, and more complicated text. We have found in our studies that English-speaking students already know Tier 1 words, and ELs may either know them from their ESL instruction or not know them at all. Tier words may be:

- Basic words that ELs may know the concept of and label in their first language, but for which they need the English label (for example, *find, search, guest, tooth*, and *answer*)

- Simple idioms and basic expressions that ELs are unlikely to know (such as *running around, give me a break*, and *hanging out*)

- Connectors such as *so, if, then, however*, and *finally*

Tier 2: Information-Processing Words

Tier 2 words have importance and utility, are in grade-level texts, and can be worked with in a variety of ways. These are words that provide precision and specificity in describing concepts students already know. Table 6.2 shows selected Tier 2 words as they relate to Tiers 1 and 3. However, it is important to note that not all word meanings lend themselves to expansions across tiers.

Table 6.2: Understanding Vocabulary Tiers

Tier 1 Word	Tier 2 Word	Tier 3 Word
house	abode	habitat
find	search	investigate

Tier 2 words include:

- Polysemous words that are characteristic of mature language users and appear frequently across a variety of content areas and domains—for example, *power, cell, radical, right, leg, tree, prime, imaginary, round, simple, expression*, and *dependent*

- Words that have instructional potential (that is, words that can be worked with in a variety of ways so that students can build rich representations of them and their connections to other words and concepts, such as the word *verb* and its expansions—*verbal, nonverbal, verbalize, verbatim*)

- Words that provide precision and specificity in describing concepts about which students already have conceptual understanding, such as *sprinted* for *run*

ELs may find it difficult to transition from a limited Tier 1 vocabulary size, which they use to communicate, to a larger and more sophisticated Tier 2 word knowledge pool. Table 6.3 illustrates ELs' likely Tier 1 expressions and selected corresponding Tier 2 academic words they need to learn at school.

Table 6.3: ELs' Likely Tier 1 Expressions and Tier 2 Words

Students' Likely Expressions	Tier 2 Word
Something someone has said	comment
Coming out	emerging
Tell me more	elaborate
To say you did something	admit
Scary	haunting
Luck	fortune

Tier 2 words for ELs generally consist of transition words, polysemous words, and cognates.

Transition Words

Some Tier 2 words are transition words that make comprehension difficult for ELs. These include *so, furthermore, on the other hand, at, into, within,* and *by.* These words are helpful when comparing and contrasting, describing, and giving examples.

Polysemous Words

Like transition words, polysemous words can make comprehension difficult for ELs. Words like *table* need to be specifically taught, because ELs may know *table* as in furniture, but not *table* as in *table of random numbers* in mathematics, or *table* as a verb, as in *table a motion* in social studies. *Trunk* is also a polysemous word; that is, it has multiple meanings: The trunk with the elephant's trunk was found under the tree trunk and put in the car trunk along with our swimming trunks (Calderón, 2007).

Cognates

Students whose first language shares cognates with English will have a head start with these words, because they will know both the concept and an approximation of the label in English. Cognate use is possible with such Romance, Latin-based languages as Spanish, Polish, Portuguese, Russian, Romanian, Albanian, Italian, and French. The Tier 2 words that should be targeted for preteaching include words that cannot be demonstrated and are *not* cognates. Table 6.4 lists English words with cognates in Spanish and Polish.

Table 6.4: Tier 2 and 3 Vocabulary in English, Spanish and Polish Cognates

English	Spanish	Polish
sum	suma	suma
factor	factor	faktor
mathematics	matemáticas	matematyka
photosynthesis	fotosíntesis	fotosynteza
computer	computador(a)	komputer

Unfortunately, we cannot rely entirely on this practice, since many EL students are not proficient enough in their first language, orally or in writing, to use word knowledge transfer as a resource for meaning. However, it is true that once they learn about the relationship of a cognate it produces an affective connection with the words and a sense of word ownership.

Tier 3 Words

These academic words in English are limited to specific content-area domains, such as social studies, math, language arts, and science. Although they are low-frequency words—for example, *isotope, peninsula, cable, osmosis,* and *hyperbole* (all cognates)—they are very important for understanding content. Literate Spanish (and other Romance

Literate Spanish speakers have a great advantage over monolingual English speakers with Tier 3 words, because many cognates are high-frequency words in Spanish but low-frequency words in English.

languages) speakers have a great advantage over monolingual English speakers with Tier 3 words, because many cognates are high-frequency words in Spanish but low-frequency words in English (for example, *democracy/democracia, round off/redondear, absurd/absurdo*).

Strategies for Vocabulary Growth

Vocabulary is at the forefront of lesson planning for English learners. An effective lesson plan will include the vocabulary essential for students to access content knowledge. Collaborative planning sessions provide teachers with valuable opportunities for the selection of that critical vocabulary and its integration across and within content areas and grade levels. Research points to less is more: students will most likely retain selected vocabulary taught in depth and breadth rather than long lists of words (August & Shanahan, 2008). Frontloading instruction by presenting students with key words prior to the lesson provides the lexical framework to comprehend content. The linguistic demands of the content areas require that teachers select strategies that will reinforce the key vocabulary before, during, and after the course of the lesson.

Calderón (2007, 2011) has proposed a seven-step process for introducing the most important and complex words or clusters of words to be used either at the beginning of a lesson, before a teacher read-aloud, or before students are to read a text:

1. The teacher reads and shows the word in the sentence from the text. This helps students remember the word in context when they begin to read, and to grasp the meaning.

2. To practice pronunciation, the students repeat the words several times with and without the teacher.

3. The teacher provides the dictionary or glossary definition(s). This exposes the students to formal English and to what they will encounter later when they are proficient enough in English to use a dictionary.

4. The teacher explains meaning with student-friendly definitions or gives an example that students can relate to

using simple language, familiar examples, pictures, props, movement, and gestures to help students comprehend the meaning (or in some cases, multiple meanings).

5. The teacher highlights an aspect of the word that might create difficulty: spelling, multiple meanings, cognates and false cognates, prefixes, suffixes, base words, synonyms, antonyms, homophones, grammatical variations, and so on. Students will later do more in-depth word study on what was highlighted.

6. The teacher engages 100 percent of the students in ways to orally use or own the word and concept (for example, Think-Pair-Share: "Turn to your partner and share how . . ." "Who wants to tell me what your partner said?" "Which do you prefer . . . ? Answer in a complete sentence."). Writing the word, drawing, or other word activities should come later, *after* reading. First, students need to use the word *orally*— several times, in a variety of ways.

7. The teacher reminds students how they will use the new word or phrase. For example, "Remember to use this word or phrase in your summaries after the reading."

These preteaching steps should provide students with an opportunity for oral production of meaning and expose them to the written word in context. Steps 1–6 should move quickly, so that no more than two to three minutes per word (or ten to fifteen minutes for all the words) are spent preteaching key vocabulary. We need to leave plenty of time for ourselves to model reading strategies, and for students to read, verbally summarize, and write.

Teachers use chart paper, blackboards, PowerPoint presentations, or whiteboards to present the seven steps. It is important that the students see the vocabulary written out. That includes the word, the sentence as they will encounter it later on during reading, the dictionary definition, a student-friendly cue, a grammatical or phonological aspect of a difficult word, and the interaction activity for step 6. The seven-step process lends itself best for teaching Tier 2 and 3 words, because those are more sophisticated and complex.

A simplified five-step version for teaching words to ELs from preschool to first grade varies slightly (Calderón, 2011). The teacher:

1. Introduces the new word in a natural setting and uses concrete objects

2. Explains the word using everyday language and provides a child-friendly definition

3. Gives examples of the word in a variety of contexts using complete sentences

4. Asks children to say that sentence to their buddy or to invent a new sentence with the new word, and share it with their buddy

5. Continues using the word at every opportunity—at home and at learning centers—and acknowledges the child's attempt at using the new word(s)

Literacy instruction centers on understanding and the communication of meaning. The teacher's role is to support students as they carry out meaningful literacy activities involving the full processes of reading and writing. As Steve Graham and Dolores Perin (2007) write:

> If students are to make knowledge their own, they must struggle with the details, wrestle with the facts, and rework raw information and dimly understood concepts into language they can communicate to someone else. In short, if students are to learn, they must read and write. (p. 2)

Meeting the Reading and Writing Needs of ELs

A reader who speaks English as a second language uses essentially the same process that a first-language reader uses. Yet the task is somewhat more difficult as the resources that first- and second-language readers bring to bear are different. The two most important differences are English language proficiency and background knowledge. By providing reading material on content familiar to students, and by building background prior to reading a text, teachers can offset reading comprehension difficulties stemming from second-language proficiency needs.

The teacher's role is to facilitate ELs' learning of key aspects of literacy by teaching them how to integrate academic vocabulary, reading comprehension, and writing with their specific content area. Thus, content teachers become reading and writing teachers by:

- Emphasizing the reading and writing practices that are specific to their subjects

- Bridging the EL's reading comprehension level, building background, and strengthening English proficiency

Proficient readers are not always proficient writers. Although reading and writing skills complement each other, they do not always go hand in hand. Many students are able to handle reading demands but may encounter difficulties with writing. ELs are in need of developing their receptive (listening and reading) and productive (speaking and writing) skills within selected texts. An important role of the teacher is to balance the receptive with the productive skills of ELs' English acquisition.

What ELs Need in Order to Comprehend Textbooks

Research points to particular elements of effective literacy programs. These elements have a powerful and dynamic interrelationship with one another and can prove to be most beneficial to improve student learning. They are not meant to be considered in isolation or as one approach to reading and writing (Biancarosa & Snow, 2004). Table 6.5 (page 120) presents these elements as instructional improvements and shows, with suggested strategies, how they would translate to EL instruction.

The focus is to ensure that students get beyond the basic literacy domains, usually related to the elementary level, to the challenging literacy of the secondary level (Biancarosa & Snow, 2004). We focus on academic language proficiency, vocabulary acquisition, reading comprehension and fluency, and writing.

The *Writing Next* report has identified specific instructional practices to improve the quality of students' writing (Graham & Perin, 2007). It poses eleven elements of effective adolescent writing instruction. A brief summary of the elements is presented in table 6.6 (page 122).

As they go through elementary, middle, and high school, students must read and write longer, more complex texts. Longer chapters are filled with new information and different structures. Students need special help in negotiating meaning in this new territory.

Table 6.5: Meeting ELs' Instructional Reading Needs

Instructional Improvements	How This Translates to EL Instruction	Suggested Strategies for ELs
Direct, explicit comprehension instruction	Uses strategies that make students aware of their own thinking processes through metacognition or the ability to recognize and repair understanding	Questioning, predicting, summarizing, engaging in think-alouds, and teacher modeling and read-alouds
Effective instructional principles embedded in content	Uses techniques unique to the content area that will facilitate understanding and from which the student can generalize to other content areas	Outlines, graphic organizers, study guides, anticipation guides
Motivation and self-directed learning	Promotes student engagement with the text by teaching self-regulating strategies that can help students become independent learners, celebrate their successes, and feel more motivated	Self-evaluation, rubrics, checklists, pocket vocabulary journals for their subject area
Text-based collaborative learning	Provides opportunities to interact with text that decentralize learning from teacher, and promotes effective collaboration among peers	Textbook walks, book talks, partner reading, buddy retell, partner summaries, team writing, cooperative learning (numbered heads together, random reporter, write around, and so on)
Strategic tutoring	Provides students with individualized instruction as per analysis of test data	Appropriate strategies that address the specific needs

Intensive writing	Provides ample opportunities for writing in conjunction with reading in order to develop critical thinking skills	Sentence combining, summarization, more vocabulary, paraphrasing, writing and editing processes
Diverse texts	Provides students with texts that present a wide range of topics at a variety of reading levels; texts must be interesting and available from a range of levels on the same topic	Texts representing a variety of cultural, linguistic, and demographic groups; high-interest and low-difficulty texts
A technology component	Serves a dual benefit as a tool or facilitator of literacy and as a topic or medium of building literacy(ies)	Support for struggling readers and writers New reading and writing demands and higher-level thinking skills
Ongoing assessment of students	Provides opportunities for authentic assessments to inform instruction through the analysis of data; provides documentation of student learning and progress	Formative assessments—teacher observations, student work samples, checklists, and student self-assessments; summative assessments—standardized tests

Integrating Vocabulary, Reading, and Writing Into Your School Improvement Plan)

School leaders play an important role in making broad changes with an academic focus and in ensuring the success of reform efforts. An EL agenda for school success needs to include milestones of implementation. A focused school improvement plan (SIP) to implement one set of strategies during the first part of the school year and an additional set in the second can form the basis of an effective quality professional development process to teach ELs and all students.

For example, equipping all students to succeed on state standards requires sustained academic vocabulary, reading, and writing instruction. While these objectives are incorporated seamlessly throughout the school year, the curriculum map shown in figure 6.2 (page 124)

Table 6.6: Effective Elements of Adolescent Writing Instruction

Elements	Strategy Instruction
1. **Writing strategies**	Explicitly and systematically teaching students the steps necessary for planning, revising, and editing their compositions so that they can use these strategies independently
2. **Summarization**	Explicitly and systematically teaching students how to summarize texts
3. **Collaborative writing**	Creating instructional arrangements for students to work together and plan, draft, revise, and edit their compositions
4. **Specific product goals**	Assigning students specific reachable goals for the writing they are to complete Identifying the purpose of the assignment (for example, " to persuade") and the characteristics of the final product
5. **Word processing**	Using computer and word-processing devices, which are particularly useful to low-achieving writers Allowing students to work collaboratively on writing assignments using personal laptop computers or to word-process a composition under teacher guidance (producing a neat and legible script and permitting the writer to add, delete, spell-check, and move text easily)
6. **Sentence combining**	Teaching students to construct more complex and sophisticated sentences through exercises in which two or more basic sentences are combined into a single sentence (an alternative approach to more traditional grammar instruction)
7. **Pre-writing**	Engaging students in activities designed to help them generate or organize ideas for their composition, such as gathering information for a paper through reading, or developing a visual representation of their ideas before sitting down to write; encouraging group and individual planning before writing; organizing pre-writing activities; prompting students to plan after providing a brief demonstration of how to do so; and assigning reading material pertinent to a topic and then encouraging students to plan their work in advance

8. Inquiry activities	Engaging students in activities that help them develop ideas and content for a particular writing task by analyzing immediate concrete data—such as comparing and contrasting cases, or collecting and evaluating evidence
	Analyzing concrete and immediate data, for example, observing peers during a specific activity
	Using specific strategies to conduct analysis, for example, asking the peers observed the reason(s) for a particular action
	Applying what was learned—for example, assigning the writing of a story incorporating insights from the inquiry process
9. Process-writing approach	Interweaving a number of writing instructional activities in a workshop environment, including emphasizing writing for real audiences; encouraging cycles of planning, translating, and reviewing; stressing personal responsibility and ownership of writing projects; facilitating high levels of student interaction; developing supportive writing environments; encouraging self-reflection and evaluation; offering personalized individual assistance, brief instructional lessons to meet students' individual needs, and more extended and systematic instruction
10. Study of models	Providing students with opportunities to read, analyze, and emulate models of good writing
	Asking students to analyze these examples and emulate the critical elements, patterns, and forms embodied in the models in their own writing
11. Writing for content area learning	Using writing as a tool for learning content material (writing-to-learn activities are equally effective for all content areas)

Source: Writing Next: Effective Strategies to Improve Writing of Adolescents in Middle and High Schools, *by Steve Graham and Dolores Perin, © 2007 Carnegie Corporation of New York. Reprinted with permission.*

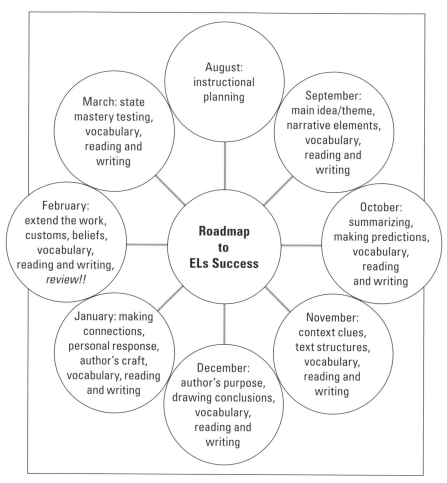

Figure 6.2: Curriculum map for teaching reading objectives.

can ensure that all objectives are taught in an equitable time frame with appropriate emphasis on explicit instruction of vocabulary, reading comprehension strategies, and writing production using academic English. Figure 6.2 illustrates one way to incorporate the four language skills to teach eighteen reading objectives.

After the completion of this curriculum map in March, the remaining months of April through June need to be devoted to reviewing reading objectives, more vocabulary development, reading and writing, and refinement of student skills.

Conclusion

ELs need strong literacy skills to succeed in school and in life. Reading for academic learning involves reading to understand, remember, and apply. Vocabulary knowledge is essential. Vocabulary is the GPS that guides ELs to success in reading and writing, which are the keys to their academic success. The pivotal role of teachers is to provide ongoing supportive feedback consistent with the implementation of instructional strategies embedded in their teaching practices. Teachers facilitate students' learning of key aspects of literacy by teaching them how to integrate academic vocabulary, reading comprehension, and writing with each specific content area. Teachers emphasize the reading and writing practices that are specific to their subjects and strengthen the English learners' reading comprehension level, writing production, and academic English proficiency.

References

August, D., & Shanahan, T. (2006). *Developing literacy in second language learners: Report of the National Literacy Panel on Language-Minority Children and Youth.* Mahwah, NJ: Lawrence Erlbaum.

August, D., & Shanahan, T. (2008). *Developing literacy in second language learners: Report of the National Literacy Panel on Language-Minority Children and Youth.* New York: Routledge.

Beck, I. L., McKeown, M. G., & Kucan, L. (2002). *Bringing words to life.* New York: Guilford Press.

Beck, I. L., McKeown, M. G., & Kucan, L. (2005). Choosing words to teach. In E. H. Hiebert & M. L. Kamil (Eds.), *Teaching and learning vocabulary* (pp. 207–222). Mahwah, NJ: Lawrence Erlbaum.

Biancarosa, G., & Snow, C. E. (2004). *A vision for action and research in middle and high school literacy* (A report from Carnegie of New York). Washington, DC: Alliance for Excellent Education.

Calderón, M. (2007). *Teaching reading to English language learners grades 6–12: A framework for improving achievement in the content areas.* Thousand Oaks, CA: Corwin Press.

Calderón, M. (2011). *Teaching reading comprehension to English learners, K–5.* Bloomington, IN: Solution Tree Press.

Calderón, M., August, D., Slavin, A., Cheung, A., Duran, D., & Madden, N. (2005). Bringing words to life in classrooms with English language learners. In E. H. Hiebert & M. L. Kamil (Eds.), *Teaching and learning vocabulary* (pp. 115–136). Mahwah, NJ: Lawrence Erlbaum.

Calderón M., & Minaya-Rowe, L. (2011). *Preventing long-term English language learners: Transforming schools to meet core standards.* Thousand Oaks, CA: Corwin Press.

Darling-Hammond, L. (2010). *The flat world and education: How America's commitment to equity will determine our future.* New York: Teachers College Press.

DuFour, R., & Marzano, R. (2011). *Leaders of learning: How district, school and classroom leaders improve student achievement.* Bloomington, IN: Solution Tree Press.

Friedman, T. L. (2005). *The world is flat.* New York: Farrar, Straus & Giroux.

Graham, S., & Perin, D. (2007). *Writing next: Effective strategies to improve writing of adolescents in middle and high schools.* New York: Carnegie of New York.

Nagy, W. E. (2005). Why vocabulary instruction needs to be long-term and comprehensive. In E. H. Hiebert & M. L. Kamil (Eds.), *Teaching and learning vocabulary: Bringing research to practice* (pp. 27–44). Mahwah, NJ: Lawrence Erlbaum.

Stahl, S. A. (2005). Four problems with teaching word meanings. In E. H. Hiebert & M. L. Kamil (Eds.), *Teaching and learning vocabulary: Bringing research to practice* (pp. 95–114). Mahwah, NJ: Lawrence Erlbaum.

Okhee Lee

Okhee Lee, PhD, is a professor in the Steinhardt School of Culture, Education, and Human Development at New York University. She completed her bachelor's and master's degrees in South Korea and received her doctorate from Michigan State University in 1989. From 1989 through 2011, she taught in the School of Education at the University of Miami.

Dr. Lee's research areas include science education, language and culture, and teacher education. Her current research involves the scale-up of a teacher professional development intervention to promote science learning and language development of English learners within a high-stakes testing policy context in science. She is a fellow of AERA and received the Distinguished Career Award from the AERA Scholars of Color in Education. She was also awarded a 1993–95 National Academy of Education Spencer postdoctoral fellowship. Dr. Lee has directed research and teacher enhancement projects funded by the National Science Foundation, the U.S. Department of Education, the Spencer Foundation, and other sources.

She has served on the editorial boards of major education research journals, including *American Educational Research Journal* and *Review of Educational Research,* as well as advisory boards for science education reform projects, including the Next Generation Science Standards.

In this chapter, Dr. Lee explores the research on the emerging discipline of teaching science to ELs and discusses which approaches, including collaborative teamwork, make science interesting, relevant, and comprehensible to ELs.

Chapter 7

Teaching Science With English Language and Literacy

Okhee Lee

The role of teachers in ensuring that all students achieve high academic standards is becoming ever more urgent and complex as a result of the growing diversity of the student population in North America, persistent achievement gaps among demographic subgroups, and the increasing demands of high-stakes testing and accountability policies across content areas for all students. Teachers of English learners face the additional challenge of helping their students develop oral and written proficiency in English while they are simultaneously learning academic content and processes (Lee, Penfield, & Buxton, in press; Wong Fillmore & Snow, 2002). Effective instruction is required regardless of whether ELs are placed in mainstream classrooms or in English for speakers of other languages (ESOL), English as a second language, or bilingual classrooms.

Research on instructional interventions to simultaneously promote science and English language and literacy has begun to emerge. This chapter addresses the state of the research on integration of science and English proficiency with ELs and describes new developments in the field fueled by emerging funding opportunities. The chapter concludes with implications for the future with regard to classroom practices, research agenda, and educational policies.

Science is used as an example of content-area instruction. However, the discussion is applicable to the content areas of English/language arts, mathematics, and social studies to the extent that reform-oriented practices across these content areas (for example, Common Core State Standards in English/language arts and mathematics) share an emphasis on conceptual understanding, problem solving, and subject-specific discourse. (See the literature review on content-area instruction with ELs by Janzen, 2008.) However, differences in epistemological foundations, pedagogical approaches, and classroom practices across content areas should also be recognized.

Integration of Science and English Proficiency

Integration of academic learning and English proficiency is necessary for various reasons. From a policy perspective, high-stakes testing and accountability demand high academic achievement of all students, including ELs (Gutiérrez et al., 2002; Wiley & Wright, 2004). From a social justice perspective, ensuring that ELs receive rich and rigorous content-area instruction—even while still developing academic language in the language of instruction (that is, English)—is a critical component of equitable education. From a research perspective, an emerging body of literature focuses on ways to support acquisition of both academic content and English proficiency (Janzen, 2008).

Content-area instruction and ESOL/ESL/bilingual education have traditionally been conceptualized as separate domains, which is problematic for the education of ELs. In terms of science instruction, many teachers, especially at the elementary level, are not adequately prepared in science disciplines or subject-specific teaching strategies (Garet, Porter, Desimone, Birman, & Yoon, 2001). In addition, teachers are often inadequately prepared to meet the learning needs of ELs and unwilling to participate in ESOL-related professional development opportunities (National Center for Education Statistics [NCES], 2001). Given this context, it should not be surprising that ELs frequently fall behind their English-speaking peers in content-area learning.

The integration of academic content and English proficiency is highlighted in reform documents related to the instruction of ELs (Teachers of English to Speakers of Other Languages [TESOL], 1997). TESOL standards (2006) target academic language proficiency in four core content areas: English/language arts, mathematics, science, and social studies. According to these standards, ELs need to develop a high level of English proficiency in content areas if they are to achieve at the same level as their English-speaking peers. Thus, instructional interventions to promote both academic learning and English proficiency are needed urgently, especially given the context of high-stakes testing and accountability policies facing today's schools, teachers, and students.

In science education, research on curricular and professional development interventions to promote proficiency of ELs in both science and English is limited, but has begun to emerge (see the review of literature by Janzen, 2008; Lee, 2005). This research highlights the role of hands-on opportunities for ELs to develop scientific understanding, engage in scientific inquiry, and construct shared meanings of science, all while acquiring English proficiency. Specific strategies that can be used in this reciprocal process are discussed in the following section.

Literacy Strategies With All Students

Literacy development requires much more than being able to speak, listen, read, and write. It involves learning to think and reason, to view and visually represent information in pictorials and graphics, and to textually represent ideas and information in words. Science activities are often predicated on students' literacy skills (Cervetti, Pearson, Bravo, & Barber, 2006; Hand, Wallace, & Yang, 2004) in the sense that they must be able to comprehend science texts and carry out directions for conducting experiments. In addition, students are expected to know how to describe, explain, and predict natural phenomena in science-specific genres of writing. They

> Literacy development involves learning to think and reason, to view and visually represent information in pictorials and graphics, and to textually represent ideas and information in words.

are expected to report science experiments in multiple formats (for example, pictorial, graphic, and textual).

Additionally, students need to code-switch from everyday uses of language, such as telling or writing stories, to the language of science (Brown & Ryoo, 2008; Brown & Spang, 2008). Science texts tend to employ certain nontechnical terms that have meanings unique to scientific contexts (for example, *matter, force, energy,* and *space*), are written in passive rather than active voice, and include nominalization of verbs or adjectives into nouns to economically summarize sentences into one abstract noun phrase (Schleppegrell, 2004). For example, instead of saying "bacteria adapt very well" and "antibiotics are available," which are more congruent with everyday ways of using language, science texts tend to convert these phrases into "adaptability of bacteria" and "availability of antibiotics," which are more abstract modes of expression (Fang, 2011). Science also involves various subregisters representing specific disciplines, including botany, meteorology, and physics, each with its own particular vocabulary and discourse patterns. Students must absorb these differences in register as they work to construct meaning in a way that is appropriate to the topic at hand.

Effective science teachers incorporate reading and writing strategies in their instruction to promote both science learning and literacy development for all students (Douglas, Klentschy, Worth, & Binder, 2006). Some of these strategies include:

- Activating prior knowledge

- Using comprehension questions about science inquiry activities or expository science texts

- Teaching academic language functions (describe, explain, predict, infer, conclude) in relation to science inquiry and process skills

- Teaching scientific genres of writing (lab reports, conference posters)

- Using graphic organizers (such as concept maps, word walls, Venn diagrams, and KWL charts)

- Selecting trade books and literature with scientific themes

- Using writing prompts

Language Support Strategies

To support ELs in learning science and developing English proficiency simultaneously, a wide range of language support strategies have been proposed. These pedagogical strategies are typically identified as ESOL strategies, but have been shown to be effective with all students (Bruna & Gomez, 2008; Fathman & Crowther, 2006; Rosebery & Warren, 2008).

Effective teachers use hands-on activities and realia (that is, demonstration of real objects or events), strategies that are especially effective with ELs. They encourage students to communicate ideas using multiple modes of representation (for example, gestural, oral, pictorial, graphic, and textual). They use nonlinguistic modes of representation (such as graphs, charts, tables, drawings, and pictures) to encourage language production, communication of ideas, and demonstration of science knowledge. They guide students to comprehend and use a small number of key science vocabulary words—both general (Tier 1), academic (Tier 2), and discipline-specific (Tier 3) (Beck, McKeown, & Kucan, 2002). They pay particular attention to those terms that are specific to ELs (Calderón, 2007, 2011). They also encourage ELs to use language in multiple contexts (*introduce, write, repeat, highlight*). In addition, they help ELs develop English proficiency by focusing on linguistic skills, including phonemes, syllables, morphemes, lexicon (vocabulary), syntax and grammar, and conventions of written English such as punctuation, capitalization, and spelling.

Discourse Strategies

Discourse strategies (that is, adjusting the level and mode of communication) can be used to enhance ELs' understanding of academic content. Unlike the language support or ESOL strategies just described, which are largely pedagogical in nature, discourse strategies focus specifically on the teacher's role in facilitating ELs' participation in classroom discourse (Gibbons, 2006). A major challenge for teachers is in how to structure activities so as to reduce the language load required for participation while maintaining the rigor of the science content and processes.

Teachers need to recognize ELs' varying levels of language proficiency and adjust norms of interaction with students accordingly—for example, by enunciating more clearly or providing longer wait time. Effective teachers also provide students with multiple redundancies of the same concepts by using synonyms or paraphrases of difficult language, repeating and rephrasing main ideas, or recasting and elaborating on students' responses (Gibbons, 2006). Furthermore, effective teachers communicate just slightly above students' level of communicative competence, thus pushing their language skills ahead a bit at a time.

Home Language Support

It is important to draw a distinction between home language instruction (that is, bilingual education) and home language support (Goldenberg, 2008). Even in the absence of bilingual education programs or fully trained bilingual teachers, teachers who share a home language with their students can use it to communicate and reinforce key science vocabulary and concepts (Hudicourt-Barnes, 2003).

Even when the teacher does not speak the students' home language, the latter can still be supported through a number of strategies, such as introducing key science vocabulary in both the home language and English, highlighting cognates as well as false cognates between English and the home language (Spanish and other Romance lexicon are often derived from Latin, the primary language of science), encouraging bilingual students to assist less-English-proficient students in their home language as well as in English, allowing ELs to write about science ideas or experiments in their home language, and inviting family and community members to participate as local experts in classroom literacy events.

Home Culture Connections

While making connections to ELs' home language is quite concrete, the notion of making connections to their cultural experiences in relation to academic content can be more abstract and subtle. Since science has traditionally been regarded as "culture-free," incorporation of home culture into science instruction has not been adequately conceptualized. Thus, science educators need a better understanding of how to articulate connections between home culture and school science (Lee, 2002; Warren, Ballenger, Ogonowski, Rosebery, & Hudicourt-Barnes, 2001).

The literature on cultural congruence indicates that students participate in classroom interactions in ways that reflect culturally based communication and interaction patterns from their home and community (Gay, 2002; Villegas & Lucas, 2002). In science classrooms, teachers need to know how various students might be more or less familiar with the expected participation norms, what interactional patterns are common among different groups of students, how these patterns might foster or limit students' participation, and how to balance a consideration of culturally based communication and interaction patterns with the dangers of stereotypes or overgeneralization based on students' cultural backgrounds. Effective teachers make the norms and expectations for classroom discourse explicit and look for opportunities to honor the full range of student discourse patterns when appropriate. For example, crosstalk (talking simultaneously with other speakers, to add to their points) is completely acceptable in some cultures, while it is considered rude and disruptive in other cultures, as it is in most North American schools.

> Since science has traditionally been regarded as "culture-free," incorporation of home culture into science instruction has not been adequately conceptualized.

The literature on funds of knowledge indicates that the lived experiences of students at home and in the community can serve as intellectual resources for academic learning (González, Moll, & Amanti, 2005; Moll, 1992). In science classrooms, effective teachers ask questions that elicit students' funds of knowledge related to science topics (Solano-Flores & Nelson-Barber, 2001). They use cultural artifacts and community resources in ways that are academically meaningful and culturally relevant. These cultural connections can be of great assistance as ELs strive to integrate prior experiences with new academic expectations. For example, Rodriguez and Berryman (2002) worked with high school students in predominantly Latino and impoverished school settings in a U.S.-Mexican border city. Using a curriculum unit on investigating water quality in their community, the students engaged in authentic activities as they explored how this topic was socially relevant and connected to their everyday lives. Having come to regard science as relevant, students saw scientific investigations as worthwhile both for themselves and for students in other schools in the region.

New Developments in the Field

Since the reviews of the literature on science education with ELs by Okhee Lee (2005) and Joy Janzen (2008), new developments have been occurring. One involves research and development projects funded by the National Science Foundation (NSF) Discovery Research K–12 (DR K–12) program. Of the 327 awards funded through this program between 2004 and 2011, thirty-two active awards (approximately 10 percent of the portfolio) address mathematics and science education for ELs either as the primary focus or as one of the student groups under investigation (Lopez-Ferrao, 2011; Martinez & Rhodes, 2011). These projects have an average of 2.5 (out of a possible five) years of funding. They focus on professional development models (nine projects), curriculum development (six projects), student learning (five projects), technology-enhanced instruction (five projects), formative assessment (four projects), scaling-up models (two projects), and a teacher preparation model (one project).

Martinez and Rhodes (2011) compared the DR K–12 projects in science education to the synthesis of the literature review between 1982 and 2004 (Lee, 2005) and the research that has been published since 2005. Lee found that few of the studies evaluated the impact of intervention programs on ELs' science achievement or English proficiency, on the achievement gaps among linguistic groups, or on the results across different levels of English proficiency. She also found that most studies used qualitative methods and tended to produce small-scale, descriptive studies conducted by individual researchers; few of the studies used either an experimental or quasi-experimental design.

Preliminary results of the portfolio analysis of the DR K–12 projects indicate new trends in research and development in science education for ELs that differ from the existing literature in important ways (Martinez & Rhodes, 2011). These projects are more likely to analyze students' science achievement results and more frequently assess changes in ELs' levels of English proficiency. These projects also address scaling-up, consequences of policy, and students' home environments—topics that have been rarely addressed in the field. A larger portion of the DR K–12 science projects are using experimental or quasi-experimental designs and mixed methods. The projects are more likely to be collecting data from at least two school districts or rural communities. Overall, the DR K–12 EL science projects compare favorably to the literature in the field and can make a valuable contribution to our understanding of science education among ELs.

Implications for Practice, Research, and Policy

With an increasingly diverse student population and a simultaneous rise in the influence of federal and state/provincial accountability systems, integration of academic content and English proficiency for ELs has become a necessity for classroom practices and educational policies. In response to this reality, the research communities in science and ESOL/ESL/bilingual education have begun to address this intersection.

Current efforts seem to focus on the integration of science, English language, and literacy. It could be that researchers are responding to the urgent needs both in the classroom and in the educational policy domains. It could also be that given the traditional disconnect between science and ESOL education, researchers are highlighting the overlaps between the two areas for classroom practices. It is important to continue efforts to find areas of integration in order to maximize the positive effects on classroom practices in both science and ESOL education. New developments in the field, fueled by emerging funding opportunities, such as the NSF DR K–12 program, indicate new trends in the research agenda for science education with ELs.

Classroom Practice

As the emerging literature indicates how science and English language and literacy can be integrated for ELs, these ideas need to be implemented and tested through classroom practices. As this emerging field of research becomes more mature, efforts could also be focused on areas that might give rise to tensions or conflicts. For example, as we have seen, English language education seeks to understand ELs' cultural backgrounds, whereas science has traditionally been considered as "culture-free." With regard to the role of vocabulary in student learning, English language education emphasizes vocabulary as a means for concept development, whereas science education tends to think of vocabulary as definitions of terms or glossary. As science and ESOL educators come together for effective education of ELs, they may identify overlaps and supports, as well as tensions and conflicts, in pedagogical approaches and epistemological assumptions.

> As science and ESOL educators come together for effective education of ELs, they may identify overlaps and supports, as well as tensions and conflicts, in pedagogical approaches and epistemological assumptions.

Research

With the growing diversity of the student population in the nation, funding agencies are supporting research and development in science education for ELs. The portfolio of the research and development projects funded by NSF's DR K–12 program presents a new direction for the research agenda. As the field becomes mature, more sophisticated treatments of English proficiency and nuanced integration of science and English proficiency will emerge. At the same time, scale-up of educational interventions will also emerge to reach ELs across a wide range of educational settings.

Educational Policy

Research on science education for ELs should be conceptualized in the context of educational policies. While the Elementary and

Secondary Education Act (formerly No Child Left Behind) mandates reporting of AYP for reading and mathematics, the same is not true for science. It is unclear how many states include science assessment results as part of state accountability or which states are including science assessment results in AYP calculation (Penfield & Lee, 2010). While science accountability policies affect all students, the impact is far greater for ELs who are under the pressure of developing English literacy and numeracy at the expense of other subject areas, including science. In addition, ELs are typically concentrated in urban schools that tend to have limited funding and resources.

An emerging educational policy involves the development of new science standards, which are comparable to Common Core State Standards in English/language arts and literacy and mathematics. Next Generation Science Standards are currently being developed by Achieve, Inc. based on a framework for K–12 science education (National Research Council [NRC], 2011). As improvements of the existing science standards (NRC, 1996), the new standards represent an ambitious goal of science learning for all students. To learn the new standards successfully, ELs need science and English language instruction that fosters their language and literacy competencies. Stanford University School of Education's "Language, Literacy, and Learning in the Content Areas for English Language Learners: Building on the Common Core State Standards and the Next Generation Science Standards Initiatives" is aimed at strengthening academic content and language instruction for ELs by delineating and fostering the language and literacy competencies that ELs need to meet the new wave of content standards across school subjects (Hakuta & Santos, 2011–2013). These two projects represent a new generation of educational policy initiatives that will inform effective science education for ELs.

References

Beck, I. L., McKeown, M. G., & Kucan, L. (2002). *Bringing words to life: Robust vocabulary instruction*. New York: Guilford Press.

Brown, B. A., & Ryoo, K. (2008). Teaching science as a language: A "content-first" approach to science teaching. *Journal of Research in Science Teaching, 45*(5), 529–553.

Brown, B. A., & Spang, E. (2008). Double talk: Synthesizing everyday and science language in the classroom. *Science Education, 92*(4), 708–732.

Bruna, K. R., & Gomez, K. (Eds.). (2008). *The work of language in multicultural classrooms: Talking science, writing science.* New York: Routledge.

Calderón, M. (2007). *Teaching reading to English language learners, grades 6–12: A framework for improving achievement in the content areas.* Thousand Oaks, CA: Corwin Press.

Calderón, M. (2011). *Teaching reading and comprehension to English learners, K–5.* Bloomington, IN: Solution Tree Press.

Cervetti, G. N., Pearson, P. D., Bravo, M. A., & Barber, J. (2006). Reading and writing in the service of inquiry-based science. In R. Douglas, M. P. Klentschy, K. Worth, & W. Binder (Eds.), *Linking science and literacy in the K–8 classroom* (pp. 221–244). Arlington, VA: National Science Teachers Association.

Douglas, R., Klentschy, M. P., Worth, K., & Binder, W. (Eds.). (2006). *Linking science and literacy in the K–8 classroom.* Arlington, VA: National Science Teachers Association.

Fathman, A. K., & Crowther, D. T. (Eds.). (2006). *Science for English language learners: K–12 classroom strategies.* Arlington, VA: National Science Teachers Association.

Garet, M. S., Porter, A. C., Desimone, L., Birman, B. F., & Yoon, K. S. (2001). What makes professional development effective? Results from a national sample of teachers. *American Educational Research Journal, 38*(4), 915–945.

Gay, G. (2002). Preparing for culturally responsive teaching. *Journal of Teacher Education, 53*(2), 106–116.

Gibbons, P. (2006). *Bridging discourses in the ESL classroom.* New York: Continuum.

Goldenberg, C. (2008). Teaching English language learners: What the research does—and does not—say. *American Educator, 32*(2), 42–44.

González, N., Moll, L. C., & Amanti, C. (2005). *Funds of knowledge: Theorizing practices in households, communities, and classrooms.* Mahwah, NJ: Lawrence Erlbaum.

Gutiérrez, K. D., Asato, J., Pacheco, M., Moll, L. C., Olson, K., Horng, E. L., et al. (2002). "Sounding American": The consequences of new reforms on English language learners. *Reading Research Quarterly, 37*(3), 328–343.

Hakuta, K., & Santos, M. (2011–2013). *Language, literacy, and learning in the content areas for English language learners: Building on the Common Core State Standards and the Next Generation Science Standards initiatives.* Palo Alto, CA: Stanford University.

Hand, B. C., Wallace, C., & Yang, E. (2004). Using the science writing heuristic to enhance learning outcomes from laboratory activities in seventh-grade science: Quantitative and qualitative aspects. *International Journal of Science Education, 26,* 131–149.

Hudicourt-Barnes, J. (2003). The use of argumentation in Haitian Creole science classrooms. *Harvard Educational Review, 73*(10), 73–93.

Janzen, J. (2008). Teaching English language learners in the content areas. *Review of Educational Research, 78*(4), 1010–1038.

Lee, O. (2002). Science inquiry for elementary students from diverse backgrounds. In W. G. Secada (Ed.), *Review of research in education,* Vol. 26 (pp. 23–69). Washington, DC: American Educational Research Association.

Lee, O. (2005). Science education and English language learners: Synthesis and research agenda. *Review of Educational Research, 75*(4), 491–530.

Lee, O., Penfield, R. D., & Buxton, C. A. (in press). Relationship between "form" and "content" in science writing among English language learners. *Teachers College Record.*

Lopez-Ferrao, J. (2011, July). *National Science Foundation: Understanding and improving ELs' STEM learning and instruction.* Panel presentation at the High-quality STEM education for English learners: Current challenges and effective practices, *STEM Forum.* Washington, DC: U.S. Department of Education Office of English Language Acquisition (OELA).

Martinez, A., & Rhodes, H. J. (2011, April). *Math and science education with English language learners: Contributions of the DR K–12 program.* Paper presented at the annual meeting of the American Educational Research Association, New Orleans, LA.

Moll, L. C. (1992). Bilingual classroom studies and community analysis: Some recent trends. *Educational Researcher, 21*(2), 20–24.

National Center for Education Statistics. (2001). *Teacher preparation and professional development: 2000.* Washington, DC: U.S. Department of Education, Office of Educational Research and Improvement.

National Research Council. (1996). *National science education standards.* Washington, DC: National Academies Press.

National Research Council. (2011). *A framework for K–12 science education: Practices, crosscutting concepts, and core ideas.* Washington, DC: National Academies Press.

Penfield, R. D., & Lee, O. (2010). Test-based accountability: Potential benefits and pitfalls of science assessment with student diversity. *Journal of Research in Science Teaching, 47*(1), 6–24.

Rodriguez, A. J., & Berryman, C. (2002). Using sociotransformative constructivism to teach for understanding in diverse classrooms: A beginning teacher's journey. *American Educational Research Journal, 39*(4), 1017–1045.

Rosebery, A. S., & Warren, B. (Eds.). (2008). *Teaching science to English language learners: Building on students' strengths.* Arlington, VA: National Science Teachers Association.

Schleppegrell, M. (2004). *The language of schooling: A functional linguistics perspective.* Mahwah, NJ: Lawrence Erlbaum.

Solano-Flores, G., & Nelson-Barber, S. (2001). On the cultural validity of science assessments. *Journal of Research in Science Teaching, 38*(5), 553–573.

Teachers of English to Speakers of Other Languages. (1997). *ESL standards for pre-K–12 students.* Alexandria, VA: Author.

Teachers of English to Speakers of Other Languages. (2006). *PreK–12 English language proficiency standards.* Alexandria, VA: Author.

Villegas, A. M., & Lucas, T. (2002). Preparing culturally responsive teachers: Rethinking the curriculum. *Journal of Teacher Education, 53*(1), 20–32.

Warren, B., Ballenger, C., Ogonowski, M., Rosebery, A., & Hudicourt-Barnes, J. (2001). Rethinking diversity in learning science: The logic of everyday language. *Journal of Research in Science Teaching, 38*(5), 529–552.

Wiley, T. G., & Wright, W. E. (2004). Against the undertow: Language-minority education policy and politics in the "age of accountability." *Educational Policy, 18*(1), 142–168.

Wong Fillmore, L., & Snow, C. (2002). *What teachers need to know about language.* Washington, DC: Center for Applied Linguistics.

Maria N. Trejo

Maria N. Trejo, EdD, began her professional career as an elementary school teacher, moved on to teach high school students, and then worked at the University of the Pacific in Stockton, California, and Washington State University, in Pullman, Washington, preparing teacher candidates. During her thirty-two-year tenure with the California State Department of Education, she implemented policy, disbursed funds to improve curriculum and instructional practices, and administered programs to support underprivileged children, underperforming populations, and English learner students. She also participated in the development of policies, examinations, and general requirements for state teacher certifications.

Dr. Trejo has served on many state and national organizations, commissions, boards, and task forces, including the Commission on Teacher Credentialing/Bilingual Assessor Agencies; National Interstate Migrant Educational Council; California County State Steering Committee of Assistant Superintendents of Curriculum, Instruction, and Staff Development; National Council of States on Inservice Education; and an expert panel for Education.com. Her unique expertise is designing professional development institutes, workshops, conferences, and international teacher exchanges. Her latest ventures have been designing and piloting webinars.

She is currently part of a team of eight national experts and associates who provide training and coaching support to teachers and administrators for preschool to grade 12 in many U.S. states, the Pacific Islands, Mexico, Ecuador, Puerto Rico, Spain, and Germany.

In this chapter, Dr. Trejo outlines the research on preschool attendance for English Learners, explains the benefits of developing skills simultaneously in English and the primary language, and shows how the loss of early learning affects ELs' future academic success, particularly in mathematics, history, and science.

Chapter 8

Linking Literacy to Content in Preschool Math, Science, and Social Science

Maria N. Trejo

Researchers affirm that children who attend high-quality early care and education programs are better prepared for kindergarten, have stronger language skills in the first years of elementary school, and are far less likely to repeat a grade or drop out of school (Copple & Bredekamp, 2009). ELs and Spanish-speaking children tend to show greater gains than any other comparable group of low-income children (Ballantyne, Sanderman, & McLaughlin, 2008). But dual-language learners (or ELs) and Spanish-speaking children are less likely to attend preschool, despite the added benefits that it promises for these groups.

Surveys conducted reveal that although many states have universal preK as a goal, they struggle to provide services for all eligible children:

- The RAND Corporation (Karoly, 2009) reported that California state-subsidized early learning programs were serving fewer than half of eligible three- and four-year-olds.

- The National Institute of Early Education Research (2010) similarly found that the state of New York was serving only 43 percent of its four-year-olds. It also found that New York was not alone in its struggle to serve all its children; Florida, Georgia, Illinois, Iowa, Massachusetts, and West Virginia were also trying to find adequate resources to provide universal preschool to all qualified children.

- The RAND Corporation (Karoly, 2009) reported that opportunities for all three- and four-year-olds were not readily available: only 13 percent of low-income children were enrolled in high-quality programs that promote school readiness and later academic achievement.

The Loss Potential of Early Learning for ELs

Key publications such as *From Neurons to Neighborhoods* (2000), *Eager to Learn* (2000), and *Early Learning Standards* (2002) have brought unprecedented awareness for practitioners and experts about early brain research, the potential of young children, and the need for pedagogical standards and strategies to improve the quality and content offered for preschool populations. Brain research over the last decade has revealed the influences of early experiences upon children's social, emotional, and cognitive development. Experts saw the potential of early childhood education as a strategy to reduce the growing achievement gap in elementary schools, and the field began to focus on early literacy as the strategy, but with not much attention devoted to other content areas. This has been a limited strategy and a loss of opportunity to further reduce the kindergarten readiness gap for children of poverty and ELs.

Exposing children to strong literacy foundations is crucial, but literacy practices alone may be insufficient if they do not include concepts of science, mathematics, and social science.

Young children master foundational skills and key concepts, develop attitudes toward preschool, and form ideas about themselves as learners very early (Shore, 2009). Exposing children to strong literacy foundations is crucial, but literacy practices alone may be insufficient if they do not include concepts of science, mathematics, and social science. A narrow curriculum limits children's ability to think and problem solve, and limits their exposure to the world and people around them. Children are goal oriented. They actively seek information and bring knowledge and experiences to the preschool settings. Teachers need to capitalize on this early capacity and curiosity.

The Importance of Early Mathematics, Science, and Social Science

Mathematics enables children to conduct the simple yet vital transactions of daily life, such as gauging distances and making change. Science helps children explore the physical properties of objects, living things, the earth, and the environment. Social science helps children relate to and get along with others and learn how others live. It helps them to develop a sense of place, to understand the rudimentary aspects of democracy, and to begin to appreciate how their neighbors work and are shaped by their environment.

Early exposure to literacy, mathematics, science, and social science develops children who ask questions, think critically, propose new ways of doing things, and make decisions based on reasoning. Comprehensive instruction also develops in children the ability to interact and work cooperatively with adults and peers, share ideas, and listen to others—skills that are basic to all other areas of learning (National Council for the Social Studies 2010).

Too many teachers shy away from teaching core content areas. It could be that teachers are challenged with the task of teaching language, since so many of their students have limited oral language skills and vocabularies. For inexperienced, unprepared, unsupported teachers, this presents a big obstacle. What should we do when our students don't speak English? ask Laurie Weaver and Catherine Gaines in *Mathematics in the Early Years* (Copley, 1999). These authors propose a pedagogical strategy modeled after the concept of "comprehensible input." Comprehensible input strategies involved teachers' modifying their language, making extensive use of manipulatives and everyday objects, and acting out and modeling whenever possible. Such strategies have helped, but they have not been enough for ELs.

In this chapter, we propose that literacy and academic vocabulary and content concepts be taught simultaneously and explicitly. We suggest that teachers not modify or simplify academic language as in the past, or overshelter instruction or experiences for young ELs. Instead, we advocate (1) that specific strategies be adapted for teaching academic vocabulary in context and (2) that children be exposed to many experiences and big ideas in key content areas.

We base the various strategies proposed on national content standards and previously published evidence-based approaches, such as the five-step ACE-LERA, the Spanish version of ExC-ELL— a vocabulary process specifically designed for ELs (Calderón, 2011):

1. Introduce the new word or phrase in a natural setting or with the use of concrete objects.

2. Explain the word using everyday language. Provide a child-friendly definition.

3. Give examples of the word in a variety of contexts. Use complete sentences.

4. Invite peer practice by asking children to use the word in a variety of peer activities.

5. Use the word at every opportunity, and acknowledge students' attempts to do so.

Mathematics

Table 8.1 (page 149) illustrates the teaching of vocabulary and concepts in mathematics using this five-step process with ELs or children who need the extra support. In the following example, children and parents are prepared to spend a day at a local market and participate in activities that help children better understand concepts of weight and measurement and learn key vocabulary.

Table 8.1: Teaching Vocabulary and Math Concepts for Weights and Measurement to ELs Using the Five-Step Process

Step	Vocabulary	Parents/ Community
1. Introduce the new word in a natural setting or with the use of concrete objects.	The teacher introduces words like *more, less, bigger, smaller, lighter,* and *heavier.*	
2. Explain the word using everyday language. Provide a child-friendly definition.	Teacher invites several children to the front of the group and says, "Luis is *taller* and *bigger* than Pedro."	Parents use the new words at home with similar games.
3. Give examples of the word in a variety of contexts. Use complete sentences.	The teacher continues to point to different pairs of children, asking, "Who is *taller?* Who is *shorter?* Is Lucy *taller* than Judy?"	
4. Continue using the word at every opportunity.	The teacher asks, "How do you know who is *shorter* or *taller?* Explain it to me." The teacher continues by measuring everyone's height and recording this information on a large piece of paper for everyone to see.	Parents go with their child to the market to point out measurements, for example.
5. Acknowledge the students' attempts at using the new word.	The teacher reaffirms children when they draw figures of different sizes and weights and use the new words in class, and again when parents come to class to share activities done at home.	Parents are invited to class to share with other children and parents.

Fundamental mathematics and science concepts, such as comparing, classifying, and measuring, can be naturally integrated beginning in preschool (Lind, 1999). Various objects can be used at school, center, or home to reinforce them. The dialog presented in the table can also be modified to include such other examples as, "Which is taller, a cat or a dog?" "What is heavier, an orange or a watermelon?" "What is more, four ice cream cones or one?" Teachers and parents can easily use classroom or everyday home objects to illustrate the concepts of weight and measurement. Children can be given real objects to see, touch, smell, or taste to help them discover each concept. Both teachers and parents can provide lots of practice for children before and after visiting different local businesses, such as the grocery or pet store.

Science

Have you ever been with a child who looks at clouds and then asks, "What keeps them up in the air?" Young children are natural explorers. They always ask, "*Why?*" They are intensely curious about everything around them.

Observation and science inquiry experiences provide ideal opportunities to expose all children, including ELs, to new words and scientific vocabulary in both English and their own language. In the National Science Education Content Standards, the National Research Council (1996) maintained that science was for all children, regardless of their age, sex, cultural or ethnic background, disabilities, aspirations, or even interest and motivation in science. Children's natural curiosity lends itself to hands-on experiences with real objects. This need not cost very much, nor do classrooms have to be equipped with many materials to involve children in basic science concepts. Consider, for example, nature walks around the school, neighborhood, or local park. Nature walks help both children and adults increase awareness of their surroundings—children love to find bugs, look at birds, feed the fish, chase squirrels, and acquire pets. Consider partnering with parents to expose children to the world around them. And because ELs are building both knowledge and vocabulary, nature walks are wonderful opportunities to teach vocabulary on the spot and to mentally collect key words to teach later in an explicit way using the five-step process. During these walks:

- Have children collect leaves of various colors, and talk about how plants make their food when the sun shines on them.

- Talk about the rainy season, the hot summers, the winter snow, and other changes we experience daily.

- Check out the clouds, and see if children can tell if it might rain. Teach them the word *predict*. Help them learn to predict by using information that they know or facts that they have.

- Teach them to say, "I predict that it will rain because . . . ," or "My prediction is . . ."

- Observe a river when it is high and when it is low, and explain what causes the difference.

During the nature walks, provide simple explanations so that children can learn from concrete experiences and continue to be curious explorers. Teachers can also mentally plan lessons during nature walks to reinforce both vocabulary and content later in class. Consider:

> Because ELs are building both knowledge and vocabulary, nature walks are wonderful opportunities for teachers and parents to teach vocabulary.

- Organizing walks so that they become sample science lessons related to physical science, life science, or earth science

- Selecting words that children encounter during their nature walks, such as *habitat, discover, color, size, shape, texture, floating, air, soil, water, sunlight, stems, leaves,* and *roots,* and concepts like recycling and conservation

- Identifying categories for presenting new vocabulary, such as plants, fish, insects, and animals that fly—to place the words in context

Social Science

Social science is one of the most diverse content areas. It includes concepts of geography, history, conservation, ecology, culture, and civics. It teaches children about people, time, and place (Ravitch, 1995). Children who come from diverse cultures—who may speak different primary languages, eat different foods, and dress differently—can be great resources for the teaching of various social science concepts, such as geography ("Where do you come from?"), language ("How do you say *friend* in Tagalog?"), and conservation

("Why do you raise your own chickens?"). A lesson such as "Exploring What My Neighbor Eats," in which each family brings a sample of what they eat for a special holiday, can expose children not only to a variety of foods, spices, smells, colors, and textures, but also to a rich culinary vocabulary and appreciation for differences.

Closely related to the area of social science is social-emotional development. Social-emotional qualities such as self-esteem; self-confidence as a learner; self-control of attention, thinking, and impulses; and initiative in developing new ideas are essential to learning at any age. Social-interaction and self-control skills are vital to learning civics or learning about people (California Department of Education, 2010).

Addressing Key Foundations in the Content Areas

The development of content-based instruction from kindergarten to grade 12 has challenged preschool educators to cover specified key concepts and to monitor children's progress along the way. The Common Core State Standards, published by the National Governors Association and Council of Chief State School Officers (NGA & CCSSO, 2010), have also stimulated conversation regarding the curriculum of early learning programs. The Common Core State Standards articulate fewer, clearer, and higher standards designed to help teachers spend more time offering in-depth instruction on each concept.

Ensuring that children enter kindergarten ready to learn is a matter of growing concern across school districts. Children's exposure to many experiences early on, their access to technology, and the emerging science of early learning compel educators to focus much more on what needs to be taught and how best to teach it. Most researchers and practitioners agree that young children's thinking is much more complex than ever imagined. Children are capable of exploring more mathematical ideas and in greater depth than has traditionally been expected. Similar findings have been reported in science as well as in history and social science (Karoly, 2009; National Institute of Early Education Research, 2010).

Yet Nancy L. Cappelloni (2011) writes, in *Kindergarten Teachers' Perception of Kindergarten Readiness,* that one in three children enters kindergarten without the skills needed to succeed in school. She found that the lack of important readiness skills among children from low-income families, ELs, and children with multiple risk factors later intensifies and predicts such academic and social problems as retention, dropout, and incidences of delinquency. Children at risk begin their school experiences with an academic readiness gap in English literacy and math.

Standards

The national councils have published selected basic concepts for early mathematics, science, and social studies that children should be exposed to prior to entering kindergarten, based on best practices and latest research. These standards were not vetted in terms of the individual needs or uniqueness of each state; therefore, educators who work with ELs in preschools should review and incorporate them as appropriate with local preliteracy and second-language acquisition curriculum.

According to *Principles and Standards for School Mathematics,* published by the National Council of Teachers of Mathematics (2010), the essential components of a high-quality mathematics program for children in grades preK–2 consists of number and operations, algebra, geometry, measurement, and data analysis and probability. Each standard describes areas and key expectations. The next section, for example, outlines the preK–12 standards for data analysis and probability.

PreK–12 Data Analysis and Probability Standards

- Formulate questions that can be addressed with data, and collect, organize, and display relevant data to answer them.

  + Pose questions and gather data about themselves and their surroundings.

  + Sort and classify objects according to their attributes and organize data about the objects.

+ Represent data using concrete objects, pictures, and graphs.

In 2011, the National Academies released *A Framework for K–12 Science Education: Practices, Crosscutting Concepts, and Core Ideas* (National Academies, 2011). This framework identifies key scientific ideas and core concepts that all children should learn by the end of high school. It encourages educators to expose students to engaging opportunities to experience how science is done.

The new document specifies core ideas in four disciplines: life science; physical science; earth and space sciences; and engineering, technology, and applications.

The authors also present three dimensions for their framework—scientific and engineering practices, crosscutting concepts, and disciplinary core ideas—and provide a sample of key learning for each:

1. Scientific and engineering practices

    • Asking questions (for science) and defining problems (for engineering)

    • Developing and using models

    • Planning and carrying out investigations

    • Analyzing and interpreting data

    • Obtaining, evaluating, and communicating information

2. Crosscutting concepts

    • Patterns

    • Cause and effect: mechanism and explanation

    • Scale, proportion, and quantity

    • Systems and system models

    • Energy and matter: flows, cycles, and conservation

    • Stability and change

3. Disciplinary core ideas

- Physical sciences

- Life sciences

- Earth and space sciences

- Engineering, technology, and the application of science

Note that the framework does not provide specifics on how to teach the big ideas or the new science concepts; that is for curriculum specialists and practitioners to decide. There are many publications that detail effective instructional practices.

David Stewart (2011), in *How to Teach Preschool Science*, makes five recommendations for teaching science to ELs and other children:

1. Begin with familiar concepts.

2. Select related topics that build on each other.

3. Choose topics that take advantage of preschool children's natural instincts.

4. Set up simple experiments using things children see around them.

5. Use everyday examples to teach about cause and effect.

Stewart also advises teachers not to simplify vocabulary: "Use appropriate vocabulary when explaining science concepts. Don't dumb down the language, because knowing the right words will help children make connections when they study more about the same concepts at a later age. If you are explaining digestion, call it digestion" (p. 2).

In her work on the *National Curriculum Standards for Social Studies: A Framework for Teaching, Learning, and Assessment to Meet State Social Studies Standards,* Michelle Herczog (2010) states that these standards offer a vision for the future of social studies education in the United States. Of the ten principles, five are most appropriate for preK to second grade. These call for educators to provide experiences for the study of:

1. Culture and cultural diversity

2. People, places, and environment

3. Individual development and identity

4. Interactions among individuals, groups, and institutions

5. The relationships among science, technology, and society

Young children learn concepts and big ideas easier than they do isolated facts. This is why a key for struggling readers is the teaching of rich academics in context.

Young children learn concepts and big ideas easier than they do isolated facts. This is why a key for struggling readers is the teaching of rich academics in context. Instruction in the early grades lends itself to thematic lesson development and to the teaching of multiple standards within each lesson. It is important to note that there is a commonality of areas across the disciplines recommended for the early grades.

Instructional Practices for ELs and Struggling Readers

In this publication, it is recommended that staff spend much more time developing thematic lessons, cover themes over longer periods of time, and include standards from multiple content areas. Figure 8.1 (page 157) shows an example using the invention of the airplane.

The comprehensive lesson shown would require a few weeks to complete, but would include all required components:

- Standards in several content areas

- Literacy and academic vocabulary skills

- Reading and writing

- Formulation of critical thinking questions and exploration of answers

- Participation of parents and community members

- Assessment points and strategies to determine the progress and level of understanding of each child

1.0 Select the big ideas to be taught and the corresponding framework.

1.1 Data analysis standard: formulating questions (mathematics)

- Students pose questions and gather data about themselves and their surroundings.
- Students sort and classify objects according to their attributes and organize data about the objects.
- Students represent data using concrete objects, pictures, and graphs.

1.2 Scientific and engineering practices: asking questions (science)

- Planning and carrying out investigations
- Analyzing and interpreting data
- Obtaining and evaluating, and communicating information

1.3 Science, technology, and society (social science)

- Provide experiences to expose children to the relationships among science, technology, and society
- Formulate questions and big ideas

2.0 Select a big topic with multiple subtopics, and opportunities for children to enjoy.

2.1 Topic: the invention of airplanes

- Introduce and read books about old and new airplanes.
- See a movie or CD about old airplanes and how they were developed.
- Help older children look up airplanes and their history on the Internet.
- Help children formulate their questions about old and new airplanes.
- Ask children:
  + Have you ever been in an airplane?
  + Do you have toy airplanes?
  + What makes airplanes fly?

Figure 8.1: A sample thematic lesson incorporating the NCSS framework: The invention of airplanes. Continued →

+ What do you think makes airplanes fly? Is it the wings, the motors?

+ Would you like to fly airplanes?

+ Who invented airplanes?

2.2   Vocabulary: select key words and idioms to teach—for example, airplane, inventor, propeller, engine, passenger, hanger, airport, pilot, cabin, steward, bigger, smaller, heavy, heavier, less, more, ticket, trip, up in the air, coming down for a landing, taking off, air museum, tarmac, terminal, models, floats, floating.

2.3   Participation of parents: invite parents to participate in the development of projects and in field trips.

•   Ask parents to help children develop paper airplanes, place them in large water containers, and see if the children can predict when the paper planes will float or sink.

•   Ask parents to read books about airplanes to their children.

•   Ask parents to come to class and share experiences from a plane trip that they have taken.

•   Share the list of vocabulary words with parents, and ask them to review or practice these with their children as they read to them or when they play or put together airplane models.

•   Ask parents to accompany their children on a trip to the air space museum, point out key elements of airplanes, use new vocabulary as appropriate, or help children to interview the museum staff.

•   After each lesson or experience, ask parents to have conversations with their children about what they are learning, what they think is going to happen next, and what else would they like to know about airplanes.

2.4   Community projects: invite community members to participate in the development of projects and in field trips.

•   Ask the staff at a local air space museum to visit the classroom, talk about the history of airplanes, show pictures, use identified vocabulary, and host a visit for the children and their parents.

•   Invite a salesperson from a local toy store to class to show various models of airplanes and various types of toys that children can learn from and assemble. Encourage the salesperson to talk about size, shape, weight, prize, and other elements associated with numbers and mathematics.

3.0 Identify assessment points and multiple means of assessment.

3.1 Classroom progress reviews

- Ask children to explain key parts of an airplane during the story reading time, or to bring an airplane model and tell the class about its parts.

- Have small groups of students put together puzzles that require their knowledge of airplanes.

- Have students draw pictures of airplanes and tell the class a story about what they draw.

- Review the list of questions that children had at the beginning of the unit and see if they can answer them.

- Ask children what they have learned about the history of airplanes and ask them if they have other new questions.

3.2 Application: authentic assessment

- Ask the parents and community members to question children about what they have learned and what else they would like to learn.

- Have groups of children and their parents develop a model airport: include airplanes, gates, towers, luggage drop-off points, check in windows, consignment stores, with various types of employees, and so on.

Professional Preparation of PreK Teachers

Early learning programs have some of the most committed, hard-working, talented educators in the United States. However, not all teachers have had opportunities to develop their expertise, and not all students have access to experienced, high-quality educators. Most teachers lack training in mathematics, science, and social studies for teaching children in grades preK–2. There is also a shortage of teachers with adequate preparation for working with ELs, children with special needs, and children at risk.

Surveys conducted by the Frank Porter Graham Child Development Institute (2006) revealed that less than 15 percent of programs offering a bachelor's or associate's degree in child development or early childhood education required an entire course or more on working with bilingual children and that the preparation received may not have included the coursework or practicum experience necessary to work with ELs. Yet numerous sources stress that teacher preparation is a crucial factor in student gains:

- The National Institute of Early Education Research (2010) has documented that nothing is more important for the improvement of children's educational gains than a well-prepared teacher.

- The International Reading Association (2005) consistently recommends that well-prepared, knowledgeable, caring preschool teachers who understand the continuum of reading and writing development staff high-quality preschool and elementary school programs.

- Research on the preparation of exemplary teachers for the early childhood years is consistent—preschool teachers do best when they have college degrees and early childhood teaching certifications (Taylor, Pearson, Clark, & Walpole, 2000).

- Legislation such as the No Child Left Behind Act (2002) (and its related initiatives *Good Start, Grow Smart*) emphasized the importance of "highly qualified" teachers.

- The National Research Council (Bowman, Donovan, & Burns, 2000), in its report *Eager to Learn: Educating Our Preschoolers,* recommended that every young child have a teacher with a bachelor's degree in early care and education.

Experts and researchers propose that professional development programs provide strong grounding on early literacy and language development because of their importance in preschool to subsequent school achievement. For content instruction in the early years, teacher development also needs to include strategies on how to:

- Integrate early exposure to mathematics, science, and social studies into the preschool curriculum

- Learn effective practice for teaching classroom vocabulary and content to children who are ELs or have limited early literacy skills

- Connect physical, emotional, and social goals in the content curriculum when appropriate

- Develop appropriate content standards for preschool

- Integrate culturally enriching academic language and literacy in the content areas

- Participate in professional development opportunities to remain up-to-date about evidence based practices

- Learn effective practices on how best to use children's primary language, home, and background to enhance their early school experiences

Michael Fullan (2010), in *All Systems Go: The Change Imperative for Whole System Reform,* maintains that "collective capacity," a hidden and uncultivated resource, can turn around schools, districts, and even government agencies. Fullan's large body of research indicates that professional learning communities, in which teachers have the opportunity to learn and work together, get results. Every school principal can point to a great teacher or a few great teachers who work in his or her campus, but most do not have a critical mass of talent. The less-experienced teachers can learn so much from their expert colleagues. When teachers work and plan together, a sense of collective responsibility and overall teacher creativity and capacity grows across campus. The best results are student growth and development.

The core message of the new standards for professional learning proposed by Learning Forward (2011) in *The Standards for Professional Learning* is that educators need to take an active role in their own continuous development and learning. Professional learning increases educator effectiveness and results for all students when it occurs within learning communities committed to continuous improvement, collective responsibility, and goal alignment.

When possible, teachers ought to be supported to plan together, develop strategies and materials jointly, and attend professional

A large body of research indicates that professional learning communities, in which teachers have the opportunity to learn and work together, get results.

development activities in teams. These practices encourage teachers to engage in ongoing self-reflection and improvement. The challenges of teaching children with wide varieties of needs do not seem so overwhelming when there is genuine support from other colleagues.

References

Ballantyne, K. G., Sanderman, A. R., & McLaughlin, N. (2008). *Dual language learners in the early years: Getting ready to succeed in school.* Washington, DC: National Clearinghouse for English Language Acquisition. Accessed at www.ncela.gwu.edu./files/uploads/3/DLLs_in_Early_Years.pdf.on November 23, 2010.

Bowman, B. T., Donovan, M. S., & Burns, M. S. (Eds.). (2000). *Eager to learn: Educating our preschoolers.* Washington, DC: National Academies Press.

Calderón, M. (2011). *Teaching reading and comprehension to English learners, K–5.* Bloomington, IN: Solution Tree Press.

California Department of Education. (2010). *California preschool curriculum framework,* Vol. 1. Sacramento: Author.

California Department of Education. (2012). *California preschool curriculum framework,* Vol. 3. Sacramento: Author.

Cappelloni, N. L. (2011). *Kindergarten teachers' perceptions of kindergarten readiness.* Accessed at www.californiakindergartenassociation.org/research on August 23, 2011.

Copley, J. V. (Ed.). (1999). *Mathematics in the early years.* Reston, VA: National Council of Teachers of Mathematics & National Association for the Education of Young Children.

Copple, C., & Bredekamp, S. (2009). *Developmentally appropriate practice in early childhood programs serving children from birth through age 8* (3rd ed.). Washington, DC: National Association for the Education of Young Children.

Frank Porter Graham Child Development Institute. (2006). *Early childhood teacher preparation programs in the United States* (National Report). Chapel Hill, NC: Author.

Fullan, M. (2010). *All systems go: The change imperative for whole system reform.* Thousand Oaks, CA: Corwin Press.

Herczog, M. M. (2010). *Using the NCSS national curriculum standards for social studies: A framework for teaching, learning, and assessment to meet state social studies standards.* Accessed at www.socialstudies.org/system/files/Images/documents/7404217.pdf on August 21, 2011.

International Reading Association. (2005). *Literacy development in the preschool years.* Accessed at www.reading.org/General/AboutIRA/PositionStatements/PreschoolLiteracyPositioP.aspx on October 31, 2011.

Karoly, L. A. (2009). *Preschool adequacy and efficiency in California: Issues, policy options and recommendations.* Santa Monica, CA: RAND.

Learning Forward. (2011). *Standards for professional learning.* Accessed at www.learningforward.org/standards/index.cfm. on August 26, 2011.

Lind, K. K. (1999). Science in early childhood: Developing and acquiring concepts and skills. In American Association for the Advancement of Science (Ed.), *Dialogue on early childhood science, mathematics, and technology* (pp. 73–83). Washington, DC: American Association for the Advancement of Science.

National Academies. (2011). *A framework for K–12 education: Practices, crosscutting concepts, and core ideas.* Accessed at www.nap.edu/catalog.php?record_id=13165 on August 20, 2011.

National Association for the Education of Young Children. (2002). *Early Learning standards: Creating the conditions for success.* Washington, DC: Author.

National Council for the Social Studies (2010). *National curriculum standards for social studies: A framework for teaching, learning, and assessment.* Accessed at www. socialstudies.org/standards/strands on August 20, 2011.

National Council of Teachers of Mathematics. (2010). *Principles and standards for school mathematics.* Accessed at www.nctm.org/standards/content.aspx?id=7564 on August 20, 2011.

National Governors Association Center for Best Practices & Council of Chief State School Officers (2010). *K–12 Common Core State Standards.* Accessed at www.corestandards.org/articles/8-national-governors-assoiation-and-state-chiefs-launch-common-state-academic-standards. www.corestandards.org on August 23, 2011.

National Institute of Early Education Research. (2010). *The state of preschool 2010: State preschool yearbook.* Accessed at www.nieer.org/yearvbook/pdf/yearbook.pdf on August 20, 2011.

National Research Council. (1996). *National science education standards.* Washington, DC: National Academies Press.

No Child Left Behind Act of 2001, Pub. L. No. 107–110. § 115, Stat. 1425 (2002).

Ravitch, D. (1995). *National standards in American education: A citizen's guide.* Washington, DC: Brookings Institute.

Shonkoff, J. P., & Phllips, D. A. (Eds.) (2000). *From Neurons to neighborhoods: The Science of early childhood development.* Washington, DC: National Academy Press.

Shore, R. (2009). *PreK–3rd: Teacher quality matters* (Policy to Action Brief No. 3). New York: Foundation for Child Development.

Stewart, D. (2011). *How to teach preschool science.* Accessed at www.ehow.com /how_8130371_teach-preschool-science.html on November 2, 2011.

Taylor, B. M., Pearson, P. D., Clark, K. M., & Walpole, S. (2000). Effective schools and accomplished teachers: Lessons about primary-grade reading instruction in low-income schools. *Elementary School Journal, 101*(2), 121–165.

Margo Gottlieb

Margo Gottlieb, PhD, is an international expert in assessment design for English learners and the creation of language development standards in preK–12 settings. She is director of assessment and evaluation for the Illinois Resource Center in Arlington Heights and lead developer for the World-Class Instructional Design and Assessment (WIDA) Consortium at the Wisconsin Center for Education Research at the University of Wisconsin-Madison. For many years, Dr. Gottlieb has consulted and provided technical assistance to governments, states, school districts, publishers, universities, and professional organizations.

Dr. Gottlieb has worked with educators in American Samoa, Brazil, China, the Commonwealth of the Northern Mariana Islands, Italy, and Mexico, and as a Fulbright recipient served as senior specialist in assessment and evaluation in Chile. As a visiting professor at the University of Guam, she helped produce English language proficiency standards. She has been invited to present in Dubai, the United Arab Emirates, the United Kingdom, Panama, and Finland, as well as throughout the United States.

Her groundbreaking bestseller *Assessing English Language Learners: Bridges from Language Proficiency to Academic Achievement* was the basis for the accompanying A Multimedia Kit for Professional Development. Dr. Gottlieb is also the author of *Assessment and Accountability in Language Education Programs: A Guide for Teachers and Administrators* (with D. Nguyen), *Paper to Practice: Using the English Language Proficiency Standards in PreK–12 Classrooms* (with A. Katz & G. Ernst-Slavit), and *Common Language Assessment for English Learners*.

In this chapter, Dr. Gottlieb explores issues surrounding common instructional assessment for ELs as a whole-school initiative, distinguishes it from other forms of assessment, and lays the foundation for the use of data derived from common instructional assessment, with its ability to embrace cultural diversity, to counterbalance data from high-stakes testing.

Chapter 9

Common Instructional Assessment for English Learners: A Whole-School Effort

Margo Gottlieb

Schoolwide assessment practices designed with English learners in mind help create a school culture that embraces linguistic and cultural diversity. To create such a successful school, there must exist a decision-making process built around reliable, valid, and fair information. Initiating and sustaining the process of gathering, analyzing, interpreting, and reporting data takes dedicated teachers and administrators. Underlying this work is the fundamental principle that schools, regardless of their location or district policy, must support the students' primary language and respect the cultural identities of the surrounding community (Miramontes, Nadeau, & Commins, 2011).

This chapter is built on the premise that common instructional assessment for English learners yields immeasurable benefits for multiple stakeholders, most importantly for students and teachers, when it is a whole-school effort. First we define common instructional assessment from a culturally responsive education perspective; then we distinguish it from other forms and explore the research roots that support assessment at the classroom level. Next, we discuss new developments in education that have contributed to having common instructional assessment serve as a counterbalance to high-stakes accountability testing. Finally, we look toward the future to envision how schools might enact common instructional assessment that highlights what English learners can do.

Culturally Responsive Teaching and Learning

The time has come for schools to be responsive to their ever-growing, linguistically and culturally diverse student populations. Barbara Bazron, David Osher, and Steve Fleischman (2005) suggest that one of the most powerful responses schools can make is to ensure that classroom instruction—and assessment—are congruent with the cultural value systems of the surrounding communities. In other words, as education professionals, we are obligated first and foremost to advance the achievement of our students. To do so, schools need to center around and reflect the muliticultural frames of reference and range of experiences of their students (Ladson-Billings, 1995).

In culturally responsive schools, everyone feels valued, secure, and safe; this inclusive environment fosters mutual trust and respect among all stakeholders (Soltero, 2011). Teachers and school leaders capitalize on the linguistic and cultural richness of their student body, in particular English learners, to construct a shared vision of students' language expectations in relation to grade-level content. Just as culturally responsive teaching recognizes the importance of including students' cultural references in all aspects of learning, so too does assessment. Table 9.1 applies the primary characteristics of culturally responsive teaching to instructional assessment.

Table 9.1: Application of Culturally Responsive Teaching to Instructional Assessment

Characteristics of Culturally Responsive Teaching	Characteristics of Culturally Responsive Instructional Assessment
Encourages participation of family members	Promotes contributions of family members to data-driven decision making

Communicates high expectations for learning	References grade-level standards in reporting results
Supports learning within a cultural context	Interprets and reports data within a cultural context
Promotes student-centered instruction	Includes student self-reflection and peer assessment
Embeds multiculturalism into the curriculum	Reshapes instructional assessment to include multicultural perspectives

How can schools prepare for culturally responsive education? First, the linguistic and cultural diversity of the student population must permeate every nook and cranny of the school—through murals, posters, photographs, signage, and original student work. Students need to identify with school as an extension of who they are and must consider it an inviting place to be. Second, culturally responsive teaching must be evident in classrooms, where it can best be planned, delivered, and captured through instructional assessment. As teachers personalize student learning through differentiation, they must capitalize on the linguistic and cultural diversity within their classrooms. Table 9.2 is a checklist of how best to do so.

Table 9.2: A Checklist for Enacting Culturally Responsive Instructional Assessment

In preparing for culturally responsive instructional assessment, we have . . .	Done!	Not Yet
analyzed the language demands of grade-level text in terms of challenges for English learners.		
identified cultural nuances and biases in instructional materials.		
included the students' linguistic and cultural experiences as background builders.		
used the community as a linguistic and cultural resource.		
created differentiated language objectives for instructional assessment tasks based on students' levels of language proficiency.		

Continued →

adapted or developed rubrics, scoring guides, or project descriptors that reflect the instructional tasks or projects for English learners.		
ensured students have a clear understanding of the language and content criteria on which their work is interpreted.		
thought about reporting assessment results to students based on the standards-referenced criteria.		

Through culturally valid assessment, we secure better and more accurate information on how schools are educating our multilingual and multicultural youth; these data inform us of student progress (Basterra, Trumbull, & Solano-Flores, 2011). However, as we shall see in the next section, by their very nature different forms of assessment have varying degrees of linguistic and cultural sensitivity.

Four Forms of Assessment

Four forms of assessment—instructional, common instructional, interim, and standardized—tend to operate simultaneously in schools (fig. 9.1). Instructional assessment and common instructional assessment are internal to the functioning of schools and represent a bottom-up effort to use home-grown data to make local decisions and contribute to personal and schoolwide accountability. Interim and standardized assessments, on the other hand, are generally externally imposed and are equated with accountability at the district, county, state, or province levels. Teachers and school leaders generally have little input into interim and standardized assessment, and there is limited presence of linguistic and cultural sensitivity.

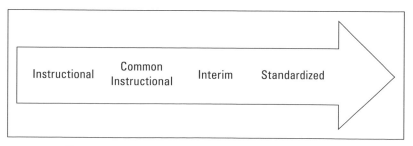

Figure 9.1: A continuum of the forms of assessment.

Since each form serves different purposes, by using them together schools can make more informed decisions. Table 9.3 contrasts the features of instructional and common assessment with those of interim and standardized achievement tests, so that you can see how these forms might complement each other.

Table 9.3: A Comparison of the Different Forms of Achievement Measures for English Learners

Instructional and Common Instructional Assessment for Measuring Academic Achievement	Interim and Standardized Achievement Tests
Designed and developed specifically for English learners	Not necessarily designed, piloted, or field tested on sufficient numbers of English learners
Crafted by educators for educators	Crafted by test developers
Have strong ties to curriculum and are representative of instruction	Have loose ties to curriculum and instruction
Consist of performance-based tasks and projects with high levels of student interaction and original student work	Items often discrete and skill-based and may represent low levels of cognitive engagement
Represent what is valued in teaching and learning	May be removed from what is valued for teaching and learning
May possess validity, but not are necessarily highly reliable for language learners	May be highly reliable but are not necessarily valid for language learners
Needed to help balance educational accountability	Dominate educational accountability

Instructional Assessment

Instructional assessment is an information-gathering process within the classroom routine in which there is a personalized interaction between teachers and students. It is designed by individual teachers to make student, group, or classroom-level decisions. The information from instructional assessment is idiosyncratic to a particular classroom culture; therefore, it is not readily transferable to other teaching situations or teachers (Gottlieb & Nguyen, 2007). Instructional assessment revolves around what teachers do every minute, day by day; it is considered a formative process that entails:

- Shared learning goals and targets between teachers and students

- Reliance on rich descriptive feedback from teachers to students

- Active involvement and engagement of students in their own learning

- Use of evidence to redirect instruction and promote student learning (Moss & Brookhart, 2009; Popham, 2008; Wiliam, 2011)

Instructional assessment should reflect the cultural makeup of classrooms. There is tremendous variability in students' historical, educational, and experiential backgrounds. Therefore, when considering instructional assessment, teachers must be aware of students' distinct characteristics, including:

- Continuity of educational experiences inside and outside the United States or Canada

- Continuity and types of language support services

- Native language literacy

- English language proficiency

- Linguistic and cultural density of the community in which students reside

- Access to resources, such as technology

Instructional assessment is unique to individual teachers. Every teacher has a teaching and management style that can't be duplicated. Every teacher has preferred ways to assess students day in and day out. Some may use checklists, others are comfortable taking anecdotal notes, still others may enjoy using video to record student performance. When we speak of instructional assessment, we acknowledge the personalization of teaching and the bond of individual teachers with their students.

Ultimately, the goal of instructional assessment is to support learning (Black & Wiliam, 1998; Stiggins, 2008), and with English learners, that learning occurs within a linguistically and culturally enriched context. Through self-reflection and peer-assessment, students can truly be participants in their own learning.

Common Instructional Assessment

In this era of educational accountability, we need to accrue a defensible body of evidence to show that our students are indeed progressing on a regular basis. How can we take the intrinsic value and benefits of instructional assessment and produce more reliable results? The answer lies in common instructional assessment.

Common instructional assessment is a consensus-building process among educators that yields a set of mutually agreed-upon measures or tasks. This form of assessment embodies a collaborative commitment and shared vision among teachers and school leaders, ideally through professional learning communities. Embedded in instruction, common instructional assessment insists on uniform procedures for collecting, analyzing, interpreting, and reporting data across multiple classrooms (Gottlieb, 2012b). By having data aggregated across classrooms, whether at a grade or department level, for a language education program or the entire school, the results are more robust, and there is greater confidence in making decisions. Thus, teachers have a voice in and help contribute to local accountability for student learning.

Professional learning communities or teams provide a venue for educators to pool their resources and expertise with the goal of improving the achievement of students. Common instructional assessment is therefore an ideal focus for professional learning communities, as it represents what teachers value and yields information that is useful, relevant, and meaningful. The entire school benefits when professional learning communities center their attention on improving the collection and use of reliable and valid data about students, especially English learners.

> By aggregating data across grade, department, language education program, or the entire school, the results are more robust and there is greater confidence in making decisions.

Common instructional assessment reflects classroom practice. Teachers are encouraged to pool their expertise and decide which culturally responsive instructional tasks best match grade-level standards. To bring equity to education, results from common instructional assessment need to offset those of standardized achievement measures. The research base sheds some light on how instructional assessment benefits schools with English learners.

Interim Assessment

Interim assessments, also known as benchmark assessments, are commercially produced measures whose primary purpose is to forecast or predict student performance on annual high-stakes tests. Given at preset intervals during the school year, there are rather stringent guidelines for administering the measures to ensure reliability of the results. Teachers generally have little to no input on the timeframe for administration or on how the data are reported and used.

Standardized Assessment

Standardized tools are either norm-referenced or criterion-referenced tests. In large part, states use criterion-referenced tests that are grounded in their academic content or language proficiency standards. In 2015, there will be a shift by the majority of states to a computer-based series of achievement measures developed by two U.S. federally funded assessment consortia and anchored in the Common Core State Standards of 2010. Two other consortia are designing achievement measures for students with severe cognitive disabilities. In parallel fashion, there is also a consortium-led, technologically driven language proficiency assessment of English learners based on its English language development standards.

The complexity of assessment for English learners, irrespective of its form, is compounded by the overlay of culture—that is, the extent to which linguistic and cultural factors shape the process of test design and test taking (Basterra, Trumbull, & Solano-Flores, 2011). Only through culturally valid assessment are we able to secure appropriate and accurate information about the performance of

English learners. Therefore, all consortia must be particularly sensitive and responsive to the unique characteristics of English learners as they craft the new generation of assessments for them.

Research at the School and District Levels

There is a growing body of research that refers to the school as a unit of analysis for examining the increased academic achievement of English learners. Claude Goldenberg and Rhoda Coleman (2011) make a strong case for the positive role of schools in advancing the academic success of these students. In particular, focus and coherence emerge as defining features of effective schools serving English learners. These traits are evident in four characteristics these schools possess:

1. Explicit academic goals around a student-centered vision for English learners

2. Reinforcement of the goals through ongoing assessment of academic progress, with an emphasis on information from instructionally informative assessments that give timely feedback (rather than standardized or high-stakes tests)

3. Leadership by school principals who consistently maintain English learners as a priority, maximize available resources for these students, and communicate this message to staff and teacher leaders, who in turn take on schoolwide responsibility for a rigorous instructional program for English learners

4. Sustained and focused professional development that centers on instructional and assessment approaches for English learners that exemplify second-language acquisition theory and practice.

In the Council of Great City Schools' 2009 report, Amanda Rose Horwitz et al. mention several contextual features and promising practices found in four urban districts that experienced gains in achievement of English learners from 2002 to 2006. Of particular interest to assessment, it is noted that "improving districts made the use of data a cornerstone of their reform strategies, significantly expanding the accessibility, quantity, and types of student data available to educators" (p. 3). Equally noteworthy in this research is a shift toward greater collaboration between the central district office and schools, with greater emphasis being placed on shared responsibility and accountability for all students. These findings underscore the value of instructional assessment as a data source that can contribute to overall school and district improvement. This research, coupled with new developments in assessment, holds tremendous promise for English learners.

New Developments

Since the mid-2000s, there has been a noticeable change in assessment practices for English learners centered around three themes: standards-based reform, the increased role of academic language, and an insistence on the use of multiple measures.

Standards-Based Reform

Standards for language learners are international in scope, having been developed in Australia, Canada, American Samoa, and the United States (Gottlieb, 2012a). Although state content standards have been part of U.S. federal legislation since 1994, the Elementary and Secondary School Act of 2002 (No Child Left Behind) ushered in a mandate for states to also have English language proficiency standards. These language standards, tied to state content standards, have become the anchor for English language proficiency testing and accountability for the growing numbers of school-aged English learners. With the widespread adoption of the Common Core State Standards in English/language arts and mathematics, we see growing unity in the standards reform movement on which future common instructional assessment will be built.

> Educators of English learners now recognize that the integration of language and content standards into every aspect of school life is the anchor for making classroom, school, district, and state decisions about student learning.

At the school and district levels, language standards have become the foundation for building curriculum for language education programs, targeting language outcomes, and developing instructional assessment for English learners. Language standards have also increased educators' clarity about the critical role of language in content classes. Educators of English Learners now recognize that the integration of language and content standards into every aspect of school life is the anchor for making classroom, school, district, and state decisions about student learning.

Academic Language

Researchers agree that students' control over and use of academic language is the greatest determinant of their academic success (Anstrom et al., 2010; Bailey, 2007; Francis, Rivera, Lesaux, Kieffer, & Rivera, 2006). It should be no surprise, then, that assessment for and of English learners across all forms has come to revolve around academic language. Defined in its broadest sense, academic language consists of the language expectations required for schooling. It encompasses the meaning, in context, of single vocabulary words and expressions, sentence forms and grammaticality, and genres and text types across multiple sentences (Bailey & Heritage, 2008; Egbert & Ernst-Slavit, 2010; Gottlieb, Katz, & Ernst-Slavit, 2009; Zwiers, 2008).

Inclusive of academic language is the unique discourse or way of constructing and communicating meaning within and across each discipline or content area (McKay, 2006; Schleppegrell, 2004; Wright, 2010). For example, the language required in telling a fairy tale is distinct from reporting the results of a scientific experiment, which in turn has no resemblance to explaining Reconstruction after the Civil War. Teachers must be aware of the language demands of their grade-level subject matter in order to explore text, promote academic discussions, facilitate classroom interaction, and frame instructional assessment.

Multiple Measures

There is wide consensus that educational decision making has to be based on a body of evidence systematically gathered over time. As Sue Brookhart (2007) has noted, multiple measures does not mean giving both the language arts and mathematics state tests or offering a state graduation test more than one time; rather, it is the use of data from a variety of forms of assessment. For English learners, this definition translates into having information from varied and complementary assessments that together reflect instruction and provide a more personalized account of student learning.

Schools that engage in common instructional assessment intentionally seek balance in the use of data from multiple measures. Although standardized and interim testing may continue to dominate the scene at the state level, in response, we must elevate the status of common instructional assessment at the school and district levels, so that local assessment data are valued. By being able to extend differentiation of instruction, especially language differentiation, to assessment, we are able to obtain more precise data on the everyday performance of English learners.

Students are a data source that is often neglected but is nevertheless extremely important. English learners, like all students, should have opportunities to engage in self- and peer assessment to reflect on the processes and products of learning (Gottlieb, 2006; O'Malley & Pierce, 1996). Self-assessment encourages students to engage in higher-level thinking by analyzing and evaluating their own work. Another of its purposes is to empower students to gradually take responsibility for and ownership of their learning. Thus, English learners gain confidence in matching learning expectations to specified, standards-referenced criteria. When extending this same process to peer assessment, students, paired with students from the same linguistic and cultural backgrounds, can use their native language to engage in academic conversations to explain and defend their work.

Usefulness of Data From Common Instructional Assessment

Information from classroom-based assessment provides the most comprehensive and personalized picture of individual students (Marzano & Kendall, 1996). Data from common instructional assessment represent what teachers feel is important in teaching and learning. Because they are customized by teachers and school leaders, data from common instructional assessment have:

- Credibility, with connections to the curriculum and its related standards

- Authenticity, since they are inspired by classroom practice

- Practicality, with potential instructional impact

Common instructional assessment lends itself to having groups of teachers and school leaders engage in joint decision making. Having teachers analyze and interpret performance data, such as oral and written language samples, to obtain inter-rater agreement on set standards-referenced criteria is an excellent professional learning activity. Results can be used to group students, plan differentiated instruction, and design student learning profiles. But more importantly, having language and content teachers work together creates a bond and promise for the education of English learners.

> Having teachers analyze and interpret performance data, such as oral and written language samples, to obtain inter-rater agreement on set standards-referenced criteria is an excellent professional learning activity.

A Whole-School Endeavor

Effective instructional assessment practices require teachers and school leaders to monitor English learners' language and content learning on an ongoing basis. By coming to understand that English learners can indeed reach grade-level expectations based on their levels of language proficiency, educators can insist on valid assessments. Common instructional assessment offers that opportunity for English learners who are being instructed in English and additional languages.

There is much work to do to make common instructional assessment a schoolwide effort. First, it is important to have a keen sense of the students' historical, educational, and experiential backgrounds. Teachers and school leaders must become familiar with the languages and cultures of their students and seek ways of translating those assets into appropriate instructional assessment practices. Second, it is foundational that teachers understand the second-language development process, know where their language learners are positioned on the second-language continuum, and be able to relate how that position affects the students' learning. Lastly, teachers must know the academic language of their discipline or grade level and use it as a vehicle for promoting educational excellence for all their students.

In his edited volume aptly named *The Teacher as Assessment Leader,* Thomas Guskey (2009) highlights the uses and benefits of formative classroom assessment across a range of instructional settings. The future holds much promise for English learners, and other students, if we are able to take these principles of instructional assessment that operate on an individual classroom level and apply them to an entire school. The acceptance and use of common instructional assessment data can then permeate the halls, reflect the school population and culture, be robust and valid, and make a school a true leader in educational reform for English learners.

Demographic trends point to the increasing presence of English learners in elementary and secondary school classrooms in the years to come. Visionary leaders who make the education of English learners a schoolwide responsibility and priority have a commitment to equity and advocacy. When common instructional assessment is integrated into a culturally responsive school, students, teachers, and the community become a united front for promoting and obtaining academic excellence.

References

Anstrom, K., DiCerbo, P., Butler, F., Katz, A., Millet, J., & Rivera, C. (2010). *A review of the literature on academic English: Implications for K–12 English language learners.* Washington, DC: The George Washington University Center for Equity and Excellence in Education.

Bailey, A. L. (Ed.). (2007). *The language demands of school: Putting academic language to the test.* New Haven, CT: Yale University Press.

Bailey, A. L., & Heritage, M. (2008). *Formative assessment for literacy, grades K–6: Building reading and academic language skills across the curriculum.* Thousand Oaks, CA: Corwin Press.

Basterra, M. d. R., Trumbull, E., & Solano-Flores, G. (Eds.). (2011). *Cultural validity in assessment: Addressing linguistic and cultural diversity.* New York: Routledge.

Bazron, B., Osher, D., & Fleischman, S. (2005). Creating culturally responsive schools. *Educational Leadership, 63*(1), 83–84.

Black, P., & Wiliam, D. (1998). Inside the black box: Raising standards through classroom assessment. *Phi Delta Kappan, 80*(2), 139–148.

Brookhart, S. M. (2007). Feedback that fits. *Educational Leadership, 65*(4), 54–59.

Brookhart, S. M. (2009). The many meanings of "multiple measures." *Educational Leadership, 67*(3), 6–12.

Egbert, J. L., & Ernst-Slavit, G. (2010). *Access to academics: Planning instruction for K–12 classrooms with ELLs.* Boston: Pearson Education.

Francis, D. J., Rivera, M., Lesaux, N., Kieffer, M., & Rivera, H. (2006). *Research-based recommendations for instruction and academic interventions.* Houston: Texas Institute for Measurement, Evaluation, and Statistics at the University of Houston for the Center on Instruction.

Freeman, Y. S., & Freeman, D. E. (2008). *Academic language for English Language Learners and struggling readers: How to help students succeed across content areas.* Portsmouth, NH: Heinemann.

Goldenberg, C., & Coleman, R. (2010). *Promoting academic achievement among English learners: A guide to the research.* Thousand Oaks, CA: Corwin Press.

Gottlieb, M. (2006). *Assessing English language learners: Bridges from language proficiency to academic achievement.* Thousand Oaks, CA: Corwin Press.

Gottlieb, M. (2012a). An overview of language education standards. In C. Coombe, S. Stoynoff, P. Davidson, & B. O' Sullivan (Eds.), *The Cambridge Guide to Language Assessment* (pp. 74–81). Cambridge, UK: Cambridge University Press.

Gottlieb, M. (2012b). *Common language assessment for English learners.* Bloomington, IN: Solution Tree Press.

Gottlieb, M., & Nguyen, D. (2007). *Assessment and accountability in language education programs: A guide for administrators and teachers.* Philadelphia: Caslon.

Gottlieb, M., Katz, A., & Ernst-Slavit, G. (2009). *Paper to practice: Using the English language proficiency standards in preK–12 classrooms.* Alexandria, VA: Teachers of English to Speakers of Other Languages.

Guskey, T. R. (Ed.). (2009). *The teacher as assessment leader.* Bloomington, IN: Solution Tree Press.

Horwitz, A. R., Uro, G., Price-Baugh, R., Simon, C., Uzzell, R., Lewis, S., & Casserly, M. (2009). *Succeeding with English language learners: Lessons from the Great City Schools.* Washington, DC: Council of the Great City Schools.

Ladson-Billings, G. (1995). But that's just good teaching! The case for culturally relevant pedagogy. *Theory into Practice, 34*(3), 159–165.

Marzano, R. J., & Kendall, J. S. (1996). *Designing standards-based districts, schools, and classrooms.* Aurora, CO: Mid-Continent Regional Educational Laboratory.

McKay, P. (2006). *Assessing young language learners.* Cambridge, UK: Cambridge University Press.

Miramontes, O. B., Nadeau, A., & Commins, N. L. (2011). *Restructuring schools for linguistic diversity: Linking decision making to effective programs* (2nd ed.). New York: Teachers College Press.

Moss, C. M., & Brookhart, S. (2009). *Advancing formative assessment in every classroom: A guide for instructional leaders.* Alexandria, VA: Association for Supervision and Curriculum Development.

No Child Left Behind Act of 2001, Pub. L. No. 107–110, § 115, Stat. 1425 (2002).

O'Malley, J. M., & Pierce, L. V. (1996). *Authentic assessment for English language learners: Practical approaches for teachers.* New York: Addison-Wesley.

Popham, W. J. (2008). *Transformative assessment.* Alexandria, VA: Association for Supervision and Curriculum Development.

Schleppegrell, M. J. (2004). *The language of schooling: A functional linguistics perspective.* Mahwah, NJ: Lawrence Erlbaum.

Soltero, S. W. (2011). *Schoolwide approaches to educating ELLs: Creating linguistically and culturally responsive K–12 schools.* Portsmouth, NH: Heinemann.

Stiggins, R. (2008). *Assessment manifesto: A call for the development of balanced assessment systems.* Portland, OR: Educational Testing Service.

Wiliam, D. (2011). *Embedded formative assessment.* Bloomington, IN: Solution Tree Press.

Wright, W. E. (2010). *Foundations for teaching English language learners: Research, theory, policy, and practice.* Philadelphia: Caslon.

Zwiers, J. (2008). *Building academic language: Essential practices for content classrooms, grades 5–12.* San Francisco: Jossey-Bass.

Alba A. Ortiz

Alba A. Ortiz is a professor of special education in the Multicultural Special Education Program and the director of the Office of Bilingual Education in the College of Education at the University of Texas at Austin. A past president of the International Council for Exceptional Children, Dr. Ortiz holds the President's Chair for Education Academic Excellence, an honor bestowed by the university in recognition of her contributions to the fields of bilingual and special education.

Dr. Ortiz has extensive experience as a speech and language pathologist, a migrant and special education instructional program specialist, and a bilingual education and special education teacher educator. She has written extensively on such topics as ELs with language and learning disabilities and prevention and early intervention for second language learners experiencing achievement difficulties.

In this chapter, Dr. Ortiz explores the essential components of response to intervention (RTI) strategies for ELs, stresses the importance of determining accurately whether low test scores are due to a lack of English proficiency or to some other disability, and explains the importance, when conducting RTI, of both prevention and early intervention.

Chapter 10

Response to Intervention for English Learners

Alba A. Ortiz

English learners experience widespread academic failure, including higher rates of retention and social promotion (Center for Policy Studies, Education Research, and Community Development [CPSER], 2011), and they are twice as likely as their English-proficient peers to be reading below grade level (National Center for Educational Statistics [NCES], 2005). This is not surprising given that, by definition, ELs have limited proficiency in English; testing them in a language they have not yet mastered results in low test scores. As straightforward as this may seem, though, general education teachers are often unable to distinguish students whose low academic performance is an artifact of limited English proficiency from those whose difficulties are associated with disabilities (Ortiz, 1997, 2002).

Bilingual education teachers have specialized expertise regarding second-language acquisition and are trained to provide culturally responsive native language and ESL instruction. They should be in a better position to accurately identify ELs whose academic struggles indicate the presence of disabilities. However, three interrelated studies of ELs who were identified as also having reading-related learning disabilities (Ortiz et al., 2012) suggest that this is not necessarily the case. Researchers examined the characteristics of ELs identified as students with reading-related disabilities by the participating district and found that available data supported a learning disability (LD) classification for only ten of forty-four students. These findings raise serious questions about the appropriateness of referrals of ELs to special education by bilingual education teachers.

Low academic achievement in general and reading-related difficulties specifically are the primary reasons for referral of ELs to special education (McCardle, Mele-McCarthy, Cutting, Leos, & D'Emilio, 2005). It is not surprising, then, that the majority of ELs in special education have reading-related learning disabilities (McCardle et al., 2005; Zehler, Fleischman, Hopstock, Penzick, & Stephenson, 2003).

> Of ELs identified as students with reading-related disabilities by participating districts, available data supported an LD classification for only ten of forty-four.

The disproportionate representation of ELs in special education (Artiles, Rueda, Salazar, & Higareda, 2005; Ortiz et al., in press) has generated substantial interest in alternatives to traditional referral and assessment processes for identifying ELs with learning disabilities. The reauthorization of the Individuals with Disabilities Education Act (2004) has given states one such alternative. Multidisciplinary teams, the group responsible for qualifying students for special education services, can now base LD eligibility on documentation of students' responses to scientific, research-based interventions. Since the IDEA reauthorization, almost every state has adopted response to intervention (RTI) to identify students with learning disabilities (Berkeley, Bender, Peaster, & Saunders, 2009).

What Is Response to Intervention?

RTI serves two primary purposes: (1) to ensure that students experiencing academic or behavioral problems in general education classrooms are provided high-quality, early intervention to resolve those difficulties; and (2) to provide an alternative to the use of IQ-achievement discrepancy formulae in the identification of students with learning disabilities (IDEA, 2004). Although implementation varies considerably, RTI models share several common elements (Berkeley et al., 2009; Greenwood, 2009):

- Schools follow a curriculum that has proven effective for the majority of children.

- Students are provided high-quality instruction based on universal design principles, and instruction is differentiated consistent with students' abilities and needs.

- Universal screenings identify students who are not meeting instructional goals.

- Struggling learners are provided increasingly intensive, research-based interventions.

- Progress in response to these interventions is continuously monitored.

General education personnel, including those who teach bilingual education and ESL, are responsible for implementing these RTI components. Whether they can achieve the goals of increasing the academic success of ELs and preventing inappropriate referrals to special education depends on whether RTI models are linguistically and cultural responsive.

Essential Components of RTI for ELs

Figure 10.1 (page 188) presents the essential components of RTI for ELs: prevention and early intervention. The figure also suggests the relationship of these components to the decision to refer a student to special education. The elements of the figure are discussed briefly in the sections that follow.

Prevention

Most RTI models begin at the level of the classroom and fail to recognize system-level issues that have an impact on the education of ELs. However, if ELs are among the lowest-achieving groups on a campus, it is important to evaluate the school climate to identify factors that may be contributing to this lack of success and to modify or adapt the core curriculum accordingly (Garcia & Ortiz, 2008; Ortiz et al., 2009). Without a positive school climate and effective

Prevention (Tier 1)

- The principal and school staff create an environment that reflects a philosophy that all students can learn and that educators are responsible for assuring that they do.
- Teachers use instructional strategies known to be effective for ELs.
- They use assessment data from multiple sources to describe student performance in the native language and in English and to differentiate instruction to meet individual needs.
- Teachers monitor student progress in the native language and in English as a second language and redirect instruction as needed.
- Students who experience achievement difficulties despite effective, differentiated instruction are provided more intensive intervention.

Early Intervention (Tier 2)

- For students who are struggling despite differentiated instruction, teachers implement more intensive interventions to address learning or behavioral concerns.
- If problems persist, they request assistance from a campus-based problem-solving team that includes members with expertise in the education of ELs.
- Students are provided individualized interventions designed by the team. Interventions may be part of a standard protocol approach and may be implemented by teachers or instructional specialists.
- Evaluate results of interventions. If problems are resolved, students continue in the core instructional program, with Tier 1 and Tier 2 interventions, as needed. If not, Tier 3 interventions are considered.

More Intensive Intervention (Tier 3)

- The RTI committee reviews information gathered during the prevention and early intervention phases. The committee tries to identify factors, other than the presence of a disability, that may explain presenting problems.
- The committee considers whether there are any other general education alternatives or interventions that might resolve presenting problems. This may include, for example, instruction provided by subject and content-area specialists, such as, reading or math specialists or after-school tutoring programs.
- If general education alternatives are exhausted, the committee may refer the student to special education.
- The special education referral committee identifies unresolved issues and develops questions that should be addressed in a special education evaluation.
- A full and individualized evaluation is requested to help determine eligibility for special education.

Source: Adapted from Bilingual Exceptional Students: Early Intervention, Referral, and Assessment *(2009), by A. A. Ortiz, P. Robertson, and C. Y. Wilkinson. Paper presented at the University of Texas at Austin BESt ERA Training-of-Trainers Conference, Austin, TX. Reprinted with permission.*

Figure 10.1: Elements of response to intervention for English learners.

instruction, teachers will be in a continual cycle of student remediation, because school and classroom contexts will be inadequate to meet student needs.

School Climate

Characteristics of schools conducive to the success of ELs include (Ortiz, Robertson, & Wilkinson, 2009):

- Strong leadership by principals with expertise specific to ELs
- High expectations for all students
- A safe, orderly environment
- Linkages across programs
- Collaborative relationships among all personnel who serve ELs
- Collaborative school, home, and community relationships
- Shared decision making
- Shared knowledge base about ELs
- Linguistic and cultural pluralism
- Well-implemented special language programs based on a common philosophy and program model
- Systematic, longitudinal evaluation of student progress and corresponding record keeping
- Well-implemented, linguistically and culturally responsive RTI
- Mechanisms for mentoring new personnel

It is beyond the scope of this chapter to discuss all of the elements of an effective school climate. While some of the elements listed apply to effective schools regardless of the student demography (for example, high expectations, a safe and orderly environment, and collaborative home-school-community relationships), some are particularly relevant to the success of ELs and are not typically found in effective school formulae. These include strong leadership by principals with expertise specific to ELs, a shared knowledge base about

ELs, well-implemented special language programs, and systematic and longitudinal evaluation of student progress.

Strong Leadership by Principals With Expertise Specific to ELs

School principals are responsible for establishing an environment that reflects the belief that *all* students can learn and, more importantly perhaps, that educators are responsible for seeing to it that they do (Ortiz, 2002; Ortiz et al., 2009). To ensure the success of ELs, campus administrators must engage educators, parents, and members of the community in discussions of the purpose and goals of special language programs (that is, bilingual education and ESL programs) and facilitate the adoption of a philosophy regarding the education of ELs and a common program model that everyone can support (Montecel & Cortez, 2002). This will help ensure the cohesiveness of programs and services within and across grades and will reduce the number of counterproductive debates about how best to educate ELs.

Shared Knowledge Base

Providing appropriate programs and services requires developing a shared knowledge base about ELs. This can be accomplished only through extensive professional development on key topics, such as native language (L_1) development and ESL (L_2) acquisition, effective L_1 and L_2 instruction, the influence of socioeconomic status on student learning, effective instruction in both the native language and English, assessment and progress monitoring, and parent-school partnerships. Principals must involve all educators on their campuses in such training to foster shared responsibility for student learning.

Well-Implemented Special Language Programs

Another key to the success of ELs is access to well-implemented special language programs. Principals must ensure that the core curricula adopted in their respective schools is effective for ELs and that it is implemented as intended. They should monitor the amount and type of native language and ESL instruction teachers provide students to avoid problems as students move across grades. For example, teachers in the early grades may teach exclusively in the native language to increase the likelihood that students will pass accountability assessments, which are also administered in the native language. However, this creates serious instructional issues for teachers in the upper grades, as ELs arrive with little proficiency in English despite having been consistently enrolled in bilingual education programs since kindergarten. To close this language gap and to prepare students for middle schools, bilingual education teachers in the upper elementary grades may decide to teach entirely in English, reasoning that students are unlikely to have access to native language instruction after elementary school. However, they fail to recognize that the switch to English-only instruction denies ELs access to knowledge and skills that are crucial to future academic success, and to content they could have acquired had they been taught in a language they understand and speak. These are examples of how lack of fidelity in implementation of the core curriculum can lead to academic failure, increasing the number of students who will need more intensive instruction such as that provided in Tiers 2 and 3 of RTI.

> The switch to English-only instruction denies ELs access to knowledge and skills that are crucial to future academic success, and to content they could have acquired had they been taught in a language they understand and speak.

Systematic, Longitudinal Evaluation of Student Progress

RTI involves systematic progress monitoring and documentation of the results of multitiered interventions provided by classroom teachers. General education teachers, including bilingual education and ESL teachers, must document attempts to resolve learning difficulties, including the outcomes of differentiated instruction and more intensive interventions. If the student is receiving services outside the general education classroom (for example, after-school tutoring or instruction provided by a reading specialist), progress resulting from these services must also be documented. In addition to analyzing an EL's current performance, educators should profile trajectories associated with language acquisition and achievement over time (Wilkinson, Ortiz, Robertson, & Kushner, 2006). This will help to pinpoint when the student first began experiencing difficulties and focus attention on discovering what interventions, if any, were attempted to resolve learning problems at specific points in time. Without a retrospective view of students' language development and academic progress, it is difficult to distinguish problems associated with a lack of timely intervention from those that suggest the presence of a disability.

A retrospective view of student performance can also help identify significant events in the child's history (such as health or medical problems, child abuse, or high mobility) that may have negatively affected his or her school experiences (Ortiz et al., 2012; Wilkinson et al., 2006). Parents who did not have the fiscal resources to do so (for example, they could not afford medical care) or did not know how to access available services may not have acted on these problems. Educators should ensure that steps are taken and interventions provided to rule out these factors as the primary cause of learning problems. To that end, school-linked health and welfare services can help ensure that families have the resources they need to meet their children's social and educational needs.

Effective Instruction

In three-tier RTI models, Tier 1 focuses on implementation of the core curriculum and on providing high-quality instruction for all students (Xu & Drame, 2008). It is expected that Tier 1 instruction will meet the needs of 85 percent of students in general education classrooms (Griffiths, Parson, Burns, VanDerHeyden, & Tilly, 2007). This also holds true for bilingual education classrooms (Brown & Dolittle, 2008).

High Expectations

Instruction for ELs must reflect high expectations for student learning and challenging language and content standards. Characteristics of instruction conducive to the success of ELs include:

- An effective core curriculum for native language and ESL instruction

- Application of universal design principles in delivery of instruction and differentiation consistent with student linguistic and cultural characteristics

- Specific skill instruction nested in the context of higher-order skill development

- Screening, assessment, and continuous progress monitoring in the native language and in English

- Instructional strategies that support language development

When teachers apply universal design concepts to the delivery of instruction, they use flexible strategies and approaches that accommodate differences in students' background characteristics, prior knowledge, learning preferences, motivation, and interests (Tomlinson, 1999). Teachers of ELs expose students to language that is meaningful and purposeful so that they develop the language required for effective social interaction, the academic language required to understand lessons and to participate effectively in academic activities, and the language skills specific to each of the subjects and content areas (Coelho, 2004). Instruction in English must be scaffolded or sheltered so that it is understandable to ELs. This might include, for example, simplifying language, using visuals, preteaching vocabulary and key concepts, or previewing lessons in English. Because language plays a key role in the acquisition of knowledge and skills, an exclusive focus on subject and content skills (for example, teaching reading without a focus on students' language proficiency and language needs) can be counterproductive (Ortiz, 2002).

> Instruction in English must be scaffolded or sheltered so that it is understandable to ELs. This might include, for example, simplifying language use, using visuals, preteaching vocabulary and key concepts, or previewing lessons in English.

Effective instruction is also culturally responsive and affirms students' cultural backgrounds, experiences, and perspectives to make curriculum and instruction personally meaningful to each student (Gay, 2002).

Linking Assessment and Instruction

Language screening, assessment, and continuous progress monitoring is an essential component of effective instruction for ELs (Ortiz & Yates, 2002). Language assessment data serve multiple purposes. They pinpoint students' communication strengths in the native language and in English. These data are used to track progress in the development of language skills, decide what skills will be taught in which language, and manage transitions from native language to English instruction. Decisions such as these cannot be based solely on the annual assessments that are required to determine whether students are eligible for special language programs (Ortiz, 2002; Ortiz & Yates, 2002).

Monitoring Progress in L_1 and L_2

In addition to supporting and monitoring language development, teachers should also teach and track progress in relation to skills that have been shown to be determinants of literacy achievement both in the native language and in English: phonemic awareness, phonics, fluency, vocabulary, and comprehension (Goldenberg, 1998; Snow, Burns, & Griffin, 1998). They should also understand the complex relationships between literacy in the native language and second-language literacy. According to Goldenberg (2010), teaching students to read in their native language promotes higher levels of reading achievement in English. However, while universal skills transfer across languages and facilitate biliteracy, relationships between language and literacy are mediated by home and school factors, including whether the native language is seen as an asset or a liability.

Given the heterogeneity of the population, bilingual education and ESL personnel should carefully examine students' language proficiency and literacy achievement. Rather than treating ELs as "two monolinguals in one" (Kester & Peña, 2002), they should develop bilingual profiles of performance based on students' combined knowledge across languages. Assessment results based on equivalent instruments and procedures, assuming these are valid for the purpose of evaluating knowledge and skills in the respective languages, provide a more accurate picture of what students know and can do in each language. They also reveal knowledge and skills that are common to both languages as well as those that are unique to each language. Students should be given credit for what they know and can do, regardless of the language in which they demonstrate those skills. Otherwise, their abilities may be underestimated, increasing the likelihood that they will be candidates for remedial or special education programs.

Comparing a student's performance in one language to his performance in the other (intraindividual differences), and comparing his performance to that of monolingual speakers of each language or to bilingual peers (interindividual differences) can help determine whether native language limitations, limited English proficiency, or both, are contributing to school failure (Ortiz, 1997; Ochoa & Ortiz, 2005). Performance that is significantly deviant from that of EL peers with similar backgrounds and comparable school histories signals the possibility that the student may have disabilities (Ortiz, 1997).

In summary, language and literacy assessment and instruction for ELs must be coordinated. Data about progress in each of these domains inform instructional decisions and help identify supports needed by students who are not progressing as expected. This might include, for example, students who are struggling to learn to read in the native language and those who are struggling with comprehension of English text because of limited English proficiency. Results of language and literacy assessments also inform decisions as to whether, or when, students are ready to exit special language programs. A guiding principle is that students should not be exited until they can be successful in classrooms where instruction is provided entirely in English (Linan-Thompson & Ortiz, 2009). Otherwise, they become candidates for remedial intervention.

Early Intervention

Of the 15 percent of students who did not progress as expected with Tier 1 instruction, 10 percent will receive Tier 2 interventions and 5 percent will likely need both Tier 2 and Tier 3 interventions

(Griffiths et al., 2007; Tilly, 2006). Tier 2 and Tier 3 interventions *supplement* Tier 1 instruction; they do not replace it.

Tier 2 instruction is typically provided for small groups of three to five students who are experiencing similar problems (Torgesen, 2006). The amount of time devoted to explicit, systematic instruction to assure mastery of critical skills and competencies varies, but interventions are typically offered three to five days per week with sessions lasting from thirty minutes to an hour (Griffiths et al., 2007). Student progress is monitored, and results are used to evaluate and redirect instruction as needed. Students who do not respond as expected to Tier 2 interventions move to Tier 3 for even more intensive instruction. Instruction is provided one-on-one or in smaller groups (that is, one to three students), and intervention sessions are longer and more focused, often concentrating on one or two specific skills at a time.

> Tier 2 instruction is typically offered three to five days per week with sessions lasting from thirty minutes to an hour.

In an RTI framework, the design and implementation of increasingly intensive interventions is typically managed through a problem-solving process or standard protocol approach (Fuchs, Mock, Morgan, & Young, 2003).

Problem Solving

In problem-solving approaches, teams of general education teachers or a team comprising general education and special education teachers and related services professionals (for example, the speech pathologist, school psychologist, and counselor), meet to pinpoint the student's problems, set priorities and goals for intervention, and design an intervention plan that is typically implemented by the student's teacher, with the support of team members (Garcia & Ortiz, 2008; Linan-Thompson & Ortiz, 2009; Ortiz, 2002). Progress is carefully monitored to identify students who might benefit from additional interventions provided through general education alternative programs and services (for example, tutoring, counseling, or instruction provided by a reading specialist). Progress data are considered in deciding whether a referral to special education is appropriate.

Standard Protocol

Schools that use a standard-protocol approach to RTI adopt an intervention or program that has clearly defined components and procedures for implementation (Fuchs et al., 2003)—for example, Success for All, Bilingual Cooperative Integrated Reading and Composition, or Reading Recovery/Descubriendo la lectura. Teachers or trained interventionists provide instruction for a specified amount of time, typically in small groups of students with similar problems. Student progress is carefully tracked to identify those who are not responding to these more intensive interventions. As in problem-solving approaches, student progress as a result of interventions is considered in deciding whether the student should be referred to special education.

Recommended Approach for ELs

Problem-solving approaches, or a combination of problem-solving and standard protocol approaches, are more appropriate for ELs because of the tremendous heterogeneity of the EL population (Garcia & Ortiz, 2008). Standard protocol approaches that involve the use of a particular program or intervention may not sufficiently accommodate factors such as students' native language and English proficiency, prior literacy instruction, the language(s) of instruction, and current performance levels across languages. Moreover, at least in initial problem-solving efforts, teachers typically have primary responsibility for implementing the interventions designed by the team. Problem-solving approaches help develop teachers' ability to respond more effectively to students' educational needs. This is an important consideration given that the majority of students do not have disabilities, and the intent of RTI is to assure that ELs receive appropriate instruction in the context of general education classrooms (Ortiz, 2002; Ortiz et al., in press). At problem-solving meetings, team members and teacher (Ortiz, Robertson, & Wilkinson, 2009):

- Review student performance and the results of differentiated instruction

- Reach consensus about the nature of the problem and set priorities for intervention

- Select or design intervention(s) to address identified priorities, specifying strategies and duration and intensity of interventions

- Determine the supports needed for successful implementation

- Determine what data will be collected to evaluate the effectiveness of the intervention and the fidelity of implementation

After the team meeting, the following occurs:

- The teacher implements the plan and reports on progress to the problem-solving team.

- If Tier 2 interventions are not successful, the student moves to Tier 3 interventions. These interventions may be provided by a content, skill, or behavior specialist.

- Tier 3 intervention may also include referral to special education.

Fidelity of Implementation

Fidelity of implementation refers to the degree to which instruction and intervention follow implementation guidelines and is an essential component of RTI (National Center on Response to Intervention [NCRTI], 2011). It is important to ensure that the RTI interventions are appropriate for ELs. To that end, evaluation should determine that interventions meet a two-pronged test (Ortiz & Yates, 2008): they must be research-based, and they must have been proven effective for ELs. The intent of RTI is compromised when interventions are based on research that did not include representative samples of ELs, when interventions are selected simply on the basis of their success with non-EL peers, or when those providing the interventions have limited knowledge about or experience in working with ELs.

More Intensive Interventions

Students who do not make expected progress with Tier 2 interventions are provided more intensive interventions in the context of general or special education programs. General education interventions may include alternative programs and services such as instruction provided by reading or math specialists outside the general education classroom (Linan-Thompson & Garcia, 2009). Instruction is typically provided in groups of one to three students and targets development of specific skills or behaviors. Tier 3 interventions may also include referral to special education.

Special Education Referral

The responsibilities of special education referral committees should be informed by data collected across the RTI tiers. A decision to request a full and individual evaluation to determine whether the student qualifies for special education signals that referral committees have decided that the student is in a school context conducive to the success of ELs, that teachers have differentiated instruction and provided more intensive interventions to address the student's difficulties, and that these efforts have nevertheless met with limited success (Garcia & Ortiz, 2008; Ortiz, 2002). It also means that interventions provided through supplementary or alternative general education support programs also failed to resolve presenting problems. Students who continue to fail despite such extensive efforts to individualize instruction and accommodate learning needs may have disabilities.

If the referral committee requests a full and individual evaluation, it should guide the assessment process by identifying issues or questions that remain unexplained even after present levels of performance, other contributing factors, and results of general education interventions have been considered (Wilkinson et al., 2006).

Is It a Difference or a Disability?

In conducting the full and individual evaluation (FIE), assessment personnel must ensure that assessments used to determine eligibility are valid and reliable for ELs, that they provide for assessment of performance across the native language and in English as appropriate, and that they generate enough information to identify students' strengths and needs (Ortiz & Yates, 2002). Results must be considered in light of data generated through the RTI process, as well as information about the student's school history and progress in the general education curriculum within and across grades (Ortiz et al., 2012; Wilkinson et al., 2006). They should also factor in parental concerns and perspectives on the child's performance at home and at school.

> Assessment personnel must ensure that assessments used to determine eligibility for special education are valid and reliable for ELs, that they assess performance across the native language and in English as appropriate, and that they generate enough information to identify students' strengths and needs.

Taken together, these data will allow the multidisciplinary team to consider the question, "Are presenting problems a reflection of linguistic or cultural difference, or are they result of a disability?" This is a complex question with no easy answers. However, research on ELs with reading-related disabilities provide some markers that can help answer it. Ortiz and colleagues (2012) suggest that the following six factors indicate the presence of learning disabilities among ELs:

1. Multiple sources confirm that students have experienced academic difficulties over time.

2. Despite consistent school histories (such as continuous enrollment, no excessive absences, and uninterrupted schooling), students' achievement scores in the appropriate language of instruction are below grade level.

3. Instruction has been differentiated without success, and students have received specialized interventions (for example, supplemental reading instruction or tutoring) and did not make adequate progress.

4. Students demonstrate two or more characteristics often associated with LD. These include problems with short-term memory, short attention span, poor fine motor skills, disorganization, difficulty staying on task, and difficulty working independently (Learning Disabilities Association of America [LDA], 2011).

5. Full and individual assessments are conducted in the native language and in English, and the results corroborate teacher and parent concerns.

6. When discrepancy formulae are used, discrepancies between IQ and achievement scores are large and correspond with teachers' reasons for referral.

In sum, to distinguish differences from disabilities, there must be sufficient evidence in school records to rule out competing factors or hypotheses that might explain learning problems. Expertise specific to the education of ELs is central to ensuring that students are not classified as having learning disabilities if their academic or behavioral problems can be explained by cultural factors, environmental or economic disadvantage, limited English proficiency, or lack of access to appropriate instruction as the cause of learning problems.

> In sum, to distinguish differences from disabilities, there must be sufficient evidence in school records to rule out competing factors or hypotheses that might explain learning problems.

Conclusion

Response to intervention has tremendous potential to help close the gap between the achievement of English learners and their non-EL peers and to help resolve the entrenched issue of disproportionate representation of ELs in remedial and special education programs. However, to meet these goals, system-level issues that contribute to student failure—including ineffective schools, curricula, and instruction—must be addressed. The first step is to ensure that the majority of ELs succeed in the core curriculum. Evaluations of RTI for ELs must then consider: (1) the cultural and linguistic responsiveness of the RTI framework, (2) the appropriateness and reliability of the screening and assessment instruments used to monitor progress associated with the native language or ESL interventions across tiers, (3) the effectiveness of problem-solving teams in addressing the needs of ELs, and (4) the availability and effectiveness of supplemental programs and services for ELs and standard protocols used with struggling learners. General educators (including principals and bilingual education and ESL teachers) will need intensive extensive professional development to fulfill their responsibilities associated with RTI (Richards, Pavri, Golez, Canges, & Murphy, 2007).

Is response to intervention the answer to improving the academic achievement of ELs and distinguishing linguistic and cultural differences from disabilities? Yes, but only if it addresses the role of school climate in student success, the implementation of culturally responsive interventions, and teacher attributes or qualifications that facilitate or hinder the academic and behavioral success of culturally and linguistically diverse students (Garcia & Ortiz, 2008). This suggests that RTI for ELs is a long-term, not a short-term, solution that begins with a clear understanding of the learner and the commitment of all school personnel to meet the needs of all students.

References

Artiles, A. J., Rueda, R., Salazar, J. J., & Higareda, I. (2005). Within-group diversity in minority disproportionate representation: English language learners in urban school districts. *Exceptional Children, 71*(3), 283–300.

Berkeley, S., Bender, W. N., Peaster, L. G., & Saunders, L. (2009). Implementation of response to intervention: A snapshot of progress. *Journal of Learning Disabilities, 42*(1), 85–95.

Brown, J. E., & Doolittle, J. (2008, May/June). A cultural, linguistic, and ecological framework for response to intervention with English language learners. *Teaching Exceptional Children, 40*(5), 66–72.

Center for Policy Studies, Education Research, and Community Development. (2011). *Research brief: Criteria for grade to grade promotion and/or retention.* Accessed at http://icee.isu.edu/Publications-All/PS&ERPublications/Gradetogradepromandreten.pdf on October 31, 2011.

Coelho, E., (2004). *Adding English: A guide to teaching in multilingual classrooms.* Toronto: Pippin Publishing Corporation.

Fuchs, D., Mock, D., Morgan, P. L., & Young, C. L. (2003). Responsiveness-to-intervention: Definitions, evidence, and implications for the learning disabilities construct. *Learning Disabilities Research & Practice, 18,* 157–171.

Garcia, S. B., & Ortiz, A. A. (2008). A framework of culturally and linguistically responsive design of response to intervention models. *Multiple Voices for Ethnically Diverse Exceptional Learners, 11*(1), 24–41.

Gay, G. (2002). Preparing for culturally responsive teaching. *Journal of Teacher Education, 53*(2), 106–116.

Goldenberg, C. (1998). A balanced approach to early Spanish literacy instruction. In R. Gersten & R. Jimenez (Eds.), *Promoting learning for culturally and linguistically diverse students: Classroom applications from contemporary research* (pp. 3–25). Belmont, CA: Wadsworth.

Goldenberg, C. (2010). Improving achievement for English learners: Conclusions from recent reviews of emerging research. In G. Li & P. A. Edwards (Eds.), *Best practices in ELL instruction* (pp. 15–43). New York: Guilford Press.

Greenwood, C. R. (2009). Introduction. In M. R. Coleman, F. P. Roth, & T. West (Eds.), *Roadmap to pre-K RTI: Applying response to intervention in preschool settings (pp. 3–4)*. New York: National Center for Learning Disabilities.

Griffiths, A-J., Parson, L. B., Burns, M. K., VanDerHeyden, A., & Tilly, W. D. (2007). *Response to intervention: Research for practice.* Alexandria, VA: National Association of State Directors of Special Education.

Individual with Disabilities Education Act, Pub. L. No. 94–142, 20 U.S.C. § 1415 (2004).

Kester, E., & Pena, E. (2002). Language ability assessment of Spanish-English bilinguals: Future directions. *Practical Assessment, Research & Evaluation, 8*(4). Accessed at http://pareonline.net/getvn.asp?v=8&n=4 on October 28, 2011.

Learning Disabilities Association of America. (2011). *Learning disabilities: Signs, symptoms, and strategies.* Accessed at www.ldanatl.org/aboutld/parents /ld_basics/ld.asp on February 29, 2012.

Linan-Thompson, S., & Ortiz, A. A. (2009). Response to intervention and English-language learners: Instructional and assessment considerations. *Seminars in Speech and Language, 30*(2), 105–120.

McCardle, P., Mele-McCarthy, J., Cutting, L., Leos, K., & D'Emilio, T. (2005). Learning disabilities in English language learners: Identifying the issues. *Learning Disabilities Research & Practice, 20*(1), 1–5.

Montecel, M. R., & Cortez, J. D. (2002). Successful bilingual education programs: Development and dissemination of criteria to identify promising and exemplary practices in bilingual education at the national level. *Bilingual Research Journal, 26*, 1–21.

National Center for Education Statistics. (2005). *Briefing on the condition of national education.* United States Department of Education Institute of Educational Sciences. Accessed at http://nces.ed.gov/whatsnew/commissioner/remarks2010/5_27_2010.asp on October 28, 2011.

National Center for Response to Intervention. (2011). *What is RTI? The essential components of RTI*. Accessed at www.rti4success.org/whatisrti on October 28, 2011.

Ochoa, S. H., & Ortiz, S. O. (2005). Language proficiency assessment: The foundation for psychoeducational assessment of second language learners. In K. W. Merrell (Eds.), *Assessing culturally and linguistically diverse students: A practical guide* (pp. 137–152). New York: Guilford Press.

Ortiz, A. A. (1997). Learning disabilities occurring concomitantly with linguistic differences. *Journal of Learning Disabilities, 30*(3), 321–332.

Ortiz, A. A. (2002). Prevention and early intervention. In A. J. Artiles & A. A. Ortiz (Eds.), *English language learners with special education needs: Identification, assessment, and instruction* (pp. 31–48). Washington, DC: Center for Applied Linguistics and Delta Systems.

Ortiz, A. A., Robertson, P., & Wilkinson, C. Y. (2009). *Bilingual exceptional students: Early intervention, referral, and assessment (BESt ERA) model*. Paper presented at the University of Texas at Austin BESt ERA Training-of-Trainers Conference, Austin, TX.

Ortiz, A. A., Robertson, P. M., Wilkinson, C. Y., Liu, Y., McGhee, B. D., & Kushner, M. I. (2012). The role of bilingual education teachers in preventing inappropriate referrals of ELLs to special education: Implications for response to intervention. *Bilingual Research Journal: The Journal of the National Association for Bilingual Education, 34*(3), 316–333.

Ortiz, A. A., & Yates, J. R. (2002). Considerations in the assessment of English language learners referred to special education. In A. J. Artiles & A. A. Ortiz (Eds.), *English language learners with special education needs: Identification, assessment, and instruction* (pp. 65–86). Washington, DC: Center for Applied Linguistics and Delta Systems.

Ortiz, A. A., & Yates, J. R. (2008). Enhancing scientifically-based research for culturally and linguistically diverse learners. *Multiple Voices for Ethnically Diverse Exceptional Learners, 11*(1), 1–23.

Richards, C., Pavri, S., Golez, F., Canges, R., & Murphy, J. (2007). Response to intervention: Building the capacity of teachers to serve students with learning disabilities. *Issues in Teacher Education, 16*, 55–64.

Snow, C. E., Burns, M. S., & Griffin, P. (1998). *Preventing reading difficulties in young children*. Washington, DC: National Academies Press.

Tilly III, W. D. (2006). Response to intervention: An overview. What is it? Why do it? Is it worth it? *The Special Edge, 19*(2), 1, 4–5.

Tomlinson, C. A. (1999). *The differentiated classroom: Responding to the needs of all learners*. Alexandria, VA: Association for Supervision and Curriculum Development.

Torgesen, J. K. (2006). *Intensive reading interventions for struggling readers in early elementary school: A principal's guide.* Portsmouth, NH: RMC Research, Center on Instruction.

Wilkinson, C. Y., Ortiz, A. A., Robertson, P. M., & Kushner, M. I. (2006). English language learners with reading-related LD: Linking data from multiple sources to make eligibility decisions. *Journal of Learning Disabilities, 39*(2), 129–142.

Xu, Y., & Drame, E. (2008). Culturally appropriate context: Unlocking the potential of response to intervention of English language learners. *Early Childhood Education Journal, 35,* 305–311.

Zehler, A. M., Fleischman, H. L., Hopstock, P. J., Penzick, M. L., & Stephenson, T. G. (2003). *Descriptive study of services to LEP students and LEP students with disabilities: Findings on special education LEP students* (Special Topic Report 4). Accessed at www.ncela.gwu.edu/resabout/research/descriptivestudyfiles/special_ed4.pdf on May 12, 2007.

Elena Izquierdo

Elena Izquierdo, PhD, is the program area chair for bilingual/biliteracy/ELL education in the Teacher Education Department at the University of Texas at El Paso. A linguist by training and an educator in practice, she earned her doctorate in linguistics and bilingual education from Georgetown University in 1995. She is a member of the national Hispanic Leadership Council (HLC) and the executive board of the Alliance for a Multilingual Multicultural Education.

Dr. Izquierdo has served as president of the Texas Association for Bilingual Education and vice president of the National Association for Bilingual Education. Additionally, as a school administrator for thirteen years, she served as a principal of the nationally recognized two-way dual-language Oyster Bilingual School and as director of Language Minority Affairs in the District of Columbia Public Schools, Washington. Her research and professional specializations focus on leadership and schooling for English learners, bilingual/EL program effectiveness, dual language education; and biliteracy. Dr. Izquierdo keynotes at national and state conferences in the areas of biliteracy and the schooling of English learners.

Dr. Izquierdo has authored or coauthored articles and book chapters in *Chicano School Failure and Success: Past, Present, And Future; Special Populations in Gifted Education: Understanding Our Most Able Students From Diverse Backgrounds; The National Journal of Urban Education & Practice;* and *Soleado: Promising Practices From the Field.*

In this chapter, Dr. Izquierdo explains the crucial element of leadership in supporting the fast-growing EL population, shows why it must be a whole-school effort, and uses research to debunk old myths, including the notion that the best way to optimize teaching and instruction for English learners is to use ESL specialists and bilingual schools.

Chapter 11

Leadership Matters for Learning English and Learning *in* English

Elena Izquierdo

The fastest-growing population in U.S. schools consists of students who are limited in their English proficiency and struggling with academic content. Districts everywhere are faced with a demographic explosion of English learners—students who are not proficient in English and require instructional support to fully access academic content in English (Francis, Rivera, Lesaux, Kieffer, & Rivera, 2006). Most of these districts are in states that traditionally have had ELs in their school communities, but other states are experiencing this rapid and large demographic shift for the first time (Lazarín, 2006).

With the advent of the No Child Left Behind (NCLB) Act of 2002, the stakes have risen significantly. NCLB requires districts and states to appropriately include ELs in state assessments. It is evident that EL performance rates are significantly behind those of their English-speaking counterparts, and whether we look at student performance rates through state assessment data or through the National Assessment of Educational Progress (NAEP), "the nation's report card," it is clear that ELs are the subgroup that is the furthest behind (Hemphill & Vanneman, 2011).

With states now accountable for showing significant annual progress in both the English-language proficiency and academic achievement of ELs, ELs must have access to the rigor—both linguistically and academically—required to meet challenging standards.

However, this practice alone is not effective because of the increase of ELs in our schools and, especially, because of the accountability mandate. We need to recognize that we have ELs who have been in our schools for many years who are not showing progress.

Schools have typically relied on the expertise of bilingual/ESL teachers to address the needs of ELs. This has been done through an array of program models provided for ELs: transitional early exit, transitional late exit, dual language, ESL content based, ESL pull out, and the general mainstream classroom (with no program support). Although there is a significant body of research that points to the most effective models (Calderón & Minaya-Rowe, 2003; Collier & Thomas, 2009; Cummins, 1981; Izquierdo, 2011b; Lindholm-Leary & Borsato, 2006), other issues compromise the quality of any program model. These include inconsistent implementation within and across program models, inconsistent implementation within and across grade levels, weak English language development models, and teachers and school administrators who lack the foundations of second-language acquisition and do not have the understanding or skills to deliver content in a way that is comprehensible to a student learning in a second language (Ballantyne, Sanderman, & Levy, 2008). At the district level, decisions about what program to provide ELs are made for various reasons, such as existing resources, varying philosophies, and personal experiences. The questions have always been: "How long does it take to learn English? How much Spanish do we use, and for how long?" These types of questions have dominated conversations looking for the "appropriate" program to use. In allowing them to do so, the more critical issues are lost. If L_1 support is implemented, it is because the "research" says it is effective, yet often attention is not given to *how* the L_1 will be utilized to optimize learning across the curriculum.

> If L_1 support is implemented, it is because the "research" says it is effective, yet often attention is not given to *how* the L_1 will be utilized to optimize learning across the curriculum.

As students transition from elementary to middle school, or from middle to high school, the challenges for them become even greater. To begin with, students feeding into the secondary grades come from various elementary program models (fig 11.1). There are marked difference in how each model manages and assigns the use of L_1 and English (L_2): initial literacy; content; percent of instruction or support used for the student's L_1; and percent of instruction or support used for the student's L_2. In some instances there is no model at all, and ELs are coming from an English-only classroom setting.

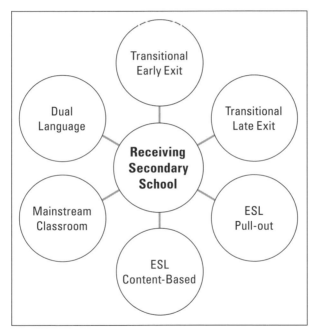

Figure 11.1: Elementary program models for ELs.

As a result, ELs feeding into the secondary years enter at various levels of development at both sides of the L_1/L_2 and content spectrum. Aside from the dual-language model, the focus of other EL programs (transitional and ESL) has been to learn English, and the primary language (L_1) support has been a means to get to English literacy through a variety of ways.

Some models have developed the L_1 more than others, while other models have focused on learning English, with the result that content learning has suffered. ELs coming from elementary school are not only at various levels of literacy in their L_1 and L_2, but are also at different levels of academic development in their content areas because of the focus of the various program models and implementation. This has created a bigger challenge for the secondary grades that generally offer some form of ESL as their program support. ELs, however, are faced with learning English and learning *in* English in order to pass their content courses and state assessments, be promoted, and ultimately graduate.

Diversity and English learners

Not all ELs are created equal! The term *English learner* leads some to assume simply that ELs need to learn English and their academic needs are essentially the same. This could not be further from the reality. Some ELs may have highly developed cognitive and linguistic skills in their native language; others are new to U.S. schools and have had a solid foundation in their L_1, or they may have had limited schooling and have academic gaps. Still others may have had interrupted schooling in their native country, a phenomenon that impacts their ability to transfer literacy skills from the first language to the second (Cummins, 1981). Secondary ELs come to the classroom with varied knowledge of English and their native language. To add to this complexity, students' language learning is influenced by their socioeconomic status, the varieties of English to which they are exposed, the approaches to language learning in their previous schooling, and the study skills they have developed over the years (Dutro & Kinsella, 2010). Although schools have many ELs new to the U.S., most are first-, second-, or third-generation U.S.-born and are products of the U.S. schooling systems (Capps et al., 2005).

> Most ELs in our schools are first-, second-, or third-generation U.S.-born and are products of U.S. schooling systems.

Regardless of the number of years in *any* of our districts, schools, or programs, these students are still not proficient in English. Some have suggested that it takes five to seven years for a student to become proficient enough to handle academic English (Collier & Thomas, 2009). This belief has generated a huge bubble in secondary schools of ELs who "despite being close to the age at which they should be able to graduate, are still not English proficient and have incurred major academic deficits" (Olson, 2010, p. 1). It is important to understand that these five to seven years have not been under optimal conditions in a prescribed bilingual/ESL type of program. Optimal conditions imply that teachers are trained in working with ELs in L_1/L_2 language, literacy, and content areas. These long-term ELs have been in and out of various instructional programs for seven years or more without having benefited from continuous and sustained instructional support and are below grade level in literacy and numeracy as well as unsuccessful on standardized tests as a result (Calderón & Minaya-Rowe, 2011).

The challenges have been in teaching for transfer and transition. Students may be learning some English, but are weak in content areas; or ELs may have achieved literacy in Spanish, but not enough English language development has taken place. It has been left up to the bilingual/ESL programs to address this situation, but just as critical is whether the receiving teachers in English-only classrooms are ready to continue the work in English language development and academic literacy. Schools need to rethink schooling for ELs and address this situation as a whole-school agenda.

School systems have never been in such distress regarding the achievement and graduation rates of ELs. For this reason, schools must reexamine how they are addressing this challenge.

How Schools Fare With the Required Tools

While schooling ELs has become an unquestionable responsibility, significant obstacles at the local school level add to the challenge: the lack of teachers and administrators who have an understanding of second-language acquisition and second-language literacy; the need to make instruction comprehensible in English through the various content areas; and an understanding of the affective, linguistic, cognitive, and sociocultural components critical to schooling ELs. The demographic shift is such that all teachers will have ELs in their classrooms, if they don't already. The majority of teachers (excluding bilingual and ESL-certified teachers) do not have the pedagogy needed to provide high-quality instruction to students who do not yet have sufficient proficiency in English and need to access academic content. Ballantyne and Sanderman (2008) uncovered the following facts:

- 29.5 percent of teachers have the training to effectively work with ELs;

- 20 states require all teachers to have training in working with ELs;

- Less than 1/6th of teacher pre-service programs include working with ELs;

- 26 percent of teachers received professional development on issues related to ELs; and

- 57 percent of teachers believe they need additional professional development providing effective education for ELs. (p. 9)

Figure 11.2 shows data from a district with a growing number of ELs coupled with an inadequate number of trained ESL practicing teachers in the feeder pattern from middle school to high school. This disparity was not enough to significantly contribute to the academic development of ELs.

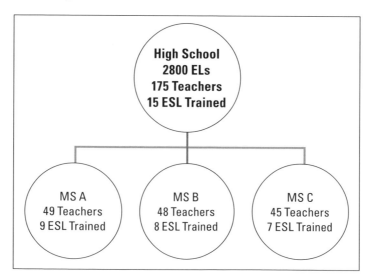

Figure 11.2: Data from a Texas school with a growing number of ELs.

The low levels of ESL teacher certification (the only support in the schools) reflected low support levels for English learners. Overall, district students with low English proficiency represented the lowest state assessment scores, and the scores regressed in the higher grades (table 11.1).

Table 11.1: Low Passing Rate of Limited English Proficient (LEP) Students in Grades 9, 10, and 11

	State	District	HS Campus Project Site	LEP
Grade 9				
Reading	92%	92%	91%	60%
Mathematics	72%	75%	79%	52%
All tests	71%	73%	76%	37%
Grade 10				
Reading	91%	91%	93%	50%
Mathematics	75%	72%	82%	51%
Science	75%	71%	80%	34%
All tests	66%	61%	71%	26%
Grade 11				
Reading	93%	92%	90%	37%
Mathematics	89%	87%	90%	49%
Science	92%	91%	91%	60%
All tests	83%	81%	81%	16%

It is important to understand that an ESL certification does not always translate into what is best for the overall achievement of ELs. Many districts are requiring teachers to seek ESL certification, but that is not enough to address the overall schooling of the

EL population. Effective professional development that provides all teachers with the understanding, knowledge, and skills needed to effectively work with ELs is quite different from a certification that is acquired in order to make the compliance mark.

Demographic trends and the demands of an increasingly global economy make it clear that educators can no longer afford to ignore the needs of struggling ELs in middle and high school. The stakes have been raised, and EL achievement must become a priority—a whole-school priority. We need to provide all teachers and administrators with the knowledge and skills to successfully address the needs of ELs in schooling in order to meet the accountability mandate, demonstrate annual and adequate English language development and academic achievement progress, and ultimately close the achievement gap. The need for effective, responsive administrators is a critical component to this transformational focus, which calls for a comprehensive review of schooling ELs that incorporates the delivery of effective instruction, ongoing assessment of the teaching and learning cycle, and evaluation (Calderón, 2007).

Learning to Lead and Leading to Learn

Principals, other administrators, superintendents, and school boards must also pay attention to the sociocultural climate in an educational setting and its effect on second-language acquisition and EL schooling. The total school context is a critical factor influencing EL academic achievement. Administrators and other school staff must commit to providing a climate that values cultural and linguistic diversity and sees ELs as a resource, not a problem. This is especially needed in schools where the demographics highlight a growing number of ELs.

> Administrators and other school staff must commit to providing a climate that sees ELs as a resource, not a problem.

A child's loss of the ability to speak and continue learning his or her home language has daunting implications for family ties and being able to socialize in the world in which the child lives. It sends children the message that the language they speak is not important, and that part of who they are is "illegal" in school. Does your school's language policy view students' L_1 as a resource? Or is the prevailing belief that the L_1 is irrelevant to academic success? A school's language policy expresses the underlying beliefs of the school's mission. It articulates the choices we have as educators and singles out the students affected by those choices (Ruiz, 1990). It can either alleviate or aggravate the stigma of social segregation that programs create.

The process of language policy is embedded in one or more of three basic orientations: (1) language as a problem, (2) language as a right, and (3) language as a resource (as cited in García, 2001). Traditional models of bilingual education that use the L_1 as a tool to get to L_2 are treating L_1 as problem and, up to a point, as a right. English language proficiency needs to be addressed, but using the student's L_1 to access curriculum is also a right until the student has learned enough English to be transitioned into an English-only classroom setting. How much support is enough? Figure 11.3 (page 216) is an example of how a language policy can affect the schooling of an EL. This student was transitioned into an English-only classroom after kindergarten, based on a two-year language policy, and this is her fourth-grade science journal entry.

Clearly, this student is struggling with linguistic and academic processes in both languages. Olsen (2010) refers to these struggling students as Long Term English learners:

> Long Term English Learners have weak academic language and significant gaps in reading and writing. For each Long Term English Learner, however, the gaps vary depending how long they remained in a specific language-learning setting, the number of changes and inconsistencies in their education, and the timing at which these changes occurred related to their linguistic development. (Olsen, 2010, p. 23)

This student's literacy development in both L_1 and L_2 will have a significant impact on her ability to succeed in academic work in middle and high school that is contingent on content literacy. However, the decision to transition the student out of L_1 support in kindergarten was made because of a language policy based on time—on how long she should receive L1 support, rather than on a determination of how the L_1 support could optimize and contribute to the literacy and academic support the child needed to succeed in the English-only classroom. Transitioning into an English-only classroom must be planned to ensure academic success. The teacher must also be ready to facilitate this transition.

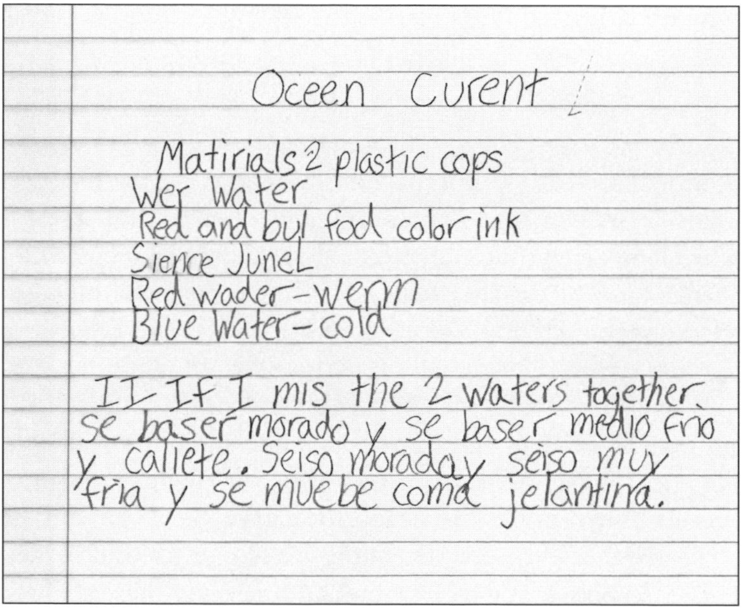
Oceen Curent

Matirials 2 plastic cops
Wer Water
Red and bul food color ink
Sience JuneL
Red wader-werm
Blue Water-cold

II If I mis the 2 waters together
se baser morado y se baser medio frio
y caliete. Seiso morada y seiso muy
fria y se muebe coma jelantina.

Figure 11.3: Journal entry of fourth-grade EL transitioned into an English-only classroom after kindergarten.

On the other hand, in more successful instances of transitioning to an English-only classroom, we neglect to recognize the enormous amount of linguistic development that transpires when an EL is effectively learning through both L_1 *and* L_2. The application of knowledge and skills from one language to another involves metacognitive processes (knowing about knowing) and metalinguistic processes (knowing about language) (Izquierdo, 2009). When an EL is learning in L_2, that student is working within and across two sets of systems, managing complex processes that facilitate the application of cognitive skills developed in one language to specific situations in the other. These processes, which are constantly taking place, are evident in the student's use of oral and written language. It is common to hear ELs using both L_1 and L_2 in a single utterance. Some educators may view this negatively. However, when you analyze linguistic occurrences, it is obvious that the reverse is true, as in the example of one EL student who was playing "ironing clothes" during play time in a kindergarten classroom. As I walked into the room, she said, "Look, Miss. I'm planching!" This child strategically code-switched and used a verb in Spanish, *planchar* (to iron), dropped the *ar* from the infinitive in Spanish, added the *ing* in English to form the present progressive, and uses it to communicate her message—in context (fig. 11.4). In fact, the activity "to iron" may have be a big event at home, and the child may have been using the verb because of its sociocultural representation. This child was demonstrating much more than appeared on the surface. She is very much aware of how language the craft of language—works.

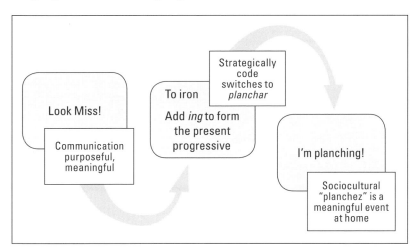

Source: "One Supana Time . . . Children Don't Know That They Know—But They Know!" *by Elena Izquieirdo. © Dual Education of New Mexico, 2011. Reproduced with permission.*

Figure 11.4: Code-switching between Spanish and English in kindergarten.

School leaders need to understand the urgency of the situation ELs are experiencing and at the same time understand how to communicate this understanding to their faculty and staff. Many attitudes about ELs and their learning are significantly influenced by educators' own perceptions about what it means to be an

"EL" in school. We must all rethink attitudes and teaching practices that have resulted in startlingly high dropout rates for ELs.

The leadership of a school needs an understanding of these challenges and their influence on schooling ELs. The content knowledge that encompasses EL schooling is key to school leaders' effectiveness (Nelson & Sassi, 2005; Stein & D'Amico, 2000; Stein & Nelson, 2003). Foundations of second-language learning, the role of the first language in literacy development in a second language, and learning in L_2 across content areas is critical to establishing the school culture needed to convey a whole-school challenge, responsibility, and direction. The need for administrators who are responsive to this transformational focus, which calls for a whole-school comprehensive review for EL schooling, is critical.

Thomas Sergiovanni and Robert Starratt (1998) assert that leadership development is shaped by a set of attitudes that provide a foundation of practice, "an educational platform" (p. 133). They also affirm that a school leader's educational platform greatly influences his or her focus and decisions. Therefore, school leaders must develop a whole-school platform that is responsive to the affective, linguistic, cognitive and sociocultural needs of its EL population. This includes understanding how all of these factors affect ELs' schooling, including their performance on standardized high-stakes assessments. For ELs to succeed, whole-school instruction must promote the acquisition of increasingly complex content knowledge across the curriculum as it integrates language development skills in listening, speaking, reading, and writing within a social context that cultivates collaboration and positive interactions among students, school leaders, and teachers.

The question has always been, "How long does it take to learn English?" Our mistake has been twofold: (1) responding to this as a time and language issue, while disregarding academic development, and (2) overlooking critical factors that affect schooling, such as the diversity of ELs and the need for whole-school readiness in order to work collaboratively toward their academic progress and achievement. A school's leadership and teaching force must collectively have an educational platform (Sergiovanni & Starratt, 1998), rooted in all aspects of EL schooling, that considers school readiness and incorporates quality, data-driven professional development.

All teachers must use strategies that promote grade-level content learning in social studies, math, science, and language arts, as well as in English language development. Students need both content and language teaching in order to succeed in the educational mainstream (Lyster, 2007). While it may seem that secondary students ought to just "pick up" English during their course of study, research indicates this does not happen (Hakuta, Butler, & Witt, 2000). Instead, the research points to the effectiveness of sheltered approaches to English instruction (Echevarria & Short, 2010). There is also ample evidence that within sheltered approaches to English instruction, there must also be explicit vocabulary development (Biemiller, 2001; Carlo et al., 2004), since vocabulary knowledge is closely tied to reading comprehension (Beck, McKeown, & Kucan, 2002).

However, mere vocabulary lists and their translations to the L1 are not enough. Academic language does not occur naturally (Schleppegrel, 2004) and needs to be taught explicitly. ELs need opportunities to use language in listening, speaking, reading, and writing in a variety of meaningful contexts, and teachers must intentionally and consistently include these opportunities in their lesson. Because many students have limited experience with academic texts, using social language as a bridge to academic language is a useful way to build on previous knowledge. Therefore, while it is clearly necessary to develop students' academic language skills, we must support teachers in using a variety of strategies, schoolwide, for guiding students in the development of academic language.

> Because many students have limited experience with academic texts, using social language as a bridge is a useful way to build on previous knowledge.

In brief, effective school leaders:

- Establish a whole-school platform that is responsive to the affective, linguistic, cognitive and sociocultural needs of their school's EL population

- Plan for whole-school professional development that is tied to the demographic needs and goals of their English learners

- Support teachers in developing the skills to intentionally, strategically, and consistently plan for and deliver content in ways that optimize the English language and academic development of their English learners in listening, speaking, reading and writing across the curriculum

- Monitor progress as evidenced through these students' collective formal and informal advancement

- Use data to drive instruction and continuous professional development for whole-school EL academic success

The challenges are great, and strong leadership is crucial. For English learners to succeed in school, leadership matters.

References

Ballantyne, K. G., Sanderman, A. R., & Levy, J. (2008). *Educating English language learners: Building teacher capacity.* Washington, DC: National Clearinghouse for English Language Acquisition.

Beck, M., McKeown, M. G., & Kucan, L. (2002). *Bringing words to life: Robust vocabulary instruction.* New York: Guilford Press.

Biemiller, A. (2001). Teaching vocabulary: Early, direct, and sequential. *American Educator 25*(1), 24–28.

Boyson, B. A., & Short, D. J. (2003). *Secondary school newcomer programs in the United States* (Research Report #12). Santa Cruz, CA: Center for Research on Education, Diversity, and Excellence.

Calderón, M. (2007). *Teaching reading to English language learners grades 6–12: A framework for improving achievement in the content areas.* Thousand Oaks, CA: Corwin Press.

Calderón, M. E., & Minaya-Rowe, L. (2003). *Designing and implementing two-way bilingual programs: A step-by-step guide for administrators, teachers, and parents.* Thousand Oaks, CA: Corwin Press.

Calderón, M. E., & Minaya-Rowe, L. (2011). *Preventing long-term English language learners: Transforming schools to meet core standards.* Thousand Oaks, CA: Corwin Press.

Capps, R., Fix, M., Murray, J., Ost, J., Passel, J., & Herwantoro, S. (2005). *The new demography of America's schools: Immigration and the No Child Left Behind Act.* Washington, DC: Urban Institute.

Carlo, M. August, D., McLaughlin, B., Snow, C. E., Dressler, C., Lippman, D. N. et al. (2004). Closing the gap: Addressing the vocabulary needs of English language learners in bilingual and mainstream classrooms. *Reading Research Quarterly, 39*(2), 188–215.

Collier, V. C., & Thomas, W. P. (2009). *Educating English learners for a transformed world.* Albuquerque, NM: Fuente Press.

Cummins, J. (1981). The role of primary language development in promoting educational success for language minority students. In California State Department of Education (Ed.), *Schooling and language minority students: A theoretical framework* (pp. 3–49). Los Angeles: Evaluation, Dissemination and Assessment Center, California State University, Los Angeles.

Dutro, S., & Kinsella, K. (2010). Issues and implementation at grades six through twelve. In F. Ong (Ed.), *Improving education for English learners: Research-based approaches* (pp. 151–207). Sacramento: California Department of Education.

Echevarria, J., & Short, D. (2010). Programs and practices for effective sheltered content instruction. In California Department of Education (Ed.), *Improving education for English learners: Research-based approaches* (pp. 251–313). Sacramento: California Department of Education.

Francis, D. J., Rivera, M., Lesaux, N., Kieffer, M., & Rivera, H. (2006). *Practical guidelines for the education of English language learners.* Houston: Center on Instruction.

García, E. (2001). *Hispanic education in the United States: Raíces y alas.* Lanham, MD: Rowman & Littlefield.

Hakuta, K., Butler, Y., & Witt, D. (2000). *How long does it take English learners to attain proficiency?:* University of California Linguistic Minority Research Institute Policy Report 2000–1. (pp. 251–313). Sacramento: California Department of Education

Hemphill, F. C., & Vanneman, A. (2011). *Achievement gaps: How Hispanic and white students in public schools perform in mathematics and reading on the National Assessment of Educational Progress* (NCES 2011–459). Accessed at http://nces. ed.gov/nationsreportcard/pdf/studies/2011459.pdf on October 28, 2011.

Izquierdo, E. (2009). Biliteracy: A journey or a destination. Soleado: *Promising Practices from the Field, 2,* 1–11.

Izquierdo, E. (2011a). One supana time . . . Children don't know that they know, but they know! Soleado: *Promising Practices from the Field, 4,* 1–11.

Izquierdo, E. (2011b). Two way dual language education. In R. R Valencia (Ed.), *Chicano school failure and success: Past, present, and future* (3rd ed., pp. 160–172). New York: Routledge.

Lazarín, M. (2006). *Improving assessment and accountability for English language learners in the No Child Left Behind Act* (Issue Brief. No 6). Washington, DC: National Council of La Raza.

Lindholm-Leary, K. J., & Borsato, G. (2006). Academic achievement. In F. Genesee, K. Lindholm-Leary, W. Saunders, & D. Christian (Eds.), *Educating English language learners* (pp. 176–222). New York: Cambridge University Press.

Lyster, R. (2007). *Learning and teaching languages through content: A counterbalanced approach.* Philadelphia: John Benjamins.

Nelson, B. S., & Sassi, A. (2005). *The effective principal: Instructional readership for high quality learning.* New York: Teachers College Press.

No Child Left Behind (NCLB) Act of 2001, Pub. L. No. 107–110, § 115, Stat. 1425 (2002).

Olsen, L. (2010). *Reparable harm: Fulfilling the unkept promise of educational opportunity for California's long term English learners.* Long Beach: Californians Together.

Ruiz, R., (2001). In E. Garcia (Ed.). *Hispanic education in the United States: Rakes y alas* (pp. 160–172). Lanham, MD: Rowman and Littlefield.

Schleppegrel, M. (2004). *The language of schooling: A functional linguistic perspective.* Mahwah, NJ: Lawrence Erlbaum.

Sergiovanni, T. J., & Starratt, R. J. (1998). *Supervision: A redefinition.* Boston: McGraw-Hill.

Stein, M. K., & D'Amico, L. (2000). *How subjects matter in school leadership.* Paper presented at the Annual meeting of the American Educational Research Association in New Orleans, Louisiana.

Stein, M. K., & Nelson, B. S. (2003). Leadership content knowledge. *Educational Evaluation and Policy Analysis, 25*(4), 423–448.

Barbara D. Acosta

Barbara D. Acosta, PhD, serves as a senior research scientist and English learner specialist for the George Washington University Center for Equity and Excellence in Education. She currently conducts evaluations of school district programs for ELs and provides professional development for state, district, and school administrators and for ESL and general education teachers.

Dr. Acosta has worked at George Mason University, the American Institutes for Research, and the University of Virginia, where she conducted applied research, evaluation, and graduate teaching in relation to the education of diverse learners. She also served as an ESL instructor for the University of Maryland English Institute and at the secondary level for the District of Columbia Public Schools. She is a cofounder of the Monsignor Oscar Arnulfo Romero University in El Salvador.

Dr. Acosta did her doctoral work in multilingual/multicultural education at George Mason University and earned a master of science degree in educational linguistics from the University of Pennsylvania. She has received the Distinguished Alumni Award from the George Mason University College of Education and Human Development and a dissertation award from the American Educational Research Association.

Kristina Anstrom

Kristina Anstrom, EdD, is the assistant director of the George Washington University Center for Equity and Excellence. She was the co-principal investigator on the *Linking Academic Language to Academic Standards Project,* funded by the Bill & Melinda Gates Foundation and is associate director of the Mid-Atlantic Comprehensive Center, which provides technical assistance to state education agencies in the mid-Atlantic states. She is also the director of a subcontract with Edvantia to provide services to state education agencies in the Appalachia region.

Dr. Anstrom has served as project director on several federally funded projects relevant to the education of English learners and literacy, including a U.S. Department of Education field-initiated research study on adolescent literacy instruction for ELs and professional development projects for teachers and teacher educators. She was also the project director for the Academic English Literature Review project and is the lead author on *A Review of the Literature on Academic English: Implications for K–12 English Language Learners.* She has authored a number of reports and articles on integrating language and content for ELs and on approaches to the instruction and assessment of ELs in mainstream contexts and is co-author of a literacy textbook for ELs titled *Keys to Learning.*

Charlene Rivera

Charlene Rivera, EdD, is a research professor at the George Washington University and is executive director and founder of the George Washington University Center for Equity and Excellence in Education. She is a nationally recognized leader in areas such as standards, assessment, state assessment policies, practices for accommodating English learners and students with disabilities, accountability, academic language, and instructional practices for teaching reading. She is widely published, with works that include books, refereed journal articles, book chapters, and scholarly reports. She co-authored the article "Test Accommodations for English Language Learners: A Meta-Analysis of Experimental Studies" in *Educational Measurement: Issues and Practice.*

Dr. Rivera serves or has served on a number of boards and technical working groups, including the Accessibility, Accommodations, and Fairness Technology Working Group of the Partnership for Assessment of Readiness for College Careers, the Gordon Commission, the Teacher Education Accreditation Council Board of Directors, the National Academies of Education Panel to Review Alternative Data Sources for Funding States Serving ELLs under Title III of the Elementary and Secondary Education Act, the National Assessment Governing Board's Technical Advisory Panel for Uniform National Rules for NAEP Testing of ELLs, and multiple state assessment technical advisory committees. She received her doctorate in education from Boston University.

In this chapter, the authors explore the idea of using communities of practice in linguistically and culturally diverse school districts to support instruction of ELs; introduce, with examples, the promoting excellence appraisal system (PEAS) framework for supporting EL education; and show why collaboration leads to schoolwide improvement.

Chapter 12

Building Communities of Practice in Linguistically and Culturally Diverse School Districts

Barbara D. Acosta, Kristina Anstrom,
and Charlene Rivera

Educators are increasingly turning to the idea of communities of practice as a promising approach for implementing change (Tackett & Cator, 2011). What does this mean for school districts whose student populations are linguistically and culturally diverse? How can educators help ensure that English learners—students who are still learning English, as well as those who are fluent in English and speak another language at home—are welcomed into the educational community, provided the right combination of support and challenge, and treated equitably? What if all educators in a district expected the same wonderful outcomes for English learners as they envision for their own children? What can be done to support communities of practice as they pursue this vision?

There is a growing recognition that to close the achievement gap educators need not only tools, programs, and strategies, but also a forum for education researchers and practitioners to share information with each other (Tackett & Cator, 2011). Communities of practice can help optimize scarce resources, reawaken a sense of cooperation and shared aims, and enhance learning for adults and children (DuFour, DuFour, Eaker, & Many, 2010). In addition, communities of practice need guidance to understand the complexities of working with students who are linguistically and culturally diverse, and to transform educational programs from pervasive "deficit" models toward an enriched, academically challenging approach for ELs.

This chapter introduces a framework for improving English learner education and illustrates how it can be used with communities of practice to help facilitate program reforms. The Promoting Excellence Appraisal System (PEAS) framework moves beyond a focus on test scores to encourage a deeper examination of how educators can cooperate to support ELs not just in their learning experiences in ESL/bilingual classes but also in content classes. Essentially, it supports ELs' access to the entire grade-level academic curriculum, to challenging coursework, including inclusion in gifted and talented, honors, and advanced placement classes, and to extra-curricular activities. In this chapter, we describe work using PEAS carried out in collaboration with two school districts and a state education agency with the goal of examining and improving district policies, programs, and services for ELs.

Splash and Ripple: A Metaphor for Improving Practice

It is helpful to visualize organizational change as a "splash and ripple" (Cox, Kozak, Griep, and Moffat, 2005). When a pebble is thrown into a lake, the immediate result is a splash, but the after effects are in the ripples, which can sometimes take off in unexpected directions. Similarly, simply providing professional development (PD) or adding a program or two may cause an initial splash but may not lead to the ripple—to the long-term effects we as educators hope to achieve. It is important to keep the pebble-throwing techniques and prevailing winds in mind as we examine factors that might affect the educational outcomes of ELs.

The George Washington University Center for Equity and Excellence in Education (GW-CEEE) developed the PEAS framework to support the transformation of instructional practice for ELs. PEAS is intended for use by district and school educators in communities of practice. We use the term *appraisal* to mean a decision-making process that supports continuous improvement in districts and schools that serve ELs. Under the guidance of university partners, the PEAS process typically begins with the formation of a district EL leadership team. University staff provide PD and coaching for this team to help them (1) understand what effective practice looks like, (2) assess the district's current needs and concerns in relation to the EL program, (3) make informed judgments about the program model(s) most appropriate to address the district's demographics and sociopolitical context, and (4) develop or reform the district's structures of support. If desired, this step can be followed by a more formal external evaluation. However, the ultimate aim is to build the district's capacity to form a professional learning community (PLC) that is knowledgeable about best practices for ELs and shares responsibility across district offices and schools for improving programs and practices for them.

If the district decides to pursue a formal appraisal, the EL leadership team is charged with working with university staff to support the appraisal process, help facilitate the collection of data, and reflect on the findings. The formal appraisal examines not only traditional measures, such as student test scores, but also what is happening across the district and in schools to support or hinder desired outcomes for students.

PEAS is organized around a set of research-based dimensions and standards of practice that serve to guide the improvement of school and district instructional policies and programs for ELs. The system:

1. Promotes a coherent, connected, and holistic approach to educating ELs within school and district settings

2. Informs the integrated development of EL-responsive instructional policies, programs, and practices

3. Describes a research-based academic learning environment supportive of ELs

4. Helps support effective partnerships with parents, families, and community members to further ELs' learning and achievement

PEAS examines student outcomes as well as district processes and structures. ELs tend to enter school with considerably lower performance than their native English-speaking peers on statewide content assessments. Effective programs produce achievement gap closure by bringing ELs up to grade level on academic content tests within five to seven years after entry into school in the U.S. (Collier & Thomas, 2009). The cross-sectional data required for purposes of federal compliance do not provide enough information to determine whether students are closing the achievement gap over time. Rather than providing snapshots of annual achievement for often shifting populations of students from year to year, university partners use the PEAS student outcome tools to examine the progress of cohorts of ELs to determine whether they are developing English and closing achievement gaps in the content areas. Ideally, if enough information is available, the team also explores whether ELs are participating at the same rate in honors, advanced placement, and college-bound courses, and whether they are completing high school, enrolling in college, and going on to successful careers at the same rates as their English-speaking peers. All of these measures provide an indication of whether district programs are achieving their goals.

Once the team determines how ELs are doing on these outcome measures and the extent to which programs are supporting or not supporting achievement gap closure, the next step is to examine district and school processes to determine where improvement is needed. This phase of the PEAS focuses on seven dimensions of practice for ELs (fig. 12.1, page 231) to determine whether sufficient supports are provided for the linguistic and cultural needs of students learning academic content through a second language.

What Do Effective Programs for ELs Look Like?

The body of research on effective programs for ELs has been evolving since the mid-1980s. The *Promoting Excellence Guiding Principles* (GW-CEEE, 2008) were developed by a team of second-language acquisition and bilingual education scholars, educators of ELs, and content and second-language assessment experts. The guiding principles represent best practices derived from research, professional wisdom, and responses to federal policy. They are the foundation of the seven dimensions of practice that make up the Promoting Excellence Appraisal System. What follows is a brief summary of the standards.

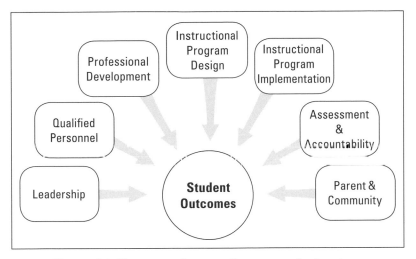

Figure 12.1: The promoting excellence appraisal system.

An effective program of support for ELs is one that is enriched, academically challenging, long-term, and integrated with programs for native English speakers. Educating ELs to high standards requires districtwide policies and procedures that hold all educators, not just ESL/bilingual teachers, responsible for their academic success. One means of holding all educators responsible for closing the achievement gap is to encourage more ESL/bilingual and general education teachers to collaborate in providing instruction that supports students' learning of English and academic content.

Research-based practice calls for educational programs in which ELs have access to the entire school curriculum. Districts and schools that are effective with ELs provide instructional curricula, materials, and resources that support these students in learning grade-level academic content (such as properly translated native language materials and English language materials controlled for linguistic complexity), and prepare teachers to adopt and use these materials. In addition, EL-responsive schools create an environment in which native English-speaking students learn academic content together with their English learner peers.

School districts must also provide services for ELs that take into account English and native language literacy, previous educational experiences, and language and cultural background and use appropriate and valid student assessment results. Districts must monitor the progress of ELs over time until school completion to evaluate the effectiveness of their instructional programs. They should support ongoing monitoring of programs and assessments to ensure their appropriateness for ELs. Districts and schools should also support ongoing, classroom-based assessment of ELs and provide professional development for teachers on research-based approaches to classroom-based assessment.

Finally, school districts that are effective with ELs provide all educators with comprehensive professional development focused on planning and delivering academic instruction that is differentiated to address students' varying English language proficiency levels. At a minimum, EL-responsive school districts provide professional development that helps content teachers understand the process of second-language development and prepares ESL and bilingual teachers with knowledge about the content they teach. Both sets of teachers learn to integrate language and content instruction (GW-CEEE, 2008).

Applying the Framework

In this section, we illustrate how we have used PEAS to help advance program improvement for districts in different contexts, with differing EL populations, needs, and goals. We describe our work with Nashville, Tennessee, an urban school district that wanted assistance to reform an existing program for its ELs. Next, we portray our partnership with the Tennessee Department of Education, which sought to develop a customized appraisal system to support districts with ELs throughout the state. Finally, we illustrate work conducted in Accomack, Virginia, a rural school district that needed help to develop a cohesive program for an emerging population of ELs.

Metropolitan Nashville Public Schools

The Metropolitan Nashville Public Schools (Metro) enroll a rich diversity of racial, ethnic, and socioeconomic groups. In 2009, approximately half of the student population was black, 33 percent white, and 15 percent Latino. The district categorizes 67 percent of its students as low socioeconomic status. In five years, the district's EL population nearly doubled from 3,988 students in 2004 to 9,734 in 2009, meaning that one in every five students was an English learner.

As home to several charities responsible for relocating refugee families, the school district had experienced a large influx of students from a wide variety of countries and varying educational backgrounds. In 2009, ELs in the district came from more than eighty different countries and spoke one hundred and twenty different languages and dialects. "We enroll children who are from countries where they have literally never been in a school or received any formal education," reported the district's executive director of English learners. "These children struggle when they arrive here and are placed in school. They do not know our language or customs" (L. Shelton, personal communication, Dec. 16, 2009).

Metro was struggling to meet the requirements of No Child Left Behind (NCLB, 2002) for its LEP[1] subgroup. In the school years 2006–2007 and 2007–2008, the district did not meet AYP for this subgroup at the high school level, and elementary and middle schools met just one benchmark for this subgroup in 2007–2008. In 2008–09, the district made AYP for LEPs for the first time. However, Metro Director of Schools Jesse Register, who was brought in to help turn around the struggling district, was not satisfied with progress in this area. The EL program became one of nine focus areas for district reform.

The district turned to the Tennessee Department of Education (TDOE) to request an appraisal of its EL programs so that it could understand the strengths of its current services and identify areas in need of improvement. For assistance, the state contacted the Appalachia Regional Comprehensive Center (ARCC), which then brought in GW-CEEE for its EL expertise. The state wanted the Metro appraisal to serve as a pilot for what would become a statewide

---

[1] While we prefer the term *English learner*, under No Child Left Behind schools and districts are required to report adequate yearly progress data using the federal term *limited English proficient* (LEP).

appraisal system that could be used with other Tennessee districts with EL populations.

At the time of the appraisal, Metro had centralized ELs into sixty-three different EL centers and two newcomer centers, with many ELs getting bussed out of their local neighborhoods. At the elementary level, most ELs received instruction in self-contained classrooms. These classrooms provided a combination of both English-language development (ELD) and content instruction through specially designed academic instruction in English (SDAIE). There were concerns that some students remained isolated from their English-speaking peers for several years. At the secondary level, there was a shortage of ESL-endorsed teachers, and many ELs were receiving instruction from teachers who were unprepared to meet their needs.

GW-CEEE led the appraisal in collaboration with the Tennessee Department of Education (TDOE), Metro Nashville, and ARCC. In addition to assessing current programs and practices, as the university partner we aimed to build both state and district capacity to understand what effective practice looks like and to initiate a process of continuous improvement of district EL programs that went beyond compliance with federal and state regulations and that involved educational stakeholders throughout the system. This collaborative process contributed to the development of several instruments, including surveys, interviews, classroom observations, and walkthroughs that benefited from the input of multiple stakeholders. Two teams of expert educators collected data in six schools.

To provide meaningful information on achievement gap closure, GW-CEEE guided the district to organize its EL data so that growth could be tracked over time. This created an opportunity to build the capacity of the state and district staff to refine their data systems and tools so they could monitor the progress of ELs longitudinally, using a cohort approach.

When we presented the results of the appraisal to the district, we reported that ELs were not growing at a sufficient rate to catch up with their English-speaking peers within the five to seven years suggested by research (Collier & Thomas, 2009). The findings on district practices provided insight into why. For the instructional dimension, the appraisal team observed a great deal of inconsistency in the implementation of effective instructional practices for ELs and few expectations for content teachers to document EL expectations in lesson plans or to indicate how lessons were differentiated to meet the needs of EL students, particularly those in secondary classrooms. Few general educators were prepared to address the needs of the English learners in their classrooms, and only a small number of them participated in EL-related professional development, which was voluntary. Although coaches were available, not everyone took advantage of their services. At the leadership level, the appraisal indicated there was little communication or coordination taking place between the EL Office and other district offices. In particular, there was limited integration of ELs' educational needs into district- or schoolwide planning and decision making.

We made three recommendations: (1) transform the district EL program from a segregated, remedial approach to educating students to an integrated, enriched approach; (2) ensure that all teachers of ELs are prepared to support high academic achievement for these students; and (3) hold all district and school personnel accountable for improving teaching and learning for English learners. Each of these recommendations was accompanied by suggested action steps (fig. 12.2).

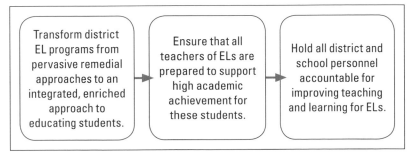

Figure 12.2: Three key recommendations for a district that enrolls ELs.

The appraisal served as the impetus for a number of changes. The district began by moving ELs back into their zoned schools, where parents would have easier access. It also transitioned elementary ELs into integrated classrooms where they now receive content instruction together with their English-speaking peers. In order to increase the participation of content teachers in EL professional development, coaches were moved from the district level to school sites. Metro is now seeking to partner with local universities to provide opportunities for both elementary and secondary content teachers to acquire an add-on ESL endorsement. In addition, the district established a multicultural family outreach department modeled after one used in Denver schools.

Many of the initial changes were made at the structural level. These organizational reforms aim to lay the groundwork for changes in instructional practice as well as in processes for coordinating and collaborating across district offices. Numerous barriers to change remain to be overcome. In particular, inclusion of the needs of ELs in the planning and implementation of initiatives and in overcoming deficit mentalities have required constant advocacy by EL staff, according to the current ESL director. Now that the state is implementing a new teacher evaluation system, school administrators feel the need for more guidance on what to look for during walkthroughs of classrooms with ELs. In addition, under the more integrated new elementary model, preparing all teachers to meet the needs of ELs has become ever more urgent.

The appraisal process appears to have helped build the district's capacity to monitor and support its programs for ELs. As the EL director suggested, "It gave us data on our EL students that we never collected before and found helpful. It opened many discussions that led to plans for improvement" (N. Chaput-Guizani, personal communication, July 8, 2011.) At the school level, teachers and administrators developed a more finely tuned appreciation for what effective practices should look like. Before the appraisal visit, teachers at one school said they thought they had been doing differentiated instruction, but feedback from the appraisal team helped them understand that their definition of and practices around differentiated instruction needed further development. Although the district still has much ground to cover, the appraisal provided compelling and clear evidence of what was needed and a roadmap the district and its schools can refer to as they plan improvement.

The Tennessee English Learner District Appraisal System

The collaborative experience of piloting the Metro appraisal was the foundation for continuing work with the TDOE to develop a system that the state could administer with other districts. The Metro appraisal had been a valuable process for both the district and the state, but it was time intensive and required outside expertise to conduct. Based on the research, the initial number of standards of practice used in the Metro appraisal was large, and the collection and analysis of data from multiple stakeholders were complex.

It was clear that more work was needed to refine a system that the SEA, with limited personnel, could implement with districts. In particular, the SEA wanted a process it could use to assess and support districts that had entered into improvement status because of a failure to meet AYP for the EL subgroup. They wanted this process to be supportive rather than punitive and simple enough to administer without outside expertise.

With the state, we collaborated to identify two to three standards of practice from each of the PEAS dimensions that the SEA felt every district needed to have in place (for example, a minimum level of practice). Building from these standards of practice, we then worked to develop a district self-appraisal questionnaire and a rubric to assess the district's current level of implementation of its EL programs. The Tennessee English Learner District Self-Appraisal (TELDSA) questionnaire can be completed in about a day. The self-assessment is designed to be flexible to different district contexts, from those with only a small number of ELs and perhaps a single ESL teacher, to larger urban districts with substantial infrastructure and resources as well as different kinds of challenges in meeting the needs of their ELs. GW-CEEE is also helping the state to develop an accompanying rubric to guide the SEA in assessing the district's level of implementation of each of the seven PEAS dimensions.

According to TDOE, the collaborative process of developing and piloting the appraisal for Metro and the subsequent TELDSA have been helpful in breaking down traditionally isolated silos in the SEA. The process also supported increased communication and cross-disciplinary learning, identifying unmet needs, enhancing shared problem solving, and reducing duplication of efforts. In addition, the SEA staff reported that they had learned new ways data could be used to help districts. This led to the development of new resources to help the state identify needs and target SEA technical assistance to districts and schools. It also provided a set of resources the state could use to assess district EL programs and help build their capacity for improvement. This collaborative process was elemental in being able to find a balance between the inherent complexities of apprais-ing the interrelated systems affecting EL programs and the need to simplify and customize the appraisal process so that it would be feasible for a state with limited resources to carry out with districts.

Accomack, Virginia

Located on a long, narrow finger of land that stretches between the Atlantic Ocean and the Chesapeake Bay, Accomack County, Virginia, is home to Chincoteague Island, famous for its wild ponies. It also houses a number of agricultural businesses and chicken-packing plants that have attracted large numbers of seasonal workers. To serve the children of this primarily migrant Hispanic population, the Accomack County Public Schools (ACPS) hired a group of ESL teachers who provided language support through both pull-out and push-in models. However, school division leaders have observed a shift to a more permanent immigrant presence. Along with the set-tling of the migrant population, the county experienced an influx of Haitian immigrants. The population of this group of immigrants increased from 6 percent to 9 percent in a five-year period, and in two elementary schools English learners made up over half of the entering student body. As a result of these changes, school division leaders recognized the need to reform their program to meet the aca-demic learning needs of the school division's growing EL population.

ACPS requested that GW-CEEE provide a technical assistance plan to help the school division identify and address reforms neces-sary for the improvement of the programs and services it provides for its EL population. The initial PEAS self-appraisal indicated that the district's programs for ELs were somewhat piecemeal and needed to be redesigned. The program was struggling to meet both the short-term goal of improving EL performance on state assessments and the long-term goal of helping students learn the language needed to speak, listen, read, and write in academic contexts. Two related challenges were to find ways to help general educators accept more responsibility for teaching ELs academic content and to improve collaboration and coordination between the ESL and general education program.

University staff worked with the district to form two levels of professional learning communities: one at the district level and another at the school level. The district EL leadership team used PEAS to conduct the initial self-appraisal and then visited the Fairfax County Public Schools, an urban district with a history of strong programs for ELs, to learn about and observe their programs. Over the next few months, university staff supported the district leadership team to develop a vision and goals for ELs using a gradual release of responsibility (that is, an "I do, we do, you do") approach. The team then presented the needs assessment, vision, and goals to the school board for approval so that they could begin implementing reforms in the following school year.

We also applied for and were awarded a small grant to implement professional development for the school-based professional learning communities (PLCs) using resources from the Doing What Works practice guide on Language and Literacy for ELs (Gersten et al., 2007). A subgroup of the district EL leadership team partnered with the university to design and implement this award, enabling each of the division's five elementary schools to form a PLC. Over a four-month period, university staff provided professional development for twenty-two PLC members, including principals, grade-level teachers, and ESL teachers. We then visited teachers in their classrooms to observe instruction and provide coaching. The project culminated with a turnkey training at the end of the school year, in which PLC members collaborated in teams of four to provide the same professional development topics to elementary peers.

The formation of PLCs at both district and school levels was critical to facilitating buy-in for needed reforms and to beginning implementation of reform practices. The project illustrates the importance of moving beyond the simple dissemination of evidence-based research to improve practice for ELs. It was clear that both district leaders and teachers needed opportunities not only to learn principles and strategies during formal professional development sessions, but also to see them modeled with lots of examples, visual support, and learning by doing. District and school leaders need opportunities to reflect on their own data, learn about evidence-based practice, observe examples of these practices, and receive coaching from university partners to formulate a cohesive vision and goals. Similarly, teachers need ample opportunities to practice, reflect, and receive feedback from peers and expert coaches. They also need structural support and encouragement from school and district leaders.

A gradual release of responsibility approach seemed to be very effective for moving PLC participants at both the teaching and leadership levels from a novice level of understanding to the point where they could develop their own instructional reforms for ELs. In addition, the leadership team's process of preparing a presentation to the school board and the teachers' process of conducting a turnkey training with peers appeared to help deepen participants' understanding of the research presented. While much work remains to be done in ACPS, the project set a solid foundation for future reforms to improve learning and teaching for ELs.

Conclusion

This chapter has illustrated how practitioners can work with university partners to improve programs and practices for ELs in a variety of contexts. The formation of communities of practice can help create buy-in from diverse stakeholders, beginning at the district leadership level and permeating the school level. This approach also helps build a sense of shared responsibility for ELs and catalyzes cross-disciplinary collaboration—a crucial process for coordinating among interrelated systems (for example, district and school leadership, curriculum and instruction, professional development, assessment and accountability, human resources, and so on) necessary to support ELs.

Our experience in working with a variety of districts both directly and through the SEA suggests that together with university partners, using the continuous improvement process, states, districts, and schools can:

- Move beyond compliance to examine whether programs are supporting student growth over time

- Use a systems approach to analyze the interlocking district and schoolwide structures that must be coordinated to support high EL achievement

- Build the capacity of a broad range of district stakeholders to sustain continuous improvement of district-wide programs and services to support ELs throughout their schooling.

- Transform pervasive deficit models to enriched, academically challenging programs so that ELs can attain the same high standards as all other students

Now that the PEAS framework has been developed, more work remains to be done to measure the effects for districts that have applied it, ideally, over several years. We plan to continue collecting data on this process to help us refine the framework as well as the processes for applying it.

References

Collier, V. P., & Thomas, W. P. (2009). *Educating English learners for a transformed world*. Albuquerque, NM: Fuente Press.

Cox, P., Kozak, S., Griep, L., & Moffat, L. (2005). *Splash and ripple: Using outcomes to design and guide community work*. Ottawa: Health Canada.

DuFour, R., DuFour, R., Eaker, R., & Many, T. (2010). *Learning by doing: A handbook for professional communities at work* (2nd ed.). Bloomington, IN: Solution Tree Press.

Gersten, R., Baker, S. K., Shanahan, T., Linan-Thompson, S., Collins, P., & Scarcella, R. (2007). *Effective literacy and English language instruction for English learners in the elementary grades: A practice guide* (NCEE 2007–4011). Accessed at www.doe.in.gov/readingsummit/docs/effective_literacy_and_english_language_instruction_for_english_learners_in_the_elementary_grades.pdf on October 31, 2011.

No Child Left Behind (NCLB) Act of 2001, Pub. L. No. 107–110, § 115, Stat. 1425 (2002).

Tackett, L., & Cator, K. (2011). *The promise of communities of practice*. Accessed at www.ed.gov/oii-news/promise-communities-practice on October 31, 2011.

The George Washington University Center for Equity and Excellence in Education. (2008). *Promoting excellence: Guiding principles*. Arlington, VA: Author.

Margarita Calderón

Margarita Calderón, PhD, is professor emerita and senior research scientist at the Johns Hopkins University School of Education. Her work has focused on effective instructional processes, two-way and dual-language programs, teacher learning communities, and professional development for schools with language-minority populations and striving adolescent readers.

For several years, Dr. Calderón has been working with the North Carolina Department of Education's Office of English Learners to train cohorts of sheltered English instruction teachers, coaches, teacher trainers, and administrators throughout that state.

Joel Gómez

Joel Gómez, EdD, is an associate professor of educational leadership at The George Washington University Graduate School of Education and Human Development, where he teaches and leads an initiative in English learner education as well as in entrepreneurship and innovation. Dr. Gómez has a doctorate in higher education administration from The George Washington University and a master's degree in Latin American studies and a liberal arts bachelor's degree from the University of Texas at Austin.

His research interests focus on the academic achievement of Latino and linguistically and culturally diverse student populations. His projects include work with the National Clearinghouse for Bilingual Education, the National Clearinghouse for English Language Acquisition, the Second Language & Culture Exposure for Children and Youth, and the South East Asia Project for English as a Foreign Language Master Teachers.

A member of the editorial board of the American Association of Hispanics in Higher Education, Dr. Gómez has served as president of the National Association for Bilingual Education and vice president of the Mexican and American Solidarity Foundation. He has presented internationally throughout North America on issues related to linguistically and culturally diverse students.

In this chapter, the authors highlight key messages from the previous chapters, further elaborate on professional learning and on what is required for it to have an impact on teachers and their ELs, and discuss some of new ways of addressing the complex issues that have risen around the education of ELs.

Chapter 13

Implementing the Change

Margarita Calderón and Joel Gómez

Schools cannot move forward toward transformation without new, profound personal learning and new ways to accomplish that learning. Personal and professional development in EL instruction has mainly been directed toward ESL and designated sheltered instruction teachers through training of trainers workshops. Dual-language and bilingual teachers may have fewer opportunities, and general education teachers probably have less opportunities, for participating in comprehensive PD on teaching and learning for ELs.

The intent of this book is to build on the schools' successes and address their gaps by providing a road map. Coherence and alignment between what already exists and what needs to be developed ensures effective implementation, continuous professional learning, and positive student outcomes. The implementation of the recommendations in this book would achieve compliance. It would also provide an opportunity to establish a more comprehensive approach to improve educational outcomes. Our recommendations are nested in evidence-based studies and grounded on observations and experiences with educational entities across the United States and in other countries.

The contributors to this book have found the following roadblocks that we must break through:

- Not enough rigor, challenge, or attention is given to ELs. As the *New York Times* wrote on October 13, 2011, "Problems arise because ELs have been an afterthought, if they're considered at all" (Otterman, 2011).

- Comprehensive year-long professional learning programs around EL instruction for all core content teachers are sparse.

- Tier 2 and Tier 3 or 4 RTI and tutoring programs that differentiate for ELs are almost nonexistent.

- As the impact of the Common Core State Standards spreads through the country, a whole-school perspective where every teacher is an EL teacher and every teacher is well prepared to teach vocabulary, discourse, reading, and writing, along with the subject-area knowledge, should be the priority in every school.

Unfeigned Professional Development

In order to integrate new instructional practices, core content, ESL and bilingual teachers need comprehensive professional programs that integrate theory, research, modeling and demonstrations of instructional methods, and coaching and feedback (Calderón, 2007a, 2007b; Joyce & Calhoun, 2010; Joyce & Showers, 2003). Follow-up activities in learning communities are necessary at the school site in order to ensure transfer from training. Researchers recommend thirty to one hundred hours of professional development a year (August et al., 2008; Edutopia, 2009; Joyce & Calhoun, 2010; Marsh & Calderón, 1989). Yet every year, schools diminish professional development on EL instruction by reducing teacher time spent on learning. They feign professional development by offering one-shot workshops without follow-up support systems or accountability for implementation.

A recent publication from the National Research Institutes (National Research Council [NRC], 2010) finds that teachers can develop declarative knowledge from training sessions but not necessarily teaching skill (procedural knowledge), much less the knowledge of how to adapt their teaching skills to a diverse group of students (conditional knowledge). There are many teachers and administrators who are skilled at citing research, albeit somewhat obsolete, about ELs who have not had the opportunity to develop procedural and conditional knowledge for effective application.

When implemented systematically, coaching helps change the culture of teaching and learning. It creates fidelity with ownership and fidelity to an innovation. It helps sustain quality implementation. When done right, coaching helps everyone become a learner—the observed and the observer. It is a vehicle for updating the curriculum. Most important, it improves student achievement (Calderón & Minaya-Rowe, 2011; DuFour, DuFour, Eaker, & Karhanek, 2010; Hord, Roussin, & Sommers, 2010).

Many schools have implemented professional learning communities. Unfortunately, most PLCs focus mainly on EL test results and on finding ways to drill to the test. In the ideal PLC, teachers do look at student data but are more intentional in their own learning and monitor each teacher's instructional delivery (Calderón, 2009; DuFour et al., 2010; Joyce & Calhoun, 2010; Knight, 2011).

> When implemented systematically, coaching helps change the culture of teaching and learning. It helps sustain quality implementation. When done right, coaching helps everyone become a learner. Most important, it improves student achievement.

Principals find it difficult to institute successful PLCs that concentrate on meeting teachers' individual needs. Just as students need differentiated approaches for learning, so do teachers. Various models of on-site learning exist (Calderón, 2007; DuFour et al., 2010; Joyce & Showers, 2003; Knight, 2011; Hargreaves & Fullan, 2009). Following are some brief examples:

- Some teachers prefer to work alone on action research, online learning, inquiry projects, and so on, but need support, specific plans, and timelines within the priority that is EL achievement.

- Other teachers need companionship, such as peer coaching, where they observe each other teach and give feedback.

- Others like to work in small groups on curriculum, lesson development, the exchange of lessons, professional book studies, video analysis, and alignment.

- Still others like to analyze student data, figure out gaps, and lay out plans for instructional interventions, including monitoring of teacher and student progress.

- PLC talk and priorities center around teachers' own learning progressions and those of ELs in regard to:

    + Linguistic development

    + Reading development

    + Writing development

    + Core concept development

    + Significant gaps in development

    + Cultural challenges

    + Socio-emotional challenges

- Teachers conduct analyses of student factors and artifacts in order to change practice.

- Core content teachers and ESL/bilingual teachers work on scaffolding lessons for ELs and on integrating each other's ideas and talents.

There might be teachers who have specific credentials to teach ELs. Nevertheless, the whole faculty and administration needs to participate in professional learning that is responsive to all students. This book has enumerated topics and dispositions to consider for the professional development of all, including the ESL/bilingual specialists. Jim Cummins outlined some of these in chapter 3, and other authors go into detail about other aspects of professional learning. The following section outlines recommendations for the content of professional learning as it relates to the integration of language, literacy, and content.

Rigorous Instruction for ELs

ELs need an integrated approach that consists of listening, speaking, reading, and writing within each content area. The four language domains are not linear. They spiral, as children and adolescents learn science, math, language arts, social studies, physical education, music, and art. All teachers need to know how to teach the following components:

- **Vocabulary**—Researchers, reading specialists, second-language-acquisition experts, and linguists agree that explicit instruction of vocabulary is necessary for students to have robust vocabularies to use throughout their daily learning routines. Whether gifted or just learning English as a second or third language, all students need explicit and varied instruction to build solid word power.

- **Reading**—Educating the full range of ELs and low-achieving students in intellectually demanding programs will require education professionals to learn new ways of teaching, with a strong focus on reading in the content areas, not just on vocabulary and second-language acquisition (August et al., 2008; Short & Fitzsimmons, 2007; Slavin & Calderón, 2001; Slavin, Madden, Calderón, Chamberlain, & Hennessy, 2009). Teaching basic reading and reading comprehension to ELs is one of the most difficult instructional endeavors for most teachers. Mainstream reading programs have not fared well for ELs. This is probably one of the reasons why there are so many long-term ELs who cannot read or learn core subject matter.

- **Writing**—Writing is the other difficult domain for ELs and their secondary school teachers. Even at the elementary level, it is rarely taught explicitly beyond the genre in language arts, although writing in science, history, or math varies considerably from the instruction given in ESL or language arts classes.

How would these components look in a professional development program?

- Vocabulary

  + Outcomes for students—Students learn vocabulary words from different tiers of vocabulary (for example, Tier 3—content words; Tier 2—connectors, polysemous, homonyms, phrasal clusters, and so on; Tier 1—basic words that trouble ELs). The selection of these words comes from the texts students read; more vocabulary is learned while students read and discuss with peers; after reading and discussions, they learn depth-of-word-knowledge and how to apply new words to different types of writing, such as summaries, reports, creative writing.

  + Training for teachers—At the workshop, the trainers model and teachers practice how to select words to teach according to their students' language and reading levels. The words range from easy to sophisticated to content-specific, concept-laden words and words that nest those concepts. Teachers learn how to explicitly preteach vocabulary and orchestrate practice with mastery through discourse protocols and word analysis activities during and after reading. Teachers also practice syntactic processing so that they can teach the ways that grammar knowledge supports reading comprehension. They bring sample student products to the next training session to discuss successes and problems.

  + Additional training for coaches and administrators—Coaches and administrators attend the training with their teachers and in a separate session learn how to observe vocabulary instructional delivery and how students apply new words. They learn to use a valid and reliable observation protocol designed specifically to record EL and teacher performance on vocabulary and discourse, as well as how to give effective feedback on the depth and breadth of word usage by teachers and students.

- Reading

    + Outcomes for students—Beginning readers learn decoding and word knowledge, fluency, and basic comprehension. Older or more advanced readers learn to apply a variety of reading strategies that support and enhance their reading comprehension and mastery of the subject domain they are studying.

    + Training for teachers—Trainers model each reading component and K–2 teachers practice at the workshop with peers how to teach phonemic awareness, phonological awareness, decoding, word knowledge, and fluency. Trainers model through "think-alouds" and effective reading comprehension strategies (using text features, examining text structures, summarizing, forming questions, monitoring comprehension, clarifying purposes for reading, and learning from reading). K–12 teachers also learn to integrate the relevant strategies that are applicable to the text students are about to read. Teachers also learn how to use effective instructional strategies such as partner reading for summarizing and cooperative learning strategies that support discussions of text with particular oral strategies (for example, for recall, paraphrasing, summarization, question formulation, and sentence-starter frames). Teachers also learn how to avoid ineffective reading strategies. SIFE teachers learn how to combine phonemic awareness, phonological awareness, decoding, word knowledge, fluency, and comprehension of content texts. All teachers learn how to set up student pairs for paired reading and how to monitor and document quality reading and application of comprehension strategies.

    + Additional training for coaches and administrators—By recording student responses on the observation protocol during teacher read-alouds, student partner reading, peer discussions, and cooperative learning activities, coaches and administrators can give specific feedback to teachers and students on the application of reading comprehension strategies. Coaches and administrators bring samples of anonymous observation protocols for discussion and feedback on their observations to their next PD session.

- Writing

    + Outcomes for students—Students focus on text structures and writing conventions to compose a variety of texts that demonstrate clear focus, the logical development of ideas in well-organized paragraphs, address to a specific audience, and appropriate language to advance the author's purpose for writing across the curriculum.

    + Training for teachers—Trainers model the development of literary, expository/procedural, and persuasive texts, or research. Literary text includes stories, poems, personal narratives, scripts, and literary responses. Expository/procedural text includes informational text, letters, analytical essays, and multimedia presentations. Persuasive text includes persuasive and argumentative essays. Teachers practice how to highlight and present features of various types of text structures with their own textbooks. They also learn to integrate writing strategies (for example, identifying main ideas and author's purpose, connecting various parts of a text), revising and editing strategies (for example, rewriting sentences, eliminating unnecessary repetitions, spelling, and grammar), and effective use of writing tools (outlines, concept maps, semantic maps, graphic organizers, and so on) as they relate to different disciplines. Teachers learn to use stratified rubrics for different proficiency levels.

    + Additional training for coaches and administrators— They learn how to record on the observation protocol the complexities of teaching writing mechanics, genre and processes in order to give precise feedback to teachers. Administrators also learn how to conduct constructive and robust teacher evaluations that continuously inform and improve teaching for ELs and other students.

Consolidation of Language, Literacy, and Content With Performance Assessment Outcomes

Mastery of core content is the main goal for all ELs. The development of academic language and literacy/biliteracy are a means to academic achievement. Language, literacy, and subject matter knowledge can be developed simultaneously when these features are addressed throughout the school year.

- **Outcomes for students**—Students keep up with core content while they learn the intricacies of academic oral discourse, communication skills, social and cooperative skills, self-evaluation and creativity.

- **Training for teachers**—Teachers learn how to integrate language, literacy, and content knowledge. They develop additional skills for critical thinking, collaboration, communication, technology, problem solving, life and career skills such as flexibility and adaptability, initiative and self-direction, social and cross-cultural productivity and accountability, leadership and responsibility. They use discourse props and activities to help students practice effective communication (for example, sentence and question starters; social protocols; and instructions on how to interrupt politely, question, and reach consensus). Teachers also learn a myriad of cooperative learning structures and technology for different learning purposes. They practice relinquishing control and empower students to become more creative in their learning, in the products and performances of that learning and in self-regulation and evaluation. They learn to assess EL learning through performance and portfolio assessment, stratified rubrics, and other differentiated testing techniques and further their reflection through observation protocols to see if their teaching is reaching all students.

- **Additional training for coaches and administrators**—Coaches and administrators learn to record effective integration of language, literacy, and content through instructional activities, discourse, and interaction patterns that facilitate learning. An integral part of professional learning, focused on ELs, prepares teachers, administrators, and coaches in how to work in collegial teams at the school, how to conduct teachers learning communities and peer coaching, give feedback, and set goals for continuous learning after each observation and coaching segment.

Coaching Institutes

From our other studies we have seen how successful schools can be when administrators and peer or specialist coaches shadow the expert coaches during class observations and participate in coaching institutes of one additional day. These institutes begin with information on how to use tools of observation, give feedback, and set goals for improvement specific to EL instruction. This is followed by actual classroom visits where the expert trainer models using an observation protocol and administrators and site coaches practice using that instrument. After each classroom observation, a debriefing session ensues for further understanding and clarification of the process. The expert trainer subsequently gives feedback to teachers as administrators, and site coaches watch, then, practice giving feedback as the expert trainer observes (Calderón, 2007a, 2007b; Calderón & Minaya-Rowe, 2011).

What Else Enables Quality Instruction?

Quality instruction is also enabled by:

- **Principal effectiveness**—Principals need to understand good instructional practices and know how to (1) observe teachers of ELs, (2) gauge how effectively teachers are using these practices, (3) be constantly aware of EL learning progressions, and (4) lead professional learning that makes it possible for teachers to master those practices embedded in their daily work. Principals, coaches and teachers need joint training on the principles of transfer of knowledge and skills from the training into the classroom. Building a community of adult learners and inspiring personal learning that focuses on EL achievement entails having administrators, coaches, teachers, and school staff work together to build the community. They need to learn together at workshops, special trainings, networks, and at the school site.

- **School improvement efforts**—The best way to improve schools is through quality professional learning that develops instructional skills to address the diverse needs of student populations in the school where they teach (Calderón, 2009; Edutopia, 2009; Joyce & Showers, 2003; Marsh & Calderón, 1989). Nevertheless, very little evidence of transfer into the classroom currently exists for the popular workshops on EL instruction. Mapping out how transfer will be measured is the critical first step in improving schools for ELs and other struggling students.

- **Central administration**—District and school administrators need to learn how to systematically monitor and measure implementation. Training should be followed by two or three instances of shadowing of experts to compare class observations and begin to collect data on implementation. The observation protocols and ancillary tools used for this purpose should generate data that can be graphed and used to track learning by the principals, teachers, and students throughout the year. District administration should set up teacher and principal support systems and continuous professional development. By this, we don't mean offering the same two-day workshops throughout the year to whoever wants to come. We mean giving the schools ten to fifteen days of professional development that goes deeply into quality instruction on oracy, literacy, and content integration, followed by another five days of coaching for each teacher and administrator. End-of-year reports should consist of an analysis of the comprehensiveness of professional development and coaching at each school, individual teacher growth data trajectories, student outcomes, and school factors that facilitated or impeded growth.

- **State-level accountability**—As Race to the Top, Title III, Title I, and similar fundings are sifted by the states, state educational agencies should be held accountable for districts showing plans, accomplishments, and learning trajectories for ELs and language-minority students. A comprehensive professional development effort, the key feature of student success, is a requirement for effective implementation of any instructional program. Most states, school districts, and schools do not document or show evidence of transfer from the training into the classroom. They should monitor and measure the teachers' implementation of the training, and correlate this with their students' learning progressions (Calderón & Minaya-Rowe, 2011; Grossman et al., 2009; Joyce & Calhoun, 2010). As our research and professional development teams travel from state to state, we find that the offices of English language instruction have not seen those moneys from Race to the Top. Yet no one holds states accountable.

Final Thoughts on Whole-School Approaches

Contributors to this text have expounded a number of worthwhile whole-school approaches for EL learners. Margarita Calderón states, "As language-minority student populations grow, either through high birth rates or the arrival of refugee children and other newcomers, all schools must be prepared to teach them." Robert Slavin reaffirms that "effective teaching of English learners is mainly a question of adapting proven approaches for students in general for the particular needs of students learning English." Margo Gottlieb discusses culturally responsive schools, and Charlene Rivera describes the benefits of communities of practice. Other authors offer a variety of content area approaches for ELs within a whole-school context. Together, these authors present a strong case for whole-school instructional approaches for ELs.

In doing so, however, a paradox arises. Do we implement whole-school instructional approaches only for ELs? Or do we implement whole-school approaches for all of the school's constituencies? Students with certain backgrounds and characteristics have been labeled in a number of ways—as LESA (limited English-speaking ability), LEP (limited English proficient), ESL (English as a second language), language minority, and bilingual, in addition to other labels. While our intentions have been good in championing learning opportunities for students with these labels, we have also served to classify and thus marginalize the same students for whom we advocate.Inherent in using these labels, or any label, is the belief that the groups to which it applies are different from members of a "superior" group and must work in an extra-special way to become like them. Because labeled students are students with an adjective preceding them, special instructional and assessment treatments are developed to wipe out the "special" label. Whether these treatments are "additive" or "subtractive," whether the treatment consists of pulling out students or providing them with academic language opportunities, these students nevertheless are on a journey to reduce a deficiency—their EL classification, a classification that we have invented and that we must now invent processes to eliminate. These processes include preassessment, ongoing assessment, postassessment, content assessment, English proficiency assessment, and other high-stakes assessments. Can a whole-school approach be successful as long as we continue to marginalize students by inventing labels for them? Will the whole-school approach become yet another failed silver bullet aimed at addressing yet another invented student label?

> Can a whole-school approach be successful as long as we continue to marginalize students by inventing labels for them? Will the whole-school approach become yet another failed silver bullet aimed at addressing yet another invented student label?

The solution is not simple. How can we best serve all students without classifying them? Part of the answer lies in the fact that current and projected demographics for North America have already redefined and transformed the whole-school population—a dynamic and evolving population for which we need to develop and implement successful whole-school instructional approaches. These instructional approaches could be oriented toward goals such as: (1) all students will speak, read, and write proficiently in at least two languages by the time they graduate from high school; (2) all graduating high school seniors will qualify to participate in postsecondary experiences; (3) all students will participate in math, science, and language arts courses with the same level of rigor and in the same sequence; (4) all students will participate equally in extracurricular activities; and (5) all students will have the same access to instructional and content expertise.

Suppose we were faced with creating a whole-school approach for all students for goal one. How would we approach it? We could start off by examining the status quo for second-language instruction under the guise of world languages, global languages, or modern languages. We would examine the extent to which the current status allows schools to meet goal one. We would discover that, indeed, schools to a large extent are not successful in meeting goal one and that, even though the U.S. is investing over $24 billion a year in second-language instruction,[1] student achievement in this area is far from acceptable. We recognize that, even though this is a huge investment in second-language instruction at the district level, it would be an even larger amount if related state level and professional development costs were factored into this equation.

In examining the status quo of second-language instructional methodologies, second-language instructional materials, and second-language assessments, we would probably ascertain that all these components would need significant revamping to allow the school to meet goal one. We would also discover that a significant number of students already have various levels of proficiency in at least two languages. In revamping professional development for second-language instruction, instructional methodologies, and instructional materials, we would ensure that these changes would take into account the advanced second-language skills of students with proficiency in more than one language. We would also establish

---

[1] In determining how much the U.S. spends on second-language instruction, we used the total student enrollment in "foreign language education" at the secondary level (about six million students), as reported in the *Digest of Education Statistics* (Snyder & Dillow, 2011). We estimated that a typical class has about twenty-five students and divided this into the six million total student enrollment to determine approximately how many teachers are involved in second-language instruction (two hundred forty thousand). We then multiplied this by one hundred thousand (the average salary per teacher is about $50,000 dollars, doubled for fringe and overhead costs) to arrive at the $24 billion estimate.

a system by which students demonstrating extraordinary mastery of a second language could receive college credit for courses taken at the secondary school level.

Recognizing that good teaching determines to a large extent student achievement and that good teaching is comprised of content mastery and instructional methodologies, we would create professional development programs for teachers based on the following principles: (1) demonstrated fluency in listening, speaking, reading, and writing in the target second language; (2) mastery of basic principles in sociolinguistic and psycholinguistic theories; (3) preparation in second-language methodologies in addition to general instructional methodologies, including classroom management, teaching and learning theories, and human growth and development; (4) mastery of a content area within a liberal arts setting; and (5) fluency in the sociocultural context of the target language. The second-language curriculum would be incorporated into the general school curriculum for RTI Tier 1 teachers. Tier 2 and 3 specialists would incorporate thematic units in the areas of math, social studies, science, and art and culture and would be integrated into second-language instructional units. Communications skills (narration, description, classification, evaluation, projection, persuasion, self expression, exposition, and so on) in the second language (or additional languages) would be aligned with the language arts curriculum.

In summary, any whole-school approaches as they exist now must be re-examined and, if necessary, retooled for existing and future whole-school populations. They must be supported by appropriate school policies, budgets, locations, staffing, curriculum, schedules, instruction, and testing; by the school climate and building; and by parent and community relations, instructional periods, and so on. Furthermore, schools must be held accountable for their success in addressing the socio-academic success of all their students. Schools must develop data-driven systems that assist them in identifying which teachers and schools need support in meeting the school's goals. They must provide a system to quickly identify and correct any deficiencies. And very importantly, school boards, schools, administrators and teachers need to be held accountable for meeting whole-school goals.

Creating and implementing whole-school approaches are not the sole responsibility of schools and school districts. State legislatures, school boards, and education agencies must enact laws, rules, and policies in support of whole-school approaches. Schools of education must prepare teachers to work successfully with all students within a whole-school setting. The federal government must hold states and school districts accountable for providing high-quality and equitable educational opportunities for all students, with corresponding socioacademic results.

> Whole-school approaches must be supported by appropriate school policies, budgets, locations, staffing, curriculum, schedules, instruction, and testing; by the school climate and building; and by parent and community relations, instructional periods, and so on.

In conclusion, the labeling game focuses primarily on the student and not on the school system. Historical antecedents demonstrate that this approach only perpetuates marginalizing students and blaming them for their "deficiencies." Current and projected demographics clearly mandate that the labeling game must end and that society must support and hold schools accountable for planning and implementing whole-school approaches for all students.

References

August, D., Beck, I. L., Calderón, M., Francis, D. J., Lesaux, N. K., & Shanahan, T. (2008). Instruction and professional development. In D. August & T. Shanahan (Eds.), *Developing reading and writing in second language learners: Lessons from the report of the National Literacy Panel on Language-Minority Children and Youth* (pp. 131–250). Mahwah, NJ: Lawrence Erlbaum.

August, D., & Shanahan, T. (Eds.). (2006). *Developing literacy in second-language learners: Report of the National Literacy Panel on Language-Minority Children and Youth.* Mahwah, NJ: Lawrence Erlbaum.

Calderón, M. (1984). Training bilingual trainers: An ethnographic study of coaching and its impact on the transfer of training (Doctoral dissertation, San Diego State University and Claremont Graduate School). *Dissertation Abstracts.*

Calderón, M. E. & L. Minaya-Rowe. (2003). *Designing and implementing two-way bilingual programs: A step-by step guide for administrators, teachers, and parents.* Thousand Oaks, CA: Corwin Press.

Calderón, M. (2007a). *Teaching reading to English language learners, grades 6–12: A framework for improving achievement in the content areas.* Thousand Oaks, CA: Corwin Press.

Calderón, M. (2007b). *RIGOR! Reading instructional goals for older readers: Reading program for 6th—12th students with interrupted formal education.* New York: Benchmark Education.

Calderón, M. (2009). Professional development for teachers of English language learners and striving readers. In L. Mandel-Morrow, R. Rueda, & D. Lapp (Eds.), *Handbook of literacy and research on literacy instruction: Issues of diversity, policy and equity* (pp. 413–429). New York: Guilford Press.

Calderón, M. (Coauthor with the Committee on the Study of Teacher Preparation Programs in the United States). (2010). *Preparing teachers: Building evidence for sound policy.* Washington, DC: National Research Council.

Calderón, M. (2011). *Teaching reading and comprehension to English learners, K–5.* Bloomington, IN: Solution Tree Press.

Calderón, M. E., & Minaya-Rowe, L. (2011). *Preventing long-term English language learners: Transforming schools to meet core standards.* Thousand Oaks, CA: Corwin Press.

Calderón, M., Slavin, R. E., & Sánchez, M. (2011). Effective instruction for English language learners. In M. Tienda & R. Haskins (Eds.), *The future of immigrant children* (pp. 103–128). Washington, DC: Brookings Institute/Princeton University.

DuFour, R., DuFour, R., Eaker, R., & Karhanek, G. (2010). *Raising the bar and closing the gap: Whatever it takes.* Bloomington, IN: Solution Tree Press.

Edutopia staff. (2009). Linda Darling-Hammond: Thoughts on teacher preparation. *Edutopia.* Accessed at www.edutopia.org/ldh-teacher-preparation on November 3, 2011.

Grossman, P. L., Brown, M. Cohen, J., Loeb, S., Boyd, D., Lanksford, H., et al. (2009). *Measure for measure: A pilot study linking English language arts instruction and teachers' value-added to student achievement.* Paper presented at the annual meeting of the American Educational Research Association, San Diego, CA.

Hargreaves, A., & Fullan, M. (Eds.). (2009). *Change wars.* Bloomington, IN: Solution Tree Press.

Hord, S. M., Roussin, J. L., & Sommers, W. A. (2010). *Guiding professional development communities: Inspiration, challenge, surprise, and meaning.* Thousand Oaks, CA: Corwin Press.

Joyce, B., & Calhoun, E. (2010). *Models of professional development: A celebration of educators.* Thousand Oaks, CA: Corwin Press.

Joyce, B., & Showers, B. (2003). *Student achievement through staff development* (3rd ed.). Alexandria, VA: Association for Supervision and Curriculum Development.

Knight, J. (2011). *Unmistakable impact: A partnership approach for dramatically improving instruction.* Thousand Oaks: Corwin Press.

Marsh, D., & Calderón, M. (1989). Applying research on effective bilingual instruction in a multi-district inservice teacher training program. *National Association for Bilingual Education Journal, 12*(2), 133–152.

National Research Council. (2010). *Preparing teachers: Building evidence for sound policy* (Report from the Committee on the Study of Teacher Preparation Programs in the United States). Washington, DC: National Academies Press.

Otterman, S. (2011 October 13). *State puts pressure on city schools over English language learners.* Accessed at www.nytimes.com/2011/10/13/education/13ell .html on October 31, 2011.

Short, D. J., & Fitzsimmons, S. (2007). *Double the work: Challenges and solutions to acquiring language and academic literacy for adolescent English language learners.* Washington, DC: Alliance for Excellent Education.

Slavin, R. E., & Calderón, M. (Eds.). (2001). *Effective programs for Latino students.* Mahwah, NJ: Lawrence Erlbaum.

Slavin, R. E., Madden, N., Calderón, M., Chamberlain, A., & Hennessy, M. (2009). *Fifth-year reading and language outcomes of a randomized evaluation of transitional bilingual education: Report to IES.* Washington, DC: Institute for Education Sciences, U.S. Department of Education.

Snyder, T. D., & Dillow, S. A. (2011). *Digest of Education Statistics 2010* (NCES 2011-015). Washington, DC: National Center for Education Statistics, Institute of Education Sciences, U.S. Department of Education.

Index

Note to index: An *f* following a page number indicates a figure; a *t* following a page number indicates a table.

Mind, Brain, & Education
Edited by David A. Sousa

Understanding how the brain learns helps teachers do their jobs more effectively. In this book, primary researchers share the latest findings in neuroscience, as well as applications, examples, and innovative strategies.
BKF358

Common Language Assessment for English Learners
Margo Gottlieb

Learn how to plan, implement, and evaluate common language assessments for your English learners. With this step-by-step guide, teachers, school leaders, and administrators will find organizing principles, lead questions, and action steps all directing you toward collaborative assessment.
BKF352

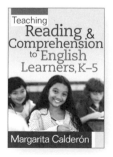

Rebuilding the Foundation
Edited by Timothy V. Rasinski

Teaching reading is a complex task without a simple formula for developing quality instruction. Rather than build on or alter existing models, this book considers how educators and policymakers might think about rebuilding and reconceptualizing reading education, perhaps from the ground up.
BKF399

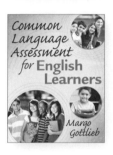

Teaching Reading & Comprehension to English Learners, K–5
Margarita Calderón

Raise achievement for English learners through new instructional strategies and assessment processes. This book addresses the language, literacy, and content instructional needs of ELs and frames quality instruction within effective schooling structures and the implementation of RTI.
BKF402